W9-BUO-380

Gilkey on Tillich

Gilkey on Tillich

Langdon Gilkey

CROSSROAD · NEW YORK

1990

The Crossroad Publishing Company
370 Lexington Avenue, New York, N.Y. 10017

Copyright © 1990 by Langdon Gilkey

All rights reserved. No part of this book may be reproduced,
stored in a retrieval system, or transmitted, in any form
or by any means, electronic, mechanical, photocopying,
recording or otherwise, without the written permission of
The Crossroad Publishing Company.

Printed in the United States of America

Library of Congress Cataloging-in-Publication Data

Gilkey, Langdon Brown, 1919–
    Gilkey on Tillich / Langdon Gilkey.
        p.   cm.
    Includes bibliographical references.
    ISBN 0-8245-0991-9
    1. Tillich, Paul, 1886–1965.   2. Theology, Doctrinal-
-History—20th century.   I. Title.
BX4827.T53G55   1989
230'.092—dc20   89-39032
                                                        CIP

*This volume
is dedicated in affection and respect
to all my colleagues
at
The Divinity School of The University of Chicago:
the deans, the faculty, the students,
and the staff
1963–1989*

Contents

Part Three: Retrospective

Abbreviations

BR   *Biblical Religion and the Search for Ultimate Reality.* Chicago: University of Chicago Press, 1955.

CB   *The Courage to Be.* New Haven: Yale University Press, 1952

DF   *The Dynamics of Faith.* New York: Harper and Row, 1957.

IOH   *The Interpretation of History.* Translated by N. A. Rasetzki and Elsa L. Talmey. New York: Charles Scribner's Sons, 1936.

LPJ   *Love, Power, and Justice.* New York: Oxford University Press, 1954.

MB   *Morality and Beyond.* New York: Harper and Row, 1963.

MSFA   *My Search for Absolutes.* New York: Simon and Schuster, 1967.

PE   *Political Expectation.* Edited by James Luther Adams. New York: Harper and Row, 1971.

TPE   *The Protestant Era.* Translated by James Luther Adams. Chicago: University of Chicago Press, 1948.

RS   *The Religious Situation.* Translated by H. Richard Niebuhr. New York: Henry Holt and Company, 1932.

SD   *The Socialist Decision.* Translated by Franklin Sherman. New York: Harper and Row, 1977.

ST   *Systematic Theology.* 3 vols. Chicago: University of Chicago Press, 1951–63.

TC   *Theology of Culture.* Edited by Robert C. Kimball. New York: Oxford University Press, 1959.

WS   *The World Situation.* Philadelphia: Fortress Press, 1965.

Preface

This volume on the philosophical theology, theology of culture, and political theology of Paul Tillich is the result of almost an entire career of dependence on and delight in his thought. I have taught courses on Tillich since I first began full-time teaching at Vassar in 1951; I note with mingled amusement and alarm that each seemingly new turn in my own thinking finds itself always prepared and all too frequently already elaborated in some aspect or another of his massive system.

As a result I have, for quite a long time, considered myself to be a "Tillichean," in part surprised and flustered by that admission, in part proud and satisfied to be in that generous tradition. In any case, as will be obvious to any attentive reader, these chapters on Tillich's theology not only stem from an affectionate recollection of him as teacher and friend, but they also represent an ever-renewed enthusiasm for his sharp, original, and ever-disturbing insights, for his unifying general grasp of things, and especially for his sense of the depth, the importance, and the scope—the terror and the healing—of the religious in life.

This was not always the case. As a young adult my interest in religion and theology had been newly quickened by a combination of the Second World War and the penetrating genius of Reinhold Niebuhr; in 1946, I came to Union Theological Seminary in New York to study for the Ph.D. with him. There, of course, I also encountered Tillich. At once I was puzzled, fascinated, and lured by his very different way of viewing existence, namely, ontologically rather than ethically as did Niebuhr. Soon I felt I was beginning to understand him; for a time I became his assistant and interpreter in his classes on systematic theology—and a devoted listener in his seminars on Augustine and Luther. I did not suspect then—nor did I for a number of years—that a new theological blood-type, if I may put it that way, was entering my arteries, one that would later become almost dominant. In any case, many of the interpretations and almost all of the cited "quotes" from Tillich's own lips, found in these pages, reach back to those shared hours in his classes.

I did not become explicitly aware of how my own modes of theological reflection were dependent on him until the mid-sixties, in fact I came to Chicago in 1963. At that point the death of God theology was slowly gestating and silently coming to birth. In various important and quite unexpected ways the theological community in America, in a sort of embattled retreat for almost two decades into its own biblical and ecclesiastical preserve, was becoming newly aware of the "world," and particularly of the claims on responsible action for justice in the world, and—what was a new awareness for me—of awareness of the persistent claims on our thinking and our truth of the world's "secular spirit." If such claims are taken with "radical seriousness"—as the new theologians were demanding—then how could one continue responsibly to speak of God? One long-time theological friend, William Hamilton, and three new ones—Paul Van Buren, Thomas Altizer, and Richard Rubenstein—were raising this question with irresistible power and devastating logic, albeit from a variety of points of view, drawing the conclusion that however one may henceforth seek to do "theology," it must be done "without God." Each of them tried to reconstruct an interpretation of Christianity (or, in Rubenstein's case, of Judaism) "without God."[1] Ironically, Tillich of all people was widely credited with being the spiritual grandfather of this theological new birth.

This new movement fascinated me. I could feel on the deepest level the power of its arguments, that is, the power of the secular spirit that spoke to all of us through it, for in many ways these, too, were my criteria of truth and value. On the other hand, my own experience had for so long (since 1939–40) and so vividly disclosed for me the faults and fissures of "modernity" that I was more lured than seriously tempted by a thoroughgoing secularity. One thing I could not do, however, was to begin to conceive how to marshal together an answer to these arguments, an answer that was lying dormant in my viscera. Heretofore, the concentration of my own modes of theology, dependent mightily on Niebuhr, was exclusively directed *negatively* in the form of a critique of the hubris and injustice of the world and *positively* at the promise of

---

1. Cf. William Hamilton, *The New Essence of Christianity* (New York: Association Press, 1961); William Hamilton and Thomas Altizer, *Radical Theology and the Death of God* (Indianapolis: Bobbs–Merrill, 1966); Paul Van Buren, *The Secular Meaning of the Gospel* (New York: Macmillan, 1963); Thomas Altizer, *The Gospel of Christian Atheism* (Philadelphia: Westminster, 1966); Richard L. Rubenstein, *After Auschwitz* (Indianapolis: Bobbs-Merrill, 1966).

redeeming and providential grace to the world's wayward inhabitants. This had been a theology relevant enough to my own recent war experiences; however, it was one apparently helpless and incapable in the face of a new need to uncover evidences of the divine reality and presence within ordinary experience and the strange uses of ordinary language. I remember being sure that while Niebuhr would have known well enough what to say, I could find no handle with which to begin. If one does not or cannot any longer start with "faith," "the Word," or even the "biblical view" (and this was what was being demanded), how *then* can one proceed in theology? How *does* one speak of God in a genuinely secular world, admitting, that is to say, only secular presuppositions? What does the word "God" mean, or refer to, in terms of ordinary experience? Is religious discourse, as they were claiming, really so unrelated to common experience, which is where the "secular" resided?

Posing these questions to myself, as I proceeded to do in both private reflection and public speeches for about a year, I began to elicit the start of an answer. Ordinary experience, "secular experience," was by no means as smooth, serene, confident, and other-directed as "official" secularism assumed. On the contrary, in the midst of ordinary experience, something quite *unordinary* continually appeared and was reflected over and over in our language about ourselves, our politics, and our world. Our ordinary experience was apparently filled with deep anxieties, anxieties on the one hand that reflected a harrowing *void* in our existence, and on the other that required an answer in terms of power, of meaning, and of hope able to overcome that threatening void. In both of these was manifest what I called a "dimension of ultimacy," an ultimacy of negation and an ultimacy of being and of meaning, which was as evident in our personal and communal life as it was in our language about that life. I found new examples from my own recent experience crowding into my mind.

When I began to work this out in a speech given at Stephens College in early 1964, I recall looking at it with great surprise and saying, "My God, that sounds like Tillich! This is Paulus's shock of nonbeing and power of being and meaning bursting through in your own theology, and you didn't even know that it was there!" That summer I wrote a long, seventy-page critique of the death of God theology followed by an attempted answer to it, a critique and an answer I now recognize as also thoroughly Tillichean.[2] To most of us *then*, however, and certainly to the new rebels, Tillich was a part of the older establishment in theology, a charter mem-

---

2. This paper on the death of God theology circulated widely from 1964 through about 1966, when I finally wrote it out in *Naming the Whirlwind* (Indianapolis: Bobbs-Merrill, 1969).

ber, so to speak, of the *Krisis* theology of the '20s and '30s, and thus
definitely of the older generation against which the revolt was being
mounted. As a consequence, it was not easy for any of us to see him
directly as a participant in *our* generation's theological problems, problems peculiar to our newly defined secular world, and thus as part of *our*
answer to that revolt. I have slowly come to see, first, how this seemingly
new issue of secularity in the '60s repeated in slightly different form his
problems in the '20s, and, secondly, how very dependent on him even
these seemingly "new" thoughts were.

In any case, when I showed this paper to him the next fall (1964), one
year before his death in 1965, to my surprise he looked a little crestfallen:
"But Langdon, I said all this years ago." Not yet knowing all that his
remark meant, I answered: "I know, Paulus. . . . But in this new situation I have *just* discovered what it means, and I have, therefore, only now
found myself saying it after you, but now in my own way."

It was, as I have noted, ironic that Tillich should have been regarded by
many as the effective predecessor and founder of this secular theology. It
was ironic because, as this volume will show, few theologians regarded
secular culture as so essentially dependent on religion ("religious substance"), as religion was in turn dependent on culture. Correspondingly,
few understood nature and culture as so permeated with the divine power
and meaning. It was, in fact, precisely as its antagonist that Tillich viewed
himself in relation to this new theology, and thus in turn he regarded that
theology as a direct repudiation of all he had tried to say. In the same
conversation, following his reading of my paper on the death of God
theology, he looked at me even more forlornly and asked, "Tell me,
Langdon, why am I so soon on the dust heap of history?"

I did not have the good sense then to remind him of what he already
knew; whatever worth they were, my answer and critique were both
thoroughly indebted to him and showed the relevance of his thought even
in this new and unexpected situation. Unfortunately, when that "answer"—expanded to be sure but still essentially Tillichean—appeared in
Naming the Whirlwind in 1969, Paulus had been gone from us for four
years. Among other things, the present volume on Tillich's thought will
show as best I can how far from "the dust heap of history" Tillich's modes
of theological thinking are.

In any case, since 1964 my reflective work, while still very much
shaped by the original influence of Niebuhr, as well as by my own
experience, has been fundamentally Tillichean in form. This continuing
dependence has been illustrated, first, in *Naming the Whirlwind* (1969);
then in the book *Religion and the Scientific Future* (1970); in the work on

the philosophy of history, on Providence, and on the concept of God in *Reaping the Whirlwind* (1976); and perhaps most especially in *Message and Existence* (1979) and *Society and the Sacred* (1981).

It was because of this list of clearly Tillichean works in theology that during 1985–86, when the centenary of Tillich's birth in 1886 was being planned and celebrated, I was asked to write several articles and to give a number of addresses summarizing and commemorating his thought. Five of the following chapters (chapters 4, 6, 8, 9 and 10) represent reworked versions of these articles and addresses on different aspects of Tillich's theology. When these were completed, I realized they represented the possible beginnings of a book-length study of Tillich, and so I went to work to fill out this original nucleus. Hence the present volume.

In this volume I quote Tillich many, many times. This is for several reasons. First, because one of the treasured legacies of Tillich's life for those who knew and worked with him was the incredible stamp that his personal presence made on each of us. His was a presence that none of us forgot, and vivid memories of his being in all its uniqueness—stories about him—accompany all our recollections and interpretations of his thought. One of the most vivid aspects of his presence, though not the only one, was his use of language. He used words unconventionally, sometimes clumsily, much more often with great imagination and subtlety, as if he had *just* come across this word and was delighted with it, holding it up before us like a jewel with different colored light within it, admiring its history, its different facets of meaning, its brilliance.

Always this exceedingly creative, often hilarious, use of words was accompanied by a characteristically unique accent, a way of speaking sounds that to us all fitted perfectly his great insight into the meanings of words and his novel use of them. This accent, to be sure, had not always been greeted with delight. When he first came to New York in 1933, Tillich's accent was apparently exceedingly heavy; and this compounded with his strange use of words—not to mention his difficult and novel ideas!—to make much of his speech fairly impenetrable. By 1946, however, when I first heard him, these barriers of speech were gone, and only the difficulty of his ideas impressed the hearer. What remained in his speech, therefore, was a voice of very deep and resonant power, a brilliant and original use of our language, and the lingering traces of that early and now charming accent—all of this making for most of us a consistent and quite fascinating synthesis with the strangeness, depth, and originality of his thought. His accent and his idiosyncratic use of words were to his friends as much a part of "Tillich" as were the insights and categories of his system. It is for this reason that in quoting him in this volume I have tried to indicate the general flavor of that accent. The *way* he said something was as much Tillich as *what* he said, and so a quote set in, say, a full-bodied American accent simply would not ring true.

I wish to express my affectionate gratitude to many members of the North American Tillich Society and colleagues in the appropriate study of his thought: particularly the late Jack Boozer of Emory University, Durwood Foster of the Pacific School of Religion, Ronald Stone of Pittsburgh Theological Seminary, Roy Morrison of Wesley Seminary, and Mary Ann Stenger of Louisville University. Gwendolyn Barnes, a colleague and helper at the Divinity School, has, with remarkably cheerful good humor and patience, typed and retyped these chapters. In particular, I would like to mention John Christopherson, presently of Hope Lutheran Church in Bozeman, Montana, who has helped me immensely with the references and has prepared the excellent index. Finally, it is with genuine affection and many exceedingly happy memories that, with mingled pride at their accomplishments, gratitude at the wonder of these "golden years" together, and regret that now in the spring of 1989 they are over, I dedicate this book to my colleagues for the past twenty-six years at the Divinity School: deans, faculty, staff, and students.

Langdon Gilkey

The Divinity School
The University of Chicago

Part One

Introduction to the System

1

Tillich's Early Political Writings

Tillich began as a political theologian, the major reflective member of a group of German socialists who perceived, in that post-war (World War I) period, the opportunity for creative and radical social change in Germany. This group named itself the "Kairos Circle" and its movement, "Religious Socialism." Although clearly they intended to help bring socialism to a deeply ailing Germany, they wished to propose a reformed or transformed socialism, a philosophically and religiously deepened form of socialist thought pruned—so they felt—of the "bourgeois errors" that orthodox socialist theory had adopted in the nineteenth century. Tillich—then thirty-five to forty-five—was the most important theorist of this movement, and his major writings from 1923 through 1933 (with the exception of *The System of the Sciences*) were devoted to formulating and advocating the principles of religious socialism.[1]

As we shall see, this represented a complex enterprise. First of all—this being Tillich—the formulation of the theory of religious socialism presupposed and so necessarily included a view of human being and of history. In this social theory, therefore, is present an early politically oriented form of the developed system with which the remainder of this volume is concerned. It will be of interest to point out not only the continuities but the surprising differences with his later thought. Secondly, as Tillich was well aware, religious socialism found itself in a very complex struggle, a war, so to speak, on several fronts at once. First of all, it must counter the

---

1. The principle documents on which this study is based are "Basic Principles of Religious Socialism" (1923), "Christianity and Modern Society" (1928), "Protestantism as a Critical and Creative Principle" (1928), and "Religious Socialism" (1930). All of these are found in *Political Expectation (PE)*. There are two further books of interest here: *The Socialist Decision* (1933; ET 1977) and *The Religious Situation* (1925; ET 1932). For further references to what Tillich meant by "religious socialism," cf. *SD*, 70f., 79, 145f.; and *PE*, 8, 47–66, 87–88, 176–80.

representatives of traditional feudal society, the residual organic, hier-archical structures and rankings of pre-bourgeois German life. Secondly, as its main antagonist, came the defenders of bourgeois liberalism, repre-senting the dominant economic rulers of capitalist Germany. And thirdly, already impatient in the wings, were the members of the rising Nazi movement, essentially anti-bourgeois and anti-feudal but appealing to and supported by aspects of each—what Tillich called "political roman-ticism." Against the traditional conservatives and the new totalitarianism, religious socialism must use rational and so bourgeois (Englightenment) arguments; against the bourgeoisie, socialism must on the one hand co-opt elements of conservative and romantic German tradition, but on the other also appeal to newer, deeper (philosophical and religious) princi-ples. This was the dilemma in which Tillich found orthodox socialism, and the theoretical vacuum which the Kairos Circle saw its new viewpoint filling.

*   *   *

Tillich begins his major statement of the religious socialist argument (in *The Socialist Decision*) with an analysis of human nature: "The roots of political thought must be sought in human being itself" (*SD*, 2). Human-ity both exists and questions itself; it is and it stands against itself; it is both being and consciousness in their unity and in their distinction (*SD*, 2–3; *PE*, 46–47). We note here *(a)* the Heideggerian or existentialist anthropology now broadened to undergird a social theory; "the two roots of all political thinking grow out of this unity"; and yet *(b)* the use of the category "being" to demarcate the finite, dependent, "thrown," and vital aspect of humanity as opposed to "spirit," consciousness, self-consciousness, and self-transcendence. The first of these, being, repre-sents our finitude and dependence, our "whence," the inescapable limits of our existence and yet the structure of our vitality and power as living creatures. Tillich refers to this "given" aspect of our humanity, now interpreted politically, as the "powers of origin": soil, blood, family, community, race, nation. These comprise our particularity, definiteness—the *there* of "being there"—and so the grounding power of our being. Social consciousness oriented to "origin," and the appeal to origin, is the root of all conservative and romantic politics (*SD*, 4).

United with being in all human being but distinct from it is the power of *consciousness*. (Consciousness is united with being even in conservative politics which represent a *consciousness* of origin.) Here human nature is able to look at itself and its world, to wonder at and to question its being and origin: "The point where man rises above 'mere being' [*sic*]" (*PE*, 12). This is where the rational and cognitive side of humanity arises: the ability to know self and world, to objectify, to analyze, and to calculate—thus the basis for science. As the seed of memory and expectation, the union of past and future, consciousness represents the capacity to plan, reassemble, and transform existence. Language and technology are its instruments; culture in all its forms is its result. It is concretely manifested in politics, the basis of rational criticism of all that is given, including the ranks and privileges, the hierarchical structures of tradition—what Tillich calls the "sacramental demonries" of traditional social life. A political theory oriented to consciousness, freedom, criticism, and planning is, therefore, "committed to the dissolution of all forms of origin" and to the "rational mastery and rational reassembling of these desacralized elements into structures serving the aims of thought and action" (*SD*, 48, 81–83, 132–33; see also *PE*, 43–44). Tillich calls this liberal and rational political consciousness "the bourgeois principle."[2] As with his later category, "technical reason," this objectivizing, analytical, instrumental consciousness, if autonomous and secular, represents the main, if not the unqualified, antagonist of most of Tillich's thought. This bourgeois consciousness remains optimistic and active because it presupposes a pre-established harmony in objective existence which guarantees order among rational self-serving entities; it also presupposes the subjective rationality of each agent to know and to understand its own self-interest. This faith in objective and subjective harmony is the basis of liberal and democratic society (*SD*, 48–50).

A third element, Tillich argues, is present in or to human being. Later he will call this the dimension of depth, the ground of reason, and the ground and power of being. Now, characteristically, it receives a political, historical, and moral (as opposed to an ontological) definition. "They [human beings] experience a demand that frees them from simply being bound to what is given" (*SD*, 4). This demand points them to the future ("whither?"); it calls for what is not yet, what ought to be, the unconditionally new. This demand is moral and therefore unconditional, the basis, in fact, of morality's unconditional claim; it arises only in relation to another person or persons, and so in community, where persons—not things—make claims on us (*SD*, 6). This demand is, finally, directed at the

---

2. Whether this principle is, in fact, the result of "the bourgeois" system of economic organization is certainly questionable, perhaps for us in ways it was not for the early Tillich. In *Systematic Theology*, Tillich labels this "technical reason" and generally seems to ascribe it to a culture oriented to science, technology, and industrialism—a "nominalist and positivistic" culture. Since the present forms of socialism seem to illustrate this consciousness as thoroughly as do the bourgeois nations, this latter view appears to be the sounder one.

fulfillment, not the abrogation, of the true origin, of our essence as humans. It is the demand for justice. Justice is thus the "true power of being," and is superior to origin (SD, 6). Tillich here seems personalistic, Jewish, moral, and temporally oriented—not unlike much biblical political theology today—and very different from the later Tillich of the system where to many these categories are deeply buried under a massive edifice of ontology. How could the Tillich we know say, as he does here, "the new being is intrinsically unontological"? (SD, 20).

Tillich calls this the prophetic (and Jewish) consciousness. It is oriented to the transcendent and not to the ideal form, as is rational criticism, although in principle it includes rational criticism as it includes and transforms the given social situation (PE, 12–13). It is, says Tillich, enunciating a theme he will repeat again and again, oriented to the transcendent, and this demand mediates to us an unconditional requirement, an ultimate seriousness. (Tillich says the seriousness of rational criticism comes only from its union with prophetic criticism [PE, 15, 20].) Since its source is the transcendent and not the particular form in which the transcendent has been realized, it can be self-critical, not identifying the transcendent with its own relative structure; hence, it is Protestant (PE, 15) or expressive of the Protestant principle.

Secondly, this consciousness is oriented to the future and not to the past, although its future goal or ideal—what is demanded—is the fulfillment of the past, of "true origin," of our essence. Prophetic consciousness is, therefore, suffused with the dialectic of demand and expectation. Tillich identifies this prophetic, transcendent element in consciousness and so in political and cultural life with theonomy: the union (in this discussion) of rational and prophetic criticism, of given situation and demanded outcome, of social fact and the ideal for that fact, of particular and universal (and in his later thought, of finite symbol and unconditional ground). We should note again how this category or dimension of the unconditional, so central to all of Tillich's thought, arises here morally and politically, and above all in a temporal framework, as demand for action for the sake of the future, of justice, and especially of the concrete new which is to come.

In any case, these are the three elements in the human situation from which proceed the three forms or, better, aspects of political consciousness, of political theory, and ultimately of political action. These are the powers of origin on which conservative and romantic politics—the politics of traditional feudal Germany and of the new national socialism—are based; the power of rational criticism, cognition, and transformation on which the bourgeois world of modern society is based; and there is the presence of prophetic demand and expectation. The relations between these three are extremely complex. Tillich's political theory represents, on one level, an effort to sort out and rearrange these relations so as to establish, over against the old and new powers of origin, *and* against the recent bourgeois secularism, a new combination of the three: religious socialism. Origin appears in two forms: traditional, conservative, class and status politics, on the one hand, and the romantic, communally oriented appeal of the Nazis to blood, race, soil, and nation on the other. In between comes the rational, prudential bourgeois spirit. This critical, rational spirit leveled and eliminated the securities and vitalities of origin within the proletariat, stripping the latter of their traditional dignity, status, and privileges, dehumanizing them and eliminating their family and national loyalties. On the other hand, bourgeois society has co-opted for itself (i.e., for the sake of bourgeois rule) the patriarchal, class, and national loyalties of origin. Thus to Tillich, present capitalistic (and democratic) culture is a "demonic" synthesis of the powers of origin and of rational, prudential consciousness thoroughly devoted to the dominance of the property-owning bourgeois class.

On the other side is socialism, or better, theonomous socialism, that is, religious socialism. Socialism is, of course, like its opposite, the bourgeois consciousness, oriented to criticism, to demand, and to the future; its aim is liberation and justice. Thus it also criticizes and refashions the traditional sacral structures of origin which have no orientation either to the future or to justice. But in principle, socialism recognizes these "powers of origin": family, person, community, nation—as essential to life's support, preservation, vitality, and meaning. No political form can be without these concrete grounds for our being (*SD*, 86–87, 99, 106, 128, 137; *PE*, 59, 68). The reason is that these powers of origin mediate directly the unconditional power to be as well as all forms of life and of meaning. Without them, rational autonomy withers. Bourgeois society has removed them and left only the autonomous reason and autonomous will, directed now at infinite power and infinite satisfaction (*PE*, 71–74). Socialism, therefore, must learn not only to criticize these traditional forms in the name of justice and liberate us from their "demonry" (*PE*, 68); it must also refashion and co-opt them, recognizing their essential place as creative bases of all human being (*PE*, 70, 74). Of course, when as a result of the desiccation of security and meaning in bourgeois society the proletariat is left empty and vulnerable, these lost powers of origin return as the "new demonry" of romantic politics: Nazism. Here blood, soil, race, and nation reappear in demonic form, that is, as destructive and demonic[3] forms of the unconditional or sacred.[4] Against this form of the powers of origin, socialism must, of course, protest (ironically alongside the bourgeois powers), first in the name of all finite cultural forms and their autonomy, and so of liberalism, of rational criticism, and of its freedom (for the truth), and in the name of the prophetic demand for justice.

The relation of socialism to the bourgeois principle is even more complex. Socialism is radically critical of the bourgeois power structure, the rule of society by the owners of the means of production. Such ownership, and the social and economic freedom to use it rationally, was made legitimate—that is, as a means to justice—through confidence in a natural harmony of social forces; where self-interest is rationally pursued, harmony will result. Socialism sees through this and thus rejects all talk of an objective harmony as well as of the rationality of the interested will (SD, 50, 69). Thus socialism unequivocally rejects the cynical "class" disposition of property and its power in the hands of owners alone, and it repudiates as well the latter's idealistic affirmation of harmony and rationality as a cover for the unlimited will of the bourgeois managers. This rejection by socialism is in the name of justice and of expectation; thus, it represents (though the socialist may not know it) an illustration for our time of the prophetic consciousness, of a temporal theonomy, and of, in fact, the kairos (PE, 38, 55, 61, 180). Also, as noted, socialism should reinterpret and refashion its relation to origins, which it mistakenly repudiated because it rightly criticized (with the bourgeoisie) the sacralization of traditional forms.

The relations of socialism to bourgeois culture are not, however, all negative. Unfortunately for its own good, socialism has adopted far too many "bourgeois errors": the worship of science and technology, the

---

3. Tillich defines demonic as the form-destroying power of the unconditional as opposed to the form-creative power of the unconditional, which is the divine (PE, 66–68, 110–11). The difference is the effect on finite and rational forms by the finite vehicles of the unconditional, in this case totalitarian, romantic forms. This corresponds to his later definition of heteronomy as an oppressive, anti-autonomous appearance of the ground of reason.

4. Note that Tillich is one of the few who saw the deeper spiritual roots of Nazism as offering in distorted form the lost necessities of social existence to an empty, anxious proletariat. Most liberal interpreters then saw Nazism as an instrument of the bourgeois rulers in order to continue their rule, and the proletarian participation in Nazism as a result of the clever propaganda of the bourgeoisie, as an intellectual error, so to speak. Tillich sees it as the almost irresistible appeal of lost primal security and meaning, a much more accurate and profound interpretation.

concentration on rational analysis and rational reassembling, the emphasis on a materialistic metaphysics, a quantitative and homogeneous interpretation of objects, and the priority of physicalist causality even in history and social sequences. It has, further, accepted the bourgeois view of human being as impelled by quantitative "needs" and satisfied by quantitative "pleasures"; it even absorbed the bourgeois confidence in pure, autonomous rationality and so its radical, anti-religious stance. For Tillich at this point, all the scientistic, positivistic, quantitative, autonomous, and atheistic elements of socialism—that is to say, its radical secularism—are part of the bourgeois principle and, therefore, alien to the real socialist principle, despite the presence of all of this in present socialist countries and despite his own insight that the original form of capitalism was a *theonomous* Calvinism (*PE*, 3–4).

Such was his disdain for bourgeois culture and his loyalty to the socialist principle that all of the faults of modern socialism, evident in both capitalist and socialist societies, were ascribed to the bourgeois principle alone. And the same faults in socialist lands were seen as deviations from the socialist principle and blamed on the bourgeois principle, although both illustrated a theonomous and a secular form. Later, while he still preferred a mixed economy, he tended to see both democratic capitalism and democratic socialism as ambiguous, to regard as fundamental a balance between economic and political power,[5] and as a consequence, to assign the basic fault to a heedless and overconfident modern rationality, an unjustified confidence in autonomy generated by scientific success, technical mastery, and industrial surpluses. As a result, instead of the bourgeois principle, he tended to blame most of this on "technical and autonomous reason."

In any case, for the Tillich of the '20s and '30s, socialism had mistakenly interpreted itself in terms of nineteenth century bourgeois culture as scientific, quantitative, economically determined, and metaphysically materialistic, as well as anti-family, anti-community, anti-national, and anti-religious (*SD*, 79–84). In doing so, it betrayed its own spiritual principle and weakened itself politically and theoretically.[6] In these writings Tillich seeks to correct these errors.

---

5. Cf. James Luther Adams's remarks in the introduction to *PE*, xix–xxx.

6. One can sense the magnitude and originality—not to mention the kairotic confidence—of Tillich's enterprise if one imagines a similar analysis of modern democratic-capitalistic society showing how, in becoming secular as it has done, it has (1) betrayed its original form in Calvinist theonomy; (2) caused by this error its own observable short-comings; and (3) might rectify them by a return to theonomy. Clearly as this shows, Tillich had earlier rejected an interpretation

For Tillich, therefore, the fundamental principle of socialism is theonomy; true socialism is religious socialism. Without this "depth"—to
use his later word—socialism falls into contradiction and is forced, so to
speak, to adopt the alien framework of bourgeois thought. Socialism
began with the radical experience of disharmony (*SD*, 89): disharmony in
the objective and economic system leading to depression and unemploy-
ment, and disharmony subjectively in the experience of alienation, vulnerability, insecurity. Even the bourgeois rulers were neither rational nor
prudential, but driven by an unlimited urge for power and for satisfaction
(*PE*, 70, 74; Tillich later uses the term, "concupiscence"). How in the face
of this visible disharmony, the actuality of estrangement, can socialist
expectation persist? Socialism "must reckon with a leap that cannot be
explained in terms of present reality" (*SD*, 69); "it contains an element of
prophetic expectation, the expectation of new being" (*SD*, 69). The
proletariat are here pictured as inwardly alienated and outwardly helpless;
how are they to be the ones to transform the world through reason?
Tillich accuses orthodox socialism of "believing in miracles" (*SD*, 73, 76).
Socialism has, through its self-misinterpretation, confined itself to immanence (*SD*, 69), to confidence in a necessitating scientific law of economic
development without demand, spiritual participation, or grounds for
autonomous action. For Tillich, this entire contradiction "cries out for"
(later "drives toward" or "raises the question of") a *religious* interpretation, a theonomous depth. The affirmation of expectation is not a description of immanent scientific laws but a mode of religious symbolism
pointing to a transcendent ground and based on faith (*SD*, 70–71). The
"new" that is to come is not an ideal utopia unrelated to the past but the
fulfillment of origin, and so hiddenly connected with it. As a consequence, proletarian action for the new is not a natural necessity but a
response to an unconditional demand; the powers of origin are not
opposed to socialist justice but its real and vital basis. Finally, the proletariat can become the vehicle of a new justice only if they remain self-
critical, conscious of the possibilities of their own ideological betrayal.
Expectation and demand, therefore, the fundamental characteristics of
"secular" socialism, point inexorably beyond the secular, and beyond the
bourgeois rational criticism, to prophetic consciousness, to a relation to
and a dependence on the transcendent (as he here terms it), or "depth" as
he later will call it. Only the transcendent as the continuing source and
ground of being, of demand, and of the unity of origin and fulfillment can

---

based on the process of *cultural secularization* and opted instead for an analysis in
terms of *economic structures*. My sense is that he later tended toward the former
mode of interpretation.

provide an intrinsic foundation for a socialist interpretation of history. Real socialism is, therefore, *theonomous* socialism; otherwise, it contradicts itself. This is a powerful argument in political theology. Nevertheless, its form (the self-contradiction of finitude in estrangement drives toward and raises the question of theonomy) reminds us inevitably of common Tillichean arguments scattered throughout Tillich's later apologetical and theological works.

This entire series of political and theological concepts is united in the category of *kairos*, the name of the circle of religious socialists. *Kairos*—if I may put it this way—is the central concept of a *temporal* (or process) *theonomy*. *Kairos* represents the unity in a specific time of the eternal and the unconditional with the historical, the finite, the particular, the concrete, and so the relative. It represents, therefore, "the fullness of time" when historical developments, reaching a point of *crisis*, prepare for something *new* (compare the later relation of the "shock of nonbeing" with the appearance of revelation). It represents also an unconditional demand, the demand for *justice* in that situation (*SD*, 140–41), for a concrete and particular justice, one related to but transformative of the given situation (*SD*, 103, 130–32). Thus *kairos* unites, first of all, past and future, old and radically new, origin and demand, being and the fulfillment of being. It also unites in temporal fashion the universal and the particular, the absolute and the relative; its coming represents the appearance of the Eternal Now in our particular historical moment, a coming that manifests the new possibilities of creation (origin) in that time (*RS*, "Introduction"), a new appearance leading toward fulfillment. Perhaps most important in these writings, it gives an ultimate and unconditional seriousness (import) to the responsibilities and possibilities of our political situation (and so to justice) (*PE*, 15–20), without either idealizing a particular social resolution (the demonic) or escaping the historical and the relative into an ideal and abstract utopia. For Tillich, then as later, utopia, while a genuine expression of possibility, represents also the danger of irrelevance or cruel fanaticism (compare "The Truth and Untruth of Utopia," *PE*, 168–74). *Kairos* thus unites with the Protestant principle of self-criticism: the transcendent source of our *kairos* (ultimate concern) energizes and makes possible a quest for justice, but the historical embodiment of the *kairos* is itself conditioned by the given situation, concrete and therefore relative, and thus subject to radical criticism as is all else in history.

In the category of *kairos*, therefore, Tillich formulates a new and very significant conception of the religious and its relation to the world. Religion here represents the transcendent meaning of the finite and all of life, not a separate area of common life (*PE*, 38, 103, 130–32). This transcendent or religious dimension is crucial to the finite as the source of its being, criticism, and possibilities; but the finite event or occasion itself is not to be identified with the transcendent: "Grace is actual in objects, not as an object but as the transcendent meaning of an object" (*PE*, 25), and "the form of grace is realized only in rational forms . . . it gives them a meaning that transcends them . . ." (*PE*, 26). Thus, "prophetic criticism transcends rational criticism and yet at the same time incorporates it within itself" (*PE*, 27). In church and culture alike, therefore, the ultimate manifests itself and gives life and meaning to those relative and cultural forms; yet they remain finite, relative, and estranged, not to be identified with the ultimate they express. Hence prophetic and Protestant self-criticism unite with the rational criticism of forms, just as the autonomous life of culture expresses and yet distorts the ultimate meanings pervasive within it.

Through this concept of *kairos*, in sum, appear in early form Tillich's most fundamental later principles of social analysis: the necessity of the transcendent for the existence and creativity of the historical; the principle of radical criticism of all historical forms (secular or religious); and finally, "all culture is actualized religion, and all religion is actualized as culture" (*PE*, 63). This is, of course, the principle of *theonomy* here expressed in terms of historical passage from origin to expectation; or, in political terms, as the historical movement through *kairos* from the given being of autonomous capitalism to a larger fulfillment of justice in religious socialism. In religious socialism, therefore, Tillich presents to us *our kairos*, a modern example of theonomy: that is to say, a theonomous society established on the ground of *our* historical conditions, namely, the modern bourgeois, autonomous, rational, and industrial culture. "Socialism is prophetism on the soil of an autonomous, self-sufficient world" (*SD*, 101, 109). This prospect of a new yet more just form of modernity was the exciting expectation of the Kairos Circle, expressed powerfully as early as 1923 but most fully in 1931–32, when *The Socialist Decision* was written. By the time the latter volume was published in 1933, however, the expectation it embodied could already be seen to be doomed. Political romanticism in Nazi form had taken over, and Tillich was forced to leave Germany for other, ironically even more bourgeois, societies.

*   *   *

In the remainder of this chapter we shall, in a more specific fashion, relate the concepts in these early political works to Tillich's later categories. Certainly the most important one, emphasized throughout this chapter, is the temporal or process meaning to theonomy which the category of *kairos* has expressed. Theonomy, the participation of the transcendent in and through the autonomy and creativity of the finite and the historical, is here a *temporal process*, achieved in the historical passage from origin through *kairos*, and through free political action in response to the *kairos*, action towards justice or fulfillment. The eternal appears not vertically but through the horizontal movement of historical time, from the immediate and the concrete past to the immediate and possible future, through the passage of what Tillich later would call destiny into enacted freedom. In these early writings even forms are temporal, emerging as new forms in each historical situation and then being replaced by newer possibilities: "Form in the spiritual and social sense is always . . . emerging form" (*PE*, 20), and "rational criticism is the criticism directed by the emerging form to the form that is passing away" (*PE*, 20; see also 98). The dynamic character of reality, even in its formal character as logos, is here unequivocally clear.

This point is not unimportant in Tillichean interpretation. Most American readers of Tillich have begun with the first volume of *Systematic Theology, The Courage to Be*, and *Theology of Culture*. In these works, theonomy has largely a vertical, almost neo-platonic implication, the presence of the unconditional ground of being in and through the finite symbol. As a consequence, to many readers the clearly dynamic, temporal, process emphasis of the third volume of *Systematic Theology* came as a surprise—to Tillicheans, a vindication of their sense that Tillich was not the static thinker that both process theologians and the later eschatological political theologians have maintained.[7] These early works which we have just reviewed show the error of the common interpretation: not only is "being" for Tillich not at all static nor the dynamic a new element, but in fact the dynamic elements of Tillich's later thought (compare *ST* I:241–52, 261–79; *ST* III, pt. IV, sec. III, pt. V, secs. I and II) represent only a mild reappearance of the fundamental motifs of Tillich's process or historical view of being. Tillich always associated his own thought with what he called "historical" rather than unhistorical interpretations of reality and with a "victory of time over space" (*PE*, 140–54); this self-interpretation takes on concrete content when we uncover the dynamic, historical character of Tillich's theonomy in these early works.

It also becomes apparent that, contrary again to the claims of process theologians, a dynamic, historical view of reality as a whole is neither dependent on the metaphysically limited character of God nor denied by a concept of God as unconditional. Nor, incidentally, did process thought

---

7. Cf. the excellent insight in Guy Hammond's *Man in Estrangement* (Nashville: Vanderbilt University Press, 1965) that Tillich's theology, far from being neo-platonic, really represents a dynamic ontology.

begin with Whitehead; in fact, Whitehead and Hartshorne represent—as Tillich's writings from 1923 show—almost (except for Teilhard) the last, rather than the first, examples of process interpretations of reality. This should have been clear from the examples of Hegel and of most nineteenth-century thinkers; it is now made clear through these early writings of Tillich. The metaphysical absoluteness and/or relativity of God, the question of the finitude of God, is a different philosophical issue than the ultimately static or dynamic character of reality as a whole.

In these early writings, especially *The Socialist Decision*, the category of "origin" is extremely significant; to my knowledge it does not appear at all after 1940. This does not mean that what origin points to or expresses vanishes; rather, the concepts involved reappear in changed form. As we have seen, origin points to our being or existence (note how differently these words are used later), the fact that we are as "thrown" and so limited, both in the fundamental conditions or limits of life but also in our concrete destiny as *here*, in this place and at this time, in this social and familial world (compare *SD*, 1–6). This aspect of our human being is, says Tillich, the source or ground of our vitality, perseverance, security, and effectiveness. Hence the "powers of origin": soil, blood, sex, family, community, nation, represent necessary principles of being or vitality in all of life and all politics. Nothing finite nor any political order can subsist for long without them (*SD*, 85–89, 98–100, 106–7, 128–30, 136–37).

In another even earlier work of 1923, "Basic Principles of Religious Socialism" (which now appears in *Political Expectation*), Tillich gives a more detailed analysis of origin and its power. Here he distinguishes "the sacramental attitude" from rational criticism, on the one hand, and prophetic criticism, on the other. The sacramental attitude is clearly the spiritual or psychological equivalent to the powers of origin. It is, he says, "the consciousness of the presence of the divine within a finite object"; here lies, he continues, "the root of sacred symbols and forms, of the sacred relationships of community and [note] justice" (*PE*, 58–59). This presence of the sacred through symbols (soil, blood, and community) and through social relations (the status, ranks, and privileges of rulers and owners) sanctifies and empowers these realities: "They owe to this character (as sacraments) their power, endurance, and invulnerability, but at the same time they owe to it the abundance of life which they mediate, and the meaning of life which they reveal" (*PE*, 59). In traditional societies, persons, and especially dominant persons, derive their "import, abundance and importance" (*PE*, 73) from these social spaces, relations, and roles, from what Tillich calls their "sacramental consecration." These persons "are" *in* their particular place, lineage, rank, and role; their power and significance are here *given,* matters of status as opposed to matters earned or contracted.

On the other hand, in traditional societies significant things, dominant persons, and significant social relations are hardly "merely" finite; as a consequence, persons are not yet *autonomous.* For it is in favor of these sacred objects, relations, and ranks that the autonomy and value of other persons are sacrificed; thus, radical injustice and exploitation result. Hence traditional societies, upheld by these "powers of origin," are also filled with "natural demonries": creaturely realities empowered by the unconditional in forms that are destructive rather than creative of other forms (*PE,* 67–74). Evident here is an early form of Tillich's important category of *participation,* the dynamic, creative, and empowering presence of the power of being in the conditioned—a participation fundamental to the being, power, and vitality of each entity and each culture, but a participation redolent with ambiguities.

This category of "sacramental consecration" as explanatory of the powers of origin is fundamental for a number of Tillich's later ideas. First of all, besides being an early form of the significant notion of participation and the ground of being, this category represents the early predecessor of the concept of *heteronomy.* Heteronomy, we recall, has two aspects: first, it represents the sacred ground of reason appearing in demonic form, a sacred tradition with unconditional authority and thus a tradition repressive of the creative autonomous forms of culture. Secondly, heteronomy appears always in stark opposition to autonomous humanism: to the principles of rational criticism and self-direction in personal and cultural life. Heteronomy, therefore, is challenged by rational criticism and prophetic criticism alike, though its main antagonist is certainly secular humanism. Tillich's favorite examples of heteronomy were the Catholic heteronomy of the late medieval and Counter-Reformation periods, and the orthodox Protestant heteronomy of the seventeenth and the early eighteenth centuries. But he recognized that secular ideologies, especially those like Nazism, which appealed to the bonds of origin, and which made ultimate claims to assent and obedience, could well represent even more demonic heteronomies. As with sacramental consecration, the sacred dimension of cultural and social life is indispensable; but it is also potentially demonic. And it is, as he noted in *The Socialist Decision,* always hovering in the wings at the end of an autonomous, rational, individual culture in which existence has been left empty and vulnerable, drained of its inherent power and meaning.

This category of sacramental consecration, secondly, is very helpful, it seems to me, in providing insight into what is meant by "liberation."

Liberation—for example, for blacks, for women, for colonial peoples—
means of course justice: equal political justice, equal rights, equal economic opportunity and pay, equal social access. But more than this is
implied, an implication carried by words like respect, dignity, integrity,
freedom, autonomy, centeredness, self-direction, and the dignity stemming from them. Here I would suggest that Tillich has helped us to see
what this "more" is, or, better, what it is that prevents equal justice both
from becoming actualized and, even if objectively realized, from representing real liberation. The problem, so it seems to me here, is sacramental consecration: the presence of unconditional value and power in one
special group, whether it be a class, a sex, a race, a rank. When this
presence is there, existence is stabilized, empowered and given meaning,
to be sure; this, of course, is the appeal of any traditional status society.
But correspondingly this sacred preference for some means inevitably that
others are systematically denied the status of full persons, centered persons capable of enacting their own unique destiny, and thus persons
capable of receiving the respect and dignity due to persons (PE, 73–79,
83–85). For the organic unity and harmony of the whole, some here are
sacrificed as autonomous persons; this sacramental consecration is therefore a "sacramental demonry" (PE, 62–79).

Patriarchalism as an ethos prevents the liberation of women even if
objective relations and possibilities are "just," because in consecrating the
male person and the male role, it drains the female person and role of
power, dignity, and autonomy. The same is, perhaps, the deepest problem
of racial imbalance; however much wealth and political power black
persons may accumulate, they feel the sacramental consecration of the
white. Hence Tillich so emphatically protested the return of any explicit
patriarchalism in political romanticism: "Socialism cannot possibly toler-
ate the restoration of male patriarchialism" (SD, 152–53). Without rational
and prophetic criticism of the sacramental consecration of leading or
ruling groups in society, there can be no liberation and so no justice.
Tillich here has, I think, helped us to understand what is deeply felt in a
social situation calling for liberation.

A closely associated subject is that of power, its relation to community,
on the one hand, and to justice, on the other (compare SD, 139–42, 80–
84). Here again we see Tillich's unusual sensitivity to both the sacramental, organic basis of life as well as the necessities of rational form—and the
unconditional claim that mediates between these two. As we might now
expect, Tillich begins his discussion of political power and of the state by
saying that "all authority is founded cultically and sacramentally: by
participation in the powers of origin" (PE, 80). Thus power adheres to
traditional ruling groups, based on family, sex, class, race, "blood." As

Tillich says, power is ultimately founded, and rulers rule, upon the recognition "for the most part unconscious, of the surpassing power of being of another" (*PE*, 53).[8] Clearly this "sacramental" base for power leads, as we have seen, to rank injustice and exploitation. As a consequence, both rational criticism (the bourgeois principle) and prophetic criticism direct an essential challenge at these inherited structures of authority.

Power, however, is necessary in any political community (*PE*, 52). First, power is necessary in order to unify the community so that it can act with one will in any given situation; only with a unified will is a community able to enact freedom (its own freedom) in history and thus shape, in part, its own destiny (*PE*, 52–53; *SD*, 138). Secondly, power is necessary to posit justice and to control or tame the inevitable presence of arbitrary and selfish will in any community.[9] Criticism, therefore, whether bourgeois criticism or prophetic criticism, cannot hope to dispense with power. Here again is the socialist dilemma. Socialism fears the sacramental basis for power, and so mistakenly flirts with anarchism; it also shares the bourgeois criticism of true traditional forms of power. How, then, is it possible to establish power *legitimately*—with a sacramental consecration that can unify the community—and yet *justly*? How can the power of being of a group be affirmed, and yet justice in its life be realized? This question, needless to say, haunts every community in history, whether traditional, democratic capitalist, socialist, communist. Tillich's answer is interesting, and like most of these early views, optimistic from today's vantage point. It shows again (1) the temporal orientation of his interpretation of culture and its movement from sacramental injustice ("being") to justice ("consciousness and conscience"). It also shows (2) how at this political stage his cultural thought is already theonomous, and (3) how on the concrete level "in theonomy being is fulfilled in justice."

Tillich's answer depends on the historical movement, which all his political thought presupposes, from being to consciousness, from origin

8. Again: "This [social power] can only be understood in terms of the social superiority of the group in question. Its superiority can be expressed in various ways: magical, military, economic, cultural, etc. The group in power, however, always has some superior qualities because of which others submit to it" (*SD*, 138).

9. "Justice can assert itself as justice only by restraint of arbitrary will, and . . . the elimination of restraint would give power to arbitrary will—thus it would mean a surrender of the theocratic to the demonic" (*PE*, 83). Thus, "justice needs for its realization a will that posits and upholds it . . . justice needs power in order to be realized" (PE, 80).

through demand, to fulfillment in justice. Again we must continue his analysis of power to understand this historical development of legitimate authority. Power, which is necessary in community, depends, says Tillich, on *assent* or *consent*, on what he will later term "participation." Force may be necessary in given situations and must always be visible. But if the sacramental power that elicits assent be gone, and if as a consequence force rather than the inner assent of the community is the basis of power, then in effect the community illustrates the struggle for power. The group still ruling has "become one of the groups fighting for power" (*SD*, 139). Thus, "power is never based on force; it is always grounded in consent, whether expressed or unexpressed or, perhaps, fragmentary" (*SD*, 139).

In a traditional society this assent depends on sacramental consecration, the traditional and numinous authority of "powers of origin." As rational and prophetic criticism appear and as the autonomous powers of judgment, assent, and decision begin to characterize all members of society, however, these sacramentally grounded forms of power no longer become viable; protest and revolution remove them. Now assent, and the power that flows from it, has a different character. In a community composed of autonomous persons, an identity of will between the rulers and the ruled becomes the necessary condition of assent. Power is now based on an eros, a participation, a common will or "love" grounded in justice: "Such consent is given because those who assent to the exercise of power consider the way in which the unified will is executed to be just. The exercise of power appears to be just when all members of a society can acknowledge that their own will is contained in the will of the whole" (*SD*, 139). Thus justice is the fulfillment of primal being, and a just society of sacramental consecration, since in an autonomous culture it is justice that elicits assent and so eros; and so "all power is based on justice" (*SD*, 140). In sum, "the development of a meaningful society, in which the possibility exists to recognize the meaningful power of being of another, or, what amounts to the same thing, the formation of a community as the unity of power and love, is the socio-ethical ideal of religious socialism" (*PE*, 53). In this coming together of power, love, and justice, there is what Tillich calls "the sacred import of creative theonomy." Here, as has been already seen, the sacral powers of origin, the rational and prophetic consciousness, and the fulfillment of being are united in love and justice. History moves from powers of origin, with their "legitimate" but unjust structures of traditional dominance, through prophetic *criticism* and *kairos*, to fulfillment based on structures of justice, the whole process being one of sacramental participation ending in the culminating sacrament of theonomy. Thus does "secular" history manifest a theonomous movement parallel to that of the *ecclesia*, namely, the movement of its catholic (sacramental) substance, through the autonomous yet prophetic principle, to fulfillment of both its sacramental and its prophetic elements—which is the fragmentary presence of the Kingdom.

A final, important theme developed in these writings and continued throughout Tillich's life was that of the principles of Protestantism and of Catholicism. Tillich's revolutionary conception of the relation of the divine to culture (really a new interpretation of the relation of the unconditional to the conditioned, the infinite to the finite) has been mentioned: the divine does not replace or transfigure (supernaturalize) the finite and "stand beside it as a separate, distinct, sacred place." Rather, the divine represents the transcendent meaning, the unconditional import of the finite, a power and meaning through which the finite exists, perseveres, and is fulfilled. Thus religion is the depth of culture, culture the expression of religion. This, of course, is the principle of theonomy: the finite remains finite and relative but becomes creative in and through the divine. As we have just seen, power, love, and justice are its results. Further, this theonomous understanding is the basis for rational and prophetic criticism, and for their unity. Prophetic criticism joins rational criticism in subjecting the finite to a critique of its hubris (*PE*, 12–13); in turn, rational criticism depends on prophetic depth for its ultimate seriousness, its transcendent meaning (*PE*, 15–20). As finite, any historical vehicle of the divine remains ambiguous and subject to estrangement, be it a natural entity, a person, a community, a movement. It is in need of criticism if it would be itself; the finite that mistakes itself for the unconditional within it is precisely the demonic. Thus each entity at once depends on, participates in, and manifests the divine insofar as it remains aware of its finitude and fallibility and points beyond itself. In this the finite entity, as Tillich's later thought will put it, becomes a true "symbol" or "medium" of revelation, an example of the New Being once manifested decisively in Jesus who is the Christ.

This understanding of the religious as theonomous (grasped originally, I believe, from the christological model) has appeared very early in Tillich's writings, at least as early as 1923; naturally, it led to a new interpretation of religious institutions, as exemplified in his essay on Protestantism in 1929. Despite the intrinsic interrelation for Tillich of finite and infinite, of culture and religion, he clearly recognizes their distinction and the actuality of their estrangement. For him, the religious, therefore, must also be represented in particular and special finite entities and communities, what he calls "religious culture" (*PE*, 27) and "the visible church" in order to become explicit and effective: "This [the unity of rational and prophet criticism] presupposes that prophetic criticism is itself supported by some being, by some religious form from which criticism proceeds" (*PE*, 22). Religious communities, therefore, are distinct but not separate from the culture they inhabit and whose "unconditional depth" or "ultimate concerns" they represent and mediate. If they are identical with the culture in its rational forms, they cease to mediate the transcendent in power and criticism; ultimately, they become empty of their own content. If they are identical with the ultimate they mediate, then their religious forms become themselves transcendent; one form of being is thus exempt from criticism, and the institution becomes demonic. Grace—the category he uses in this connection—"is something present but not something objective. It is actual in objects, not as an object but as the transcendent meaning of an object" (*PE*, 25).[10]

This fundamental viewpoint leads, then, to the interpretation of Catholicism and Protestantism.[11] Catholicism represents, in the form of religious institution, the sacramental consecration we have seen in Tillich's interpretation of culture: here the divine is immediately present within the powers, rites, and officiants of the institution itself. Thus Catholicism represents an unequivocal and direct union of the sacred and the finite religious form, or as Tillich terms it, a "tangible" or "visible" form of grace (*PE*, 33). In one sense, this is the power and validity of Catholicism: "Grace is only grace if grace is present" (*PE*, 30); without the Catholic substance, "there is no church at all" (*PE*, 10). On the other hand, as we have noted, when the medium is identified too closely with the divine it represents, then a finite form itself is made unconditionally sacred and authoritative—and that is the demonic. "A form of grace that has been objectively fixated raises the forms in which it appears—the rational forms that it absorbs into itself [for example Thomism]—above the level of change" (*PE*, 37). But the forms of grace, if not grace itself, are

---

10. The similarity with Barth in roughly the same period, despite all their differences, is striking. In neither does anything finite, even or especially the church, and proclamation within the church, "possess" grace. Grace is there in judgment and (for Barth) promise, (for Tillich) transcendent meaning. Thus for both the prophetic category is "anticipation," expectancy, awaiting in faith its promise if one looks beyond one's self and one's community—and all the vehicles of grace—for its coming (*PE*, 26–27).

11. It should be recalled that these essays (1925–35) precede Vatican II by more than thirty years and follow shortly upon the sharp condemnation of Catholic modernism in the 1920s. The Catholicism that Tillich knew was Vatican I Catholicism at its zenith: rigidly neo-Thomist, dogmatic, rational, and legalistic, and essentially hierarchical, even ultramontane. There was as yet no visible sign of the startling appearance of "grace" in the early 1960s! It is surprising, therefore, that Tillich's analysis of pre-Vatican II Catholicism was as positive as in fact it was—more positive than that of most liberal Catholics at present.

historical; "the form of grace always strives for realization in the changing historical forms." Hence Catholicism has not been able, as Protestantism has, to take "the step toward doing away with the objectification of the holy" (*PE*, 39); nor has it been able "to strengthen the prophetic as opposed to the priestly element in the churches" (*SD*, 145), and thus begin to unite itself with new movements of cultural reform. After Vatican II, however, with the new element of prophetic criticism (as well as rational and historical criticism) of the church's means of grace, there has appeared in Catholicism precisely what Tillich then missed, namely, the union of Catholic substance with new movements of cultural reform.

Correspondingly, Protestantism represents, at its best, "prophetic criticism," a retention of the presence of grace always subjected to the criticism of its finite forms: "It is the continual task of prophetic criticism to fight against the confusion of the form of grace with religious culture" (*PE*, 27). Thus, conscious of the relativity of its own forms as well as those of culture, Protestantism is open to uniting the secular, economic, and political with their transcendent meaning, and so mediating to a culture moving toward socialism its own theonomous meaning. The secular movement of sacramental, political empowerment toward justice which we have traced above can, therefore, receive its religious complement in the appearance of Protestantism. Because of its understanding that the religious represents the transcendent meaning of the finite and not a separable objectification of grace, Protestantism is able to unite the drive toward social justice with an acknowledgment of unconditional religious meaning; thus, it can help to create the theonomy made possible by our *kairos*. So Tillich and his circle hoped in the late '20s.

Tillich also saw the temptation implicit in Protestantism. Because here there was no objective, visible form of grace and no established sacral priesthood, Protestantism was always vulnerable to identification with its culture. Its acknowledgment and expectation of grace could become identical with the rationality and goodwill of culture. "Where a visible form of grace is lacking, religious life becomes subject to political and social forces and cannot avoid secularization" (*PE*, 9); thus, "Protestantism is always exposed to the danger of becoming secularized" (*PE*, 33). This virtual identity with its surrounding culture has occurred over and over in many forms of what we usually term "mainline" Protestantism—or, to escape that danger, there appears Protestant fundamentalism, the transformation of a gospel of expectation and promise into a supernatural messsage of trans-historical redemption. Tillich might well have surveyed the current situation of Protestantism with the unwelcome chagrin of an unhappy prediction now thoroughly confirmed: those forms of Protestantism that have united themselves with rational criticism have become virtually identical with their cultural surroundings and have lost influence; other forms of Protestantism have appeared in violent fundamentalist reaction to the autonomous principles of modern culture. The two things he did not predict were (1) the appearance of theocratic fundamentalism intent on a heteronomous conquest of secular humanist and liberal culture—in the name of bourgeois and Christian values, and (2) the rebirth of a theonomous (that is, a critical and yet sacramental) Catholicism as perhaps the most viable form of modern Christianity—though the principles of his interpretation certainly made room for such eventualities.

* * *

We have come to the end of our summary and commentary on Tillich's early political writings. As is evident almost three quarters of a century later, the great hopes in these works for a Kairos embodying a religious socialism in the 1920s and early 1930s were never fulfilled. Instead, the dark forces of political romanticism prevailed, and out of them a renewed split between a nascent capitalism and a firmly established communism appeared. As Tillich said in 1950: "My own personal feeling is that today we live in a period in which the Kairos, the right time of realization, lies far ahead of us in the invisible future, and a void, an unfulfilled space, surrounds us" (*PE*, 180).

This did not mean that Tillich lost interest in either the political or the historical. As a part of the thought embodied in the following chapters, he continued to develop the most significant interpretation of religion and culture in this century and one of the two or three great theological interpretations of history in our time. As was the case with his great American colleague, Reinhold Niebuhr, however, the immediate unity or even identity of theological interpretation with a concrete political program, represented in his early "religious socialism," seemed less and less viable to him.

2

Introduction to Tillich's Thinking: The Drive to Unity and the Need for Ontology

Tillich's mature thought is strange to us. It has always struck us as Anglo-Saxons and especially as Americans, as a little bit alien, unexpected, and thus puzzling. Here is a *religious* thinker who writes philosophically and, to most of us, "abstractly"; here is a philosopher dominated by religious interests, and yet who seems, if we listen a moment, to be talking directly about us. It is, therefore, hard to know what he is saying, to fit it into the ways we usually think religiously, philosophically, and even personally. This introductory chapter to Tillich's systematic thought is designed to soften that strangeness a bit, to explain why the mature Tillich expresses himself the way he does, and to outline as briefly as possible some of the main principles of his thought. These principles appear everywhere in his later thinking as its guiding presuppositions or assumptions; although they are rarely discussed directly, it is their consistent presence that makes everything he wrote and said a part of his "system."

Tillich as Ontologist: The Category of Being

The strangest part of Tillich's thought, which continually meets with objection, is certainly its *ontological character.* First, it is philosophical in its fundamental character even when it speaks of us as persons and of God; secondly, as philosophical it uses, in talking of us or of God, the concept of *being* as its basic category or word. And that is strange! For Tillich, ontology means what "metaphysics" means for Whitehead (and for Aristotle)—the study of what it means for anything *to be* insofar as it

23

is.[1] Thus everything that is, in any way that it is, illustrates that "structure of being" which an ontologist seeks to discern, to uncover, and to explicate. As ontological, therefore, Tillich's theology is, throughout, a way of thinking concerned with the *being* of things and the *being* of God, their most fundamental nature or structure and so the way they are and behave. Thus is Tillich's thought philosophical, ontological, and apparently abstract. Why does he write that way? As we shall see, there are several reasons why Tillich is ontological as a thinker and as a theologian; why, that is, he uses so persistently the category of being.

1. The unity of object and subject, matter and spirit, the "real," and the merely psychic

For Tillich, one of the most disastrous characteristics of the modern cultural situation is its dualism, its universal and apparently self-evident assumption that reality is split into fundamentally unconnected blocks or areas. There is a dualism between us and God: we are ourselves, and God is a vast personal self; a dualism between us as personal selves and "nature," the inorganic world around us and in us; a dualism between body and psyche; and in culture between natural science and the humanities. In religious and moral speech, therefore, we speak only of selves and persons, and possibly of God as a "person" over there. Most Protestants beginning the study of Tillich are thus baffled: all the language about God and humans familiar to them in church has suddenly vanished, and quite literally they do not recognize what Tillich says as speech about religion or Christianity at all.

On the other side, in science we speak of the inorganic in terms of material entities and mathematical formulae, a realm totally void of "spirit" and so utterly distinct from the language appropriate to persons, morals, and religion. Thus religion has little to do with the "real world" of science, technology, and industry. Correspondingly, science has little to do with social theory and ideologies, moral issues, ethical judgments, and, of course, religion. Philosophy, which is supposed to provide bridges between all of these widely separated realms, has *nothing* to do, except possibly distinguish different language games! All this is usually blamed on poor Descartes, who merely expressed in the seventeenth century the growing gulf between the material, extended, external "reality" known by the natural science of Galileo, on the one hand, and the "internal," inquiring "reality" of thinking which he experienced in him-

---

1. For Tillich's reasons for preferring the word "ontology" to the word "metaphysics," cf. *ST* I:20; *BR*, 6–7; and *ST* II:10–12.

self as a scientist and philosopher, on the other. Modern culture, dominated by science and technology and yet remaining political, moral, and in part religious, continues this commonly assumed dualism. The only difference is that much of the intellectual community, despite its science (or because of it), has quietly dropped Descartes's other substance, namely thought or inward spirit, as itself either a part of the realm of extension, or "subjective" and therefore quite unreal.

To Tillich, this dualism of the common person, and its intellectual counterparts, represents a disastrous error. Such a dualism between external matter and inward spirit, inorganic and personal being, summed up in material nature, personal self, and personal God, makes it impossible to understand our personal life in the body, our common life in family and community, our varied and essential relations to nature in us and around us, and the nature of God as "ground" of nature and of ourselves.[2] Such an unreconciled dualism, of course, also makes knowing and so science, not to mention the purposive use of knowledge in technology, inconceivable; in science and technology alike body, sense, cognitive mind, and decisive purpose (and responsibility) are mysteriously intertwined in some deeper unity. For cultural and religious reasons alike, therefore, some mode of thought, some "category," must penetrate below the distinction of matter and spirit, inorganic and personal, nature, person, and God to express their essential unity as well as their differences. And for Tillich this category is that of *being*. For all *are* in their various ways; they illustrate a common structure of being that is similar and in some way "analogous" in each realm; and thus all illustrate a fundamental unity of some sort which our experience assumes and illustrates and thought, therefore, can express. Being, therefore, is a category that assumes that both matter and spirit are real as its central aspects; it is a category that makes it possible for us to think of these different realms as traits of a common world as well as distinguishable realms within it—which is, after

---

2. One notes that radical criticism of the common dualism assumed in our culture is common among other philosophical contemporaries of Tillich. One could say that the thrust of Whitehead's metaphysical construction was as much directed at what he called the "bifurcation of reality" into matter and psyche as it was the predominance of the category of unchanging substance (cf. A. N. Whitehead, *Process and Reality* [New York: Macmillan, 1929], pp. 43–44, and especially *Science and the Modern World* [New York: Macmillan, 1925], chaps. 3, 4, and 5). Also interesting is Keiji Nishitani's argument that the "impersonal and blind" cosmology of modern science weakens the credibility of the personal God of Christianity and makes a Buddhist view more relevant (cf. Keiji Nishitani, *Religion and Nothingness* [Berkeley: University of California Press, 1982], chaps. 2 and 3).

all, our experience. Thus being is "beyond" both, and so at first it appears to us as "abstract," although in fact an inorganic realm void of all cognitive spirit to know of it, and a "personal" self void of inorganic and living organic body, are even more abstractions distant from the lived unities of our experience.

2. The unity of life and the disciplines

Closely connected with this impulse in Tillich's thought towards unity of matter and spirit, and inorganic reality with organic and psychological reality, was an even more evident drive toward cultural unity, unity of the various separated ("estranged") facets of our common life. Tillich was well aware of the well-known diversity of the university, a diversity resulting in mutual strangeness, the inability to speak together and to comprehend one another (except, as he once remarked, at "ze bar of ze faculty club, ze comptroller's office where ze checks are located, and ze sports field"). But he saw as few did the way this *cultural* fragmentation reflected and encouraged a fragmentation of the everyday *existence* of persons in that culture. I recall him illustrating this fragmentation one time as follows:

> I drive my car after breakfast to ze supermarket to buy goods to feed my body; I stop in at my lawyer's to make my will; at ze library to get a book for my mind; I have just time for my appointment with my analyst about my unconscious; and before it closes I attend an opening at ze gallery—for my "spirit." On ze way home I pay for a prescription for my liver and buy a journal on current events to see vat happens in history. Then I arrive at home to sit quietly in my chair before I eat. All day I have tended my body, the mortality of my being, my thinking, my psyche, my aesthetic, and my historical spirit—and finally my body again. *I* am the being who does all this. Thus there is some unity hidden somewhere in all of these diversities; but in the university and in the languages of culture, all these aspects of me— and of everyone else—are abstracted out, reshaped in new terms, and made to be so separate and distinct as to become quite out of touch with one another. Personally and actually each of us *lives* this unity, just as a culture as a whole lives its unity as long as it lives. But we cannot now express this unity in language, and so we cannot *think* it; soon we will hardly be able to feel it. Unity at some level is necessary for the being of any organism, of a person, and of a cultural community—none, no level, can bear to live through the incoherence of falling apart.

Tillich often referred to the psychological terror of "falling apart into pieces" (*ST* II:61), of losing one's center as a spiritual being. He deplored, as we shall see, the separation of cognition from emotion and commitment, of thought from feelings and affirmations, of means from ends; the disjunction of science from morals, technology from art, business and politics from social theory—and all from philosophy and religion—horrified him; and he feared continually the separation and conflict of the ontological polarities that make up and constitute whatever is. As a consequence, like Hegel before him, he searched for unity on existential, cultural, and theoretical levels, and thus for categories within which all of these diverse aspects could be united. Such uniting categories cannot, without grave imbalance, appear in any *special* discipline or science (which is *ontic*, dealing with *one* realm of being); it must locate itself in some discipline applicable to all special disciplines alike. This discipline for him is ontology, the inquiry into what it is for *anything* or *any* realm of beings to be; ontology searches for the structure common to *all* these aspects and fields. The category common to all was, for Tillich, being— for all, in chemistry, in psychology, in economics, in art, in gymnastics, and even in religion, "are" and thus share in being.[3] Just as *estrangement* (disunity with that to which we belong) is for Tillich the first name for evil, and as *reconciliation* (return of the estranged) is the primary signal of redemption, so *unity* is perhaps the central drive of his thought. The first requirement of unity, as our argument shows, is to establish a level of discourse below and yet within the special diversities of life. For him, the category demanded by this requirement is the category of being.

3. *Being, philosophy, and unity*

Tillich's thought thus expresses a deep consciousness of unity in all of existence accompanied by a sharp awareness of the threat and often the reality of disunity, of estrangement. This unity covers all the apparently antithetical aspects of our existence: nature and history, objects and subjects, world and self, scientific and personal being, objectivity and commitment, and so on. It includes as well a deep unity of all beings, at whatever level they may exist, with their infinite ground, a unity often lost in a separation of God from the world or a loss of God entirely, and the consequent loss of world and of self. For Tillich, this unity with the infinite ground of all is the basis of the unity of each being, and each realm of being, with the others. This for Tillich is the essence of religion. Since the expression of this unity by definition transcends the terms of the

---

3. Tillich's assumption that being is the best category with which to explicate this underlying and uniting ontological or metaphysical realm is, of course, debatable. Whitehead agreed with Tillich that speculative thought must "descend" below the relatively abstract special areas of experience and of the disciplines to "actuality"—below precisely the dualities that Tillich had found. For Whitehead, however, the category of "becoming" was preferable to that of being.

special disciplines, and of the special areas of life, it seems abstract, out of touch with direct experience. But clearly the separate areas are themselves abstractions. To take them as separate is naive; to take them as unrelated is dangerous. Correspondingly, the one entrance into the unity of life is through a category common to all.[4]

Being refers, then, to the common structure and the common ground of subjects and objects, world and self; it transcends and includes impersonal, scientific ways of thought and "personal," spiritual ones. Far from excluding the personal and reducing all discourse to the "impersonal," as its critics assume, an ontological approach sets these aspects of reality into "being," as effective parts of reality. Instead of denying the reality of the personal, or of separating it from nature and the inorganic, Tillich includes it as essential to the structure of being, which is, after all, the way we experience our own being.

As soon as one begins to read Tillich, one notices that *being* does not mean what at first we expect it to mean. Generally we assume that being represents an abstraction from the varied *objects* of our sensory experience and so of our knowledge, what they all have in common as objects that are taken to be real. This is accurate enough for the classical tradition in philosophy and for its central category of "substance." But this is not what being means for Tillich. Certainly it means "what is real" (or "actual" in Whitehead's terms); but as we have seen, objects and experience are not alone that which is real. *Subjects,* knowers as well as known, are also "real," and real *as knowers.* This is, of course, what Hegel showed when he insisted that Spirit, Consciousness, or Mind is what is above all real. But again Tillich disagrees: consciousness and thought are real aspects of being, but for him being precedes and founds consciousness, not the reverse. Tillich is not an idealist, and "being," while inclusive of consciousness, is a far richer category than conscious experience; in fact, being manifests itself in and through all dimensions of actuality, inorganic, organic, psychic, and spirit (*ST* III:17–30).

Where, then, in experience does "being" appear if not directly from

---

4. Readers familiar with Whitehead will notice the significant similarity of interest, if not in the precise means to fulfill it. For Whitehead, to take the results of the special sciences, especially of physics, as defining unambiguously the reality out there and so as providing the fundamental and uniting mode of discourse about all of experience, is "the fallacy of misplaced concreteness," that is, taking the abstraction of one field as the actuality common to all. And again, metaphysics (Tillich's ontology) provides categories appropriate to that actuality and so is capable of being the "critic of abstractions." Cf. *Science and the Modern World,* esp. pp. 72ff.

either known objects or knowing subjects? From Kierkegaard and then Heidegger, Tillich derives his answer: reality or actuality appears more directly in our awareness of ourselves as *existing* beings, in our awareness of our own being (our "being there," *Dasein*) from the inside. In us, being is "present to itself," aware of itself, its body, its environment, its space and time, its future. Here the inorganic, the organic, the psychic, and what even transcends these, are wedded together in our awareness of our own being. Tillich once said:

> We can in a sense, and in a real sense, know a tree, all about a tree. But because we can only study it from the outside, we can never know what it means to be a tree. Its own being—the mode of being it represents—remains strange to us. We do, however, know what it is to be a human: we can experience our own being, and the structure of our being "from the inside." Thus must we begin there if we would ask about being: "Man is the entrance into being" in the sense that for us it is our experience of our own being that establishes our most direct touch with the character of the being that manifests itself all around us.[5]

Those who know Kant, Kierkegaard, and Heidegger will recognize an unexpected lineage in this passage, a lineage that has, so to speak, re-established the category of being on a new basis in twentieth-century thought. In our experience of ourselves, as moral subjects, as deciding selves, as *Dasein* projected toward death, and now in Tillich as "finite freedom," we experience being directly in ourselves. The origin, therefore, of the category of being lies not in our external experience of objects but in our inner awareness of ourselves as existing subjects. In that sense it is "personal" to the core; but at the same time it is never separated from the body of the self, from the world of the self, that is, from the experience of our bodily actuality in the world (the "withness of the body" of Whitehead), and it includes our "thrownness" into the world from our past, our impulsion into a future, and our inescapable boundedness by nonbeing. In the unity of the self in its world as both an object and a subject, the "being" of the self becomes a category that can, in principle, unite the fragmented life of modernity.

4. *Being, nonbeing, and religion*

So far we have given what might be called the *philosophical* grounds for Tillich's use of the category of being; that is, as presenting us with the conditions for understanding actuality and our actuality. Now let us turn

---

5. Cf. as references for this point: *ST* I:62, 168–69; and especially *BR*, 11–14.

to the even more important *religious* grounds for the centrality of this category and so for the philosophical approach to theology that goes with it. To most of us in Protestant America, religion has to do with two issues: our moral behavior and the state of our soul, whatever that state may be. The concerns of religion, therefore, begin and end with our so-called "spiritual" existence, with the ups and downs of our psyches, our personal behavior with regard to individual virtues and vices, and our hope for a possible personal future after death. One notes at once how much this interpretation of religion, limited to issues of psychic and moral relevance, leaves out: issues of our body (health and disease); issues of our social persona (success, failure, and meaningful goals of life); and especially issues of our community (its peace, justice, and career in history). It leaves out the world, history, nature, and most of what makes up the self. No wonder modern culture has wondered about the relevance as well as the credibility of religion!

Now, while psychic and moral matters also are to Tillich assuredly religious concerns, nevertheless, religion has for him a much wider scope. Religion is an issue of our entire being, of the whole of what we are: our bodily health; our psychic health (unconscious and conscious); our spiritual health (anxieties, loneliness, meaninglessness, despair); our inescapable limits, most notably "having to die"; and especially the social and moral career (and its religious career, too) of our wider communities, that is, with history and its prospects for justice. All that we are, body, psyche, mind, will, community, vocation—all this is relevant to religion for Tillich; in other words, the *whole* of our being, and the *world's* being in all the aspects of both.[6]

Tillich expresses this relation of religion to the whole of our being and the world's being in three important formulae: First, religion, he says, is *ultimate concern;* the concerns which are ultimate have to do with our *being* and our *nonbeing,* issues that extend far beyond the moral and even the psychic spheres. Especially in his analysis of the relation of our finitude to our deepest anxieties, we shall see how this understanding of religion enlarges our sense of its scope and importance into areas that, on the one hand, surely need "rescue," and yet areas, on the other, that are not usually thought of as "religious." For as we have seen, our being and our nonbeing point to crises and strengths that include all of ourselves: body, psyche, mind, spirit, and wider community.

---

6. For references to Tillich's effort to "widen" the scope of the religious beyond its usual limitations, morals, and institutions, cf. *ST* I:11–12, 14; II:80–86; III:94–106, 151–61; *PE*, 55–65, 185–91; *TC*, 3–9; *MSFA*, 130–32; *MB*, 13–64.

Second, religion has to do inescapably with the *structure* of our being:[7] religious problems represent a *distortion* of our structure; religious answers represent a *renewal* of the structure of our being, in effect, the New Being. Because the religious itself (our ultimate concerns) arises from the fundamental *structure* of our being, religion must be interpreted and understood with the help of an understanding of that structure. Since in ontology we examine the structure of our being, in ontology we open up an understanding of religion (of issues of our being and nonbeing). It is, then, the better to interpret genuine religion, as well as the better to understand actuality philosophically, that Tillich uses this category.

Third, the religious dimension of our existence—that which concerns our being and our nonbeing, the ups and downs of our essential structure—characterizes, permeates, and dominates *both* our individual and our social existence. All of finite being for Tillich is *polar;* that is, each self is internally related to its natural environment and in our case also to its social world. Individuals *are* real individuals by participating in communities, and communities *are* real communities because there are autonomous and creative individuals in them. Thus, just as material concerns (food, shelter, security, disease) affect individuals and communities alike, and in both directions, so spiritual health and spiritual disease run back and forth from communities to individuals and the reverse. The religious issues of individual life, therefore, appear and reappear—perhaps originally appear—in communal life, whether we are speaking of the religious community (the churches) and their individuals, or of society and culture and their individuals. The ills and strengths of a given community's existence: its sins and its virtues, its deep anxieties and its courage, its injustice, its suffering, and its death, on the one hand, and its drive towards justice and reconciliation, on the other—these communal strengths and ills affect, shape, and even dominate each individual's existence. Individuals live in history *through* their communities: there they suffer, there they sin, and there they may be creative, caring, and redemptive.

As we shall see throughout this volume, Tillich's thought moves naturally and easily from an analysis of our individual finite being, on the one hand, to our social and historical being in communities, on the other, and

---

7. Tillich says that philosophy is concerned with the *structure* of our being and theology with the *meaning* of our being (cf. chap. 3). The point of this paragraph is to argue that the meaning of our being is intertwined with the structure of our being as (to follow Augustine) sickness and health are intertwined with the order of our life and our bodies.

it moves as easily in the other direction as well. It is no accident that Tillich's career began in the '20s and the '30s with a dominant and passionate involvement, personally and intellectually, in the Religious Socialist Movement, and that his personal stance of active protest against the Nazi Regime in 1934 arose over the "social" issue of the exclusion of Jews from the German universities.

When Tillich came to this country in 1936 as a refugee and immigrant, such active participation in public political life seemed both inappropriate and unwise. Even in the late '40s, he often confessed a sense of bewilderment and "not quite at-homeness" in the American political scene, which is no wonder! But from the late '30s through the '50s he remained a staunch democratic socialist in conviction, and a thinker devoted to "political theology" in conferences, conventions, and local actions. As his bibliography of articles and addresses shows, during this period he wrote constantly on political and social issues. His later theological analyses of reason, finitude, and existence interpret for us the social and historical traumas and conflicts of history as fully as they do our individual anxieties and disasters.

Certainly in the late '40s and '50s he became a leader of that decade's new theological concerns of existentialism, psychoanalysis, and the interpretation of art. From the vantage point of the liberationist '70s and '80s, this has seemed hopelessly individualistic and passive. Many contemporary Europeans, newly inspired by liberationist concerns, interpret this as Tillich's easy acceptance of American individualism and privatism. Quite to the contrary, Tillich frequently said that one reason he "felt at home" at Union Theological Seminary was that the overriding assumption there, even in the '40s and '50s, of the relevance of Christian faith to political renewal and reform (the legacy of the earlier Social Gospel) was "similar to the assumption that had motivated *us* in the religious socialist world of the 1920s." Present-day European liberationist theologians should reread the European theology—Protestant (post-Bultmannian and dogmatic Barthian) and Catholic alike—of that post-war period of the '40s and '50s. It is not irrelevant to note further that even in 1951, Tillich wrote out a new set of lectures on "the political meaning of Utopia"[8] and delivered them in Berlin on his first return to Germany. The present volume will seek to reflect both of these concerns with regard to the religious: individual anxiety and serenity, on the one hand, and social injustice, disintegration, and social renewal, on the other. The first principles of Tillich's mode of thinking theologically are, therefore, (1) his

---

8. *PE*, 125–80.

ontological way of proceeding, (2) his use of the category of *being*, and (3) the inclusiveness of his theological interests, his concern for the *whole* of our being and that of the world, thus for natural, personal, and historical being alike.

3

The Theonomous Character of Thought: Reason and Revelation

The second cluster of principles that pervade and characterize Tillich's mode of thinking concerns his understanding of reason and culture, on the one hand, and of religion and so of revelation, on the other. Unless we understand somewhere near the outset what his view of these are—for they are not what most of us usually think of reason, culture, and religion—we will have a difficult time with Tillich.[1]

For Tillich, true thinking unites two sets of "polarities"[2] at present separated in our cultural life, and, as always for Tillich, separation of those things that belong together spells serious trouble. There is, on the one hand, the polarity of the cognitive and the emotive, the objective and the involved, knowledge and eros; on the other, there is the polarity of human reason or spirit and its divine ground or its depth. All creative thinking and understanding represent for him a union, however fragmentary, of these two sets of polarities.

Correspondingly, whenever emotion and cognition fall apart, or thought and its religious depths are estranged, then culture flounders and disintegrates and the demonic eventually makes its appearance. The union

---

1. As will become evident, the following discussion represents a commentary on, and explication of, the section entitled "Reason and Revelation," in *ST* I:71–152.

2. This word, while useful here, is not strictly accurate. For Tillich, polarity means two apparent opposites that are, nevertheless, *interdependent*, mutually essential for one another. While this concept holds for the cognitive and the emotive, it does not in the same way hold for reason and its ground. For Tillich, the divine ground is not dependent *in the same way* on its finite creatures.

of all of these is what Tillich terms "ontological reason," and it is also what he means by "theonomy" or "theonomous thinking." Their disunion is one main evidence, though not the only one, of the estrangement of our actual historical existence, of "the Fall." Ideal thought, therefore, unites these: eros and commitment with objective thought, active spirit with depth; or, in another set of terms, creative thought unites religious substance (the depth of a culture's life) with a culture's autonomous forms, and thus forms a unity in tension among its cultural forms rather than a separation and conflict of them. When religious substance and cultural forms separate, trouble is brewing; when they unite, a culture is healthy, creative, and growing.

As we shall see, Tillich assumes and explicates this view of intellectual, spiritual, and cultural existence (of thought, science, morals, politics, and art) throughout his analysis of culture; it is, one might say, one fundamental presupposition of that analysis, of a "theology of culture." Nevertheless, his most explicit explanation of this view of creative thinking appears in relation to his definition and description of *theology* as a union of philosophical inquiry and religious witness. Theology, for him, is the clearest example—almost a sort of paradigm—of theonomous thinking. The reason is that, more explicitly than in other modes of thinking (natural science, political and economic theory, psychology, humanistic inquiry, and so on), theology raises questions about the relations of these two sets of polarities. Thus, in becoming conscious of its own structure, it makes the union of cognition and emotion, objectivity and eros, ends and means, and the union of thought and its depths explicit. These same unities characterize science, social science, and philosophy as well; each of these becomes impossible if these unities do not hold. Nevertheless, all this can remain quite hidden, even denied, in these cultural disciplines, which tend to see themselves as "objective," on the one hand, and purely "autonomous," on the other. Thus Tillich introduces his understanding of reason, of creative thinking and doing, and the essential relation of these to their divine depths, in presenting his understanding of theology and its method in part one of his *Systematic Theology.*

Reason as the Unity of Eros and Logos

Reason to Tillich is the creative, culture-producing power of human being (and so of being). He inherits from Hegel and from classical German philosophy the notion of reason as the spiritual power productive of *all* of culture. Thus reason for him is not exhaustively defined, as modern scientific culture defines it, in terms of scientific inquiry, logical analysis and organization, systems management, and the development of rational means—that "objective" and "neutral" investigative, analytical, and organizing capacity of mind, which we associate with reason. For Tillich, reason is also that power that creates, shapes, and reshapes cultural life in all its aspects: artistic and literary power, political insight and comprehension, technical and economic imagination, moral and spiritual intuition, and the ability to make pragmatic and practical judgments. Yet reason is more than problem solving, pragmatics. It is even more than theory construction; it is also "wisdom." Reason is thus as close to art as it is to science, as both understand very well; it is as evident in creative social, political, and moral judgments as in technical advances and business administration. It is through the work of reason that political and economic institutions are established, shaped, and reshaped; that the social customs and ordinary rules of behavior are devised and interrelated; that cities are planned, built, and decorated; and that works of memory, imagination, morals, and religion are orally transmitted, fashioned and refashioned, organized and finally set down. Reason is the culture-producing power in human being.

In each of these powers of reason there is manifest a polarity of rationality and emotion, of objectivity and subjectivity, of detachment and involvement, of organizing and intent. As always, if one of these poles becomes weak and vulnerable, the other weakens as well. Without commitment or eros to truth, scientific objectivity is impossible; without clear and valued ends, means destroy themselves; without presuppositions held by intuitive vision or faith, thinking cannot even begin much less persevere. The problem is not, for Tillich, that modern culture has separated *reason* as logical and scientific thinking from emotions and ends; it is rather that reason has been defined as purely the former, as what he terms "technical reason" (*ST* I:53–54, 56, 72–74). Thus, stripped of commitment and valuing, reason is estranged from itself. There can be no objective thought, no scientific inquiry, without commitment to that mode of thinking, a commitment that neither the promise of grants nor even of fame can dissolve: objectivity itself depends upon the love of it, that is to say, on intense subjectivity.[3] Creative thought—and science is an excellent example of this, as are literature, art, and philosophy—thus combines emotive and decisive elements with logical and empirical ele-

---

3. The many recent cases of important scientists, and well-regarded teams of researchers, overlooking, denying, even changing evidence for the sake of funds well illustrates Tillich's point that *moral* commitment to "integrity" is a necessary *condition* for "objective" science.

ments. This is what Tillich calls "ontological reason" (*ST* I:72–73, 75, 77), and it characterizes every aspect of any cultural activity that is creative.

For Tillich, the polarity of commitment and eros, involvement and objective rationality, is complemented by the polarity of union and distance, participation and detachment. Without a measure of *distance* from the object there can be no knowing: the subject must detach itself in order to know its object; complete union without distinction obliterates knowing. Scientific culture has well understood this point, and so it has viewed detachment, spiritual separation from its object, as the most essential requirement of valid knowing and so of reason. Again Tillich agrees and yet disagrees. All knowing must, in a sense, also "participate" in its object and so unite with it: be impelled or drawn toward it, respect it and its own integrity; in fact, be "grasped" by it and thus shaped by it, if the object is to be genuinely known. Total distance destroys knowledge. Knowledge, in fact, is for Tillich an aspect of the universal drive to reunion with the objective world from which we are separated; and correspondingly, different sorts of knowledge represent different modes of participation of the subject of knowing in the objects known. When, for example, persons are to be known, the participatory side of the cognitive relation becomes utterly necessary; love is a requirement for true understanding. For this reason, certain kinds of knowing can transform and even heal: knowledge by participation of the self in itself (as in therapy) effects a healing reunion with one's self; participating knowledge of a community and its values reshapes an isolated individual into a member, a citizen; knowledge through love of the other tranforms both; and knowledge through ultimate concern for the good "converts" the knower into an image of the good.[4]

As a consequence, if knowing seeks to strip itself of these emotive and participatory elements, to relate itself only externally to its objects, and thus to shape itself as pure, unconcerned detachment distantiated from its objects, from purposes, and from ends of any sort (I suppose the ideal of the "pure observer" and of "a value-free science"), then knowledge will in the long run be destroyed. Without participation in the objects of knowledge, real relations to them weaken and disappear; as a consequence, our always fallible certainty about what we know becomes increasingly vul-

---

4. Tillich referred continually to the Platonic source for these notions and reminded his students that most theologians regarded this interpretation of knowing (as participation and thus as transforming) as "Greek" and thus as damaging, if not lethal, for any valid theology. As is evident, at this point Tillich was not only thoroughly Greek but also Augustinian.

nerable. Knowledge depends upon, and drives toward, a deep level of unity between subject and object. Otherwise, the object separates from and can never be known by the subject.

Furthermore, without the subject's commitment to the integrity of its object and to ends that include that integrity, knowledge becomes *controlling knowledge* (*ST* I:97). Controlling knowledge is evident when, for example, science (as "objective") becomes the instrument of industrial and commercial expansion, an expansion dominated only by desire for profit and so intent on *control* through what it knows; then we speak of "exploitation." Such exploiting knowledge becomes even more demonic when knowledge is used to dominate persons, as in the use of "science" by totalitarian regimes. In each case, knowledge destroys rather than understands its object. Knowledge is always power, and power will be used, *unless* it is controlled by the knower and controller himself or herself. In other words, unless knowing is *self*-controlled by union, by commitment to truth and the good, by respect, justice, and love, knowledge leads to ruthless exploitation: of nature, of community, and of others. Tillich expressed these thoughts many decades ago in the '20s and into the '30s, long before the effects of controlling reason and scientific expertise (then becoming evident in their *political* use) were apparent on animals, on plants, on ecosystems, and on all of nature's resources. This knowledge, undirected by its own "rational" eros and by rational ends, manipulates its objects because it is itself not *self*-controlled, undirected by wisdom. As a consequence, reason so defined is itself driven—by greed and self-love (concupiscence). "Technical reason" rules the world, but technical reason itself is ruled by the world's irrational goals of wealth, power, and pleasure.

The so-called complete detachment of reason is, for Tillich, only a momentary "detachment," as in the brief moments of a laboratory experiment. For it is, so to speak, a detachment within a parenthesis, a parenthesis itself ruled by outside forces. In the end reason, even the most objective technical reason, is not at all detached from all ends, but is itself the servant of some other set of goals and purposes, as when large corporations or the Pentagon hire scientists and their laboratories. If these ends, which direct the use of reason, lie quite *outside* the scope of reason, then there is little ground for hope. Modern technical culture, having identified reason with a technical rationality devoid of ends and thus unrelated to justice and love, is itself dominated by controlling knowledge. Reason is here *techne* and not *wisdom*, a split that makes a reason so defined move toward that which at first represents its very opposite, namely the demonic.

Reason and the Ground of Reason

As with all finite being, human reason has a depth or a ground, a ground that transcends reason and yet is present and active within the power of reason: an ultimate, unconditional, sacred dimension. This ground provides the essential *bases* for reason, the conditions that make the creative exercise of reason in cultural life possible. It is the unity of subject and object in the infinite ground of both that makes possible the correlations of being and of thought, of external object and inquiring subject, that represent the conditions of knowledge. And it is the presence of order (logos), encompassing both objective world and rational self, that provides the further condition for the relevance of *logical method* in the subject to the *patterns* exhibited by the objects. Thus confidence in knowledge, the awareness that we know, is based on apprehension of this ground of unity, a confidence in the harmony present in all our experience and so an assurance of the ultimate relevance of thought to being; it is our awareness of this uniting ground that establishes the "correlation" between what is inquired about and the inquiry that inquires. Without that assumed unity of being and of thought, the acids of skepticism erode the sense of the reality of our knowing, and certainty becomes infinitely elusive.

Correspondingly, an ultimate concern for *truth* itself, and thus for the integrity of both inquiry and inquirer, is basic for the possibility of science, as we have just noted. Here again aspects of the unconditional—the unconditional unity of thought and being, on the one hand, and the unconditional value of truth, on the other—represent the presuppositions of reason as cognitive, as knowing. In the aesthetic realm the unconditional ground of reason is present as *beauty itself*, the import or aesthetic grasp of reality expressed in and through each work of art. In legal, political, and moral reason the unconditional is represented by *justice itself*, the normative form of communal relations that makes any actual legal, political, or communal structure of relations possible. Again, however wayward actual courts may be, there *are* no courts and there is no law—except arbitrary power—if *all* judges can be bought. Lawyers and politicians, to be sure, work for money; for many that remains the "bottom line." But again, if *all* can be bought or bribed, if in none is there a concern for justice, for order, for freedom, and for equality, then these political institutions wither and communal life becomes impossible. Institutions exist as corrupted, to be sure; but unless they also embody an essential (normative) structure of truth, beauty, and justice, they cannot persist. If there is no concern for art, but only for the money or fame received through art, there will be no art. Institutions, and with them culture itself, depend on the presence within those institutions of *ultimate concern*, commitment to the unconditional structures and norms that make cultural arts and their institutions—however unjust, unlovely, or inefficient they may be—possible at all. Institutions depend essentially on technical reason and creative imagination; however, they also depend on the *meaning* or *worth* of participation in them. Without commitment to that meaning, the institution quickly disintegrates. It is the depth of reason that mediates and so communicates that ultimate and unconditional meaning necessary to all of culture and so permeating all of creative communal life. It is this, or an aspect of this, that Tillich calls the "religious substance" of each culture's life, its relation to the depth of reason (*ST* III:157–61; *TC*, 40–51; *TPE*, 55–65).

The awareness of this unconditional depth or ground of cultural life—of creative human reason—is universal, as culture is universal. Each culture embodies a vision of what is real, of how truth is uncovered, known and appropriated, of what is beautiful, and of what is of value or meaning, and it incarnates in its life a mode of commitment to that symbolic understanding and its implications. The embodiment of the culture's vision becomes explicit in its *myths*, and the arts, sagas, and crafts expressive of those myths. The community identifies itself with this vision, or the realities expressed there, by the *cults* of the community. Thus for Tillich the divine ground—the unconditional power of being and of meaning—manifests itself universally in and to all of human existence; it is through the myths and the cults of culture that that manifestation is expressed.

In each culture, this infinite ground is grasped in significantly different form: one way, for example, in each tribal community, another way in Greek cultural life, another way in China, and so on. In each case it is *this* particular vision of reality, of truth, of beauty, of goodness, or of value, which forms the culture and represents its essential core: its vision of what is, of what is true, and of what is of value. Thus this fundamental vision, this response to the manifestation of being-itself, constitutes for each culture its "religious substance": that is, (1) that culture's grasp of reality, truth, beauty, and value (and so the union of reality, truth, and value for that culture); and (2) correspondingly, the way the culture structures the meaning and the meanings of corporate and individual life, its "ultimate concerns," or its ways of uniting reality and the good. For Tillich, every creative culture has as its core such a religious substance: a vision (not his word) of reality, truth, and value that animates all of its life and is expressed in all of the works, the social structures, and the arts of that culture. This vision is articulated and borne by symbols fundamental to that culture's life (its self-understanding or its rhetoric); further, this vision establishes and grounds all the special arts and disciplines: cognition, the arts, the vocations, and the crafts of its common life, and it gives significance to each role *(Beruf)* and pattern of behavior.

In this sense, for Tillich each culture is "theonomous" at its creative outset, inspired and directed by its own vision of reality, truth, and value—and their unity—which vision grounds and directs its significant expressions, institutions, and roles. The most recent example of this (as we shall see later) is for Tillich the Enlightenment in the West, a creative vision of reality as orderly and harmonious (compare Newton, Spinoza, and Descartes), of truth as objective, rational, and later empirical, and of goodness as united to reason in justice, autonomy, and freedom. This is, let us note, not just a vision of what was thought to be *ideal*, though it was also that. (This is an *observer's* interpretation.) It represented for all who participated in it a vision of what *is*, of *reality*, of what was most real in all of existence. This most real that was also harmonious and orderly was called Nature, and Nature was conceived to be in the closest unity with Reason; furthermore, both of them together—Nature and Reason—defined justice for persons, for society, and for all of history. That this vision was important, there can be no question; all it did was to start two revolutions! Thus the important symbol of "natural law," as crucial for the development of seventeenth- and eighteenth-century science as it was for the political establishment of this country and of Republican France, was a symbol of this powerful unity of reality, truth, and value, a unity that represented the "religious substance" of Enlightenment culture. Insofar as Enlightenment science, politics, morals, and religious thought presupposed that reality, as a whole, was characterized by the principle of "pre-established harmony," a universal principal relevant to inquiry, to economics, to politics, to morals, and to religion alike, the Enlightenment was "theonomous." It was a culture established on a particular manifestation of the ground of all as "rational," a vision expressed through the major symbols of the culture, representing, therefore, the "religious substance" of the culture.

The divine and unconditional ground of reason is, as is obvious, an aspect of *essential reason* for Tillich, as a relation to the divine ground is central, even definitive, for all finite being whatsoever. This relation to the divine is, therefore, not only present in so-called "religious" cultures, that is, in those archaic cultures where the religious substance of the culture is expressed in clearly religious myths and cults and preserved by religious institutions. "Secular" cultures, where explicit religion becomes a subordinate or even an unimportant aspect of the culture instead of its dominant center, still possess and live, for Tillich, from a religious substance, as the examples of the Enlightenment itself or of recent communist Russia show. The religious dimension of a culture's life, therefore, its religious substance, represents an essential component of its self-interpretation and self-understanding, as essential to it as the meanings establishing and governing its political, economic, social, and psychological characteristics. As a consequence, in order to understand the dynamics of that culture, its strengths and its major perils, it is as necessary to analyze fully this religious substance as it is to uncover and delineate its economic or political structures. This, incidentally, represents the main role of what Tillich termed a theology of culture, namely, the explication of the religious substance of a society's life and, so to speak, the career of that substance in the historical development of that culture. For Tillich, the principle explanatory factor in the rise and fall of a given culture is the career of its religious substance.

For Tillich, therefore, the religious dimension of culture, the relation of reason to its ground, is essential and not peripheral to culture, to its creativity, on the one hand, and its weakening and destruction, on the other. Myth and cult, as we noted, represent explicitly this dimension embodied implicitly in all its cultural life. Myths organize the religious substance of a culture into a coherent cluster of religious symbols, expressive of its ultimate vision and of its ultimate concerns; or, more precisely, myths are expressive of the sacred "powers" that have established and now preserve that culture (that give it power, order, and possibility), and they are expressive of the appropriate behavior we should manifest, we who are related to the cosmic environment. Correspondingly, cult gives communal or collective expression to this religious substance, and thus, as Durkheim said, common cultic action invigorates and reinvigorates the spiritual power latent within that religious substance. A culture whose modes of rational understanding and of praxis are in touch with its own ultimate convictions or vision, a culture where myth and reason interpenetrate and mutually support as well as criticize each other, is healthy—this is "theonomy." A culture, however, that is scornful of its own mythic, symbolic substance, or worse, that denies such a substance exists, is in that measure destructive of the sources of its own life and strength, of its own instruments for self-criticism, and its own grounds for hope. Such a culture—anxious, skeptical, empty of ends, of confidence, and of principles of unity—is in danger of a "takeover" by an alien mythology.

This scenario represents, in fact, the way Tillich interprets the career of modern Western culture.[5] The Enlightenment begins with an electrifying vision of autonomous reason over against the religious heteronomy of the late medieval culture. In the latter, myth and cult—and the relationship to the unconditioned—became hardened and unyielding, gradually separating themselves from the developing autonomous life of the late medieval period and thus appearing more and more "over against" the latter and repressive of it. In reaction, a new "religious substance" appeared, the "theonomous" vision of the identity of Nature and Reason, of the "harmony" of Nature's laws with autonomous Reason and with universal justice. Slowly, however, the exclusively *autonomous* themes in this vision expanded: nature as natural law separated itself from mind; reason disengaged itself from imagination, from eros, and from commitment; and "objective reality" became void of intentions or of values. As a consequence, nature as reality became viewed as merely mechanical and blind, "mindless"; the active autonomous intellect (the inquiring rational subject) is distinguished more and more radically from its passive, determined object (the natural system of the world); and thus integrity and justice became subjective, "preferences." As the objective world becomes void of inward meaning, so the self, therefore, disappears in unreal subjectivity; it becomes empty of real purposes and secure values; skepticism grows, ends waver. Externally an apprehension of fatedness appears, internally an apprehension of emptiness, unreality, and isolation. A sense of the transience and especially the meaninglessness of existence: rootless, relative, and brief, hovers over the culture, expressed especially in its drama and its art. As the power and reality of autonomy thus diminish and then disintegrate through the very expansion of autonomy, the scene is set for the return of a revitalized myth and cult that will give order and meaning back to the external world and reality and purpose back to the empty, isolated self. Hence arise the power of the new "religious" mythologies in the twentieth century which are representative of oppressive heteronomies *against* autonomy. They portray a world structured by intense meanings and tasks; thus, they give to the empty self new belief, new vital tasks, a "place" in community, and unconditional purposes for life, provided the self surrenders its autonomy. The power of these new heteronomies or "ideologies" cannot, Tillich feels, be understood unless we see the essential need of creative reason for its own

---

5. The major references for Tillich's view of the career of modern culture, a view explicated in the following paragraphs, are the discussion of autonomous reason in *ST* I:81–94, of the development of modern culture in *The World Situation* and *The Religious Situation*, and chaps. 3, 4, and 16 in *The Protestant Era*.

unconditional ground, the forming of creative cultural and communal life on unconditional meanings and tasks, and the consequent emptiness of an unqualifiedly autonomous culture set in an externally meaningless world.

The attempt of culture to become thoroughly secular, therefore, is, for Tillich, a mistake. The rejection of myth and cult in the name of rational autonomy will only prepare the way for the reappearance of these "religious" aspects of culture in some demonic nationalistic, economic, racist, or even religious form, a return that overwhelms rational, moral, and artistic autonomy. Most dangerous of all, this reappearance of heteronomous ideology or religion can, as Japan, Germany, and Stalinist Russia (not to mention fundamentalist America) show, unite itself to "technical reason," to science, technology, and industrial rationalism, and threaten autonomy, rationality, and religion everywhere. Correspondingly, for religion to seek to separate itself from cultural reason, and especially from the criticism that a mature culture in all fields brings to bear on religion, will lead it to become heteronomous, superstitious, and (if it can become theocratic) repressive. For Tillich, a religious community separate from (or, worse, against) culture is as much an alienation from itself as is a culture without religion: the separation of church and culture is fatal to both and in both a sign of the Fall (*TC*, 42).

The Religious Dimension or Revelation

As is evident from this discussion of reason, "revelation" is a category of universal relevance to Tillich (*ST* I:108–13). It represents the way he understands the appearance of the depth or ground of reason, or more precisely, the manifestation of the religious substance, the theonomous depth, of any culture's life. That is to say, as we have seen, each culture begins "theonomously" with a vision of being-itself, of reality, truth, and value, of authentic nature, authentic community, and authentic human being; this vision is structured symbolically (myth) and enacted communally (cult), and it expresses the norms and meanings of that culture's life as well as what "really is" to it. This beginning represents, for Tillich, a self-manifestation, a "revelation," of the divine ground. A creative minority is "grasped" by this vision (or hierophany, as Eliade would put it), and the culture's career begins. Thus in its most pervasive meaning in Tillich, revelation is universal, associated with the rise of cultures everywhere.

The religious substance of a culture is manifested to it in its developing life. As the presupposition of all thought and action alike, it is not empirically established by or argued to in the process of that life; nor is it "discovered" as one discovers an unknown lake or range of mountains. Finally, it does not appear inductively in the doing of the culture's various tasks, as if it appeared out of a long process of trial and error. For all that a culture does, and the way it is done, presupposes this substance. In this sense, all creative thought and praxis are *theonomous:* dependent on a religious substance (a set of fundamental symbols or presuppositions, a "pre-understanding" concerning reality, truth, and value), which is expressed in and through the science, philosophy, literature, art, and praxis of the culture. Thought does not, because it cannot, argue to the unconditional ground; rather, to be thought or action at all, it must presuppose the presence of that ground. "Religion is the substance of culture, culture the form of religion" (*TPE*, 57; *TC*, 42; *ST* III:158). As one consequence, there is what Tillich calls a "theological" element in all thinking, and so in each philosophy, a "mystical a priori" (*ST* I:9) with which reflective thinking begins, namely, the ontological, epistemological, and ethical presuppositions essential to its development and characteristic of its epoch in time and its locus in space. For philosophy, as does all else in culture, lives from and expresses the fundamental religious substance, the vision that animates its culture's life. One task of the religious community within each culture, or possibly at its center, is to express, criticize, and re-express again—in its myth, cult, and its reflection of both—the religious substance of the culture in which it dwells.

In the earliest cultures (archaic cultures) religion and society are inextricably joined. Each facet of the culture (its crafts and social structure) stems from some mythic event or revelation. The order of its homes and towns is a "sacred" order established by divine powers, and all its "knowledge" (pre-science, pre-philosophy, pre-social theory) is "religious" in character, as are its moral and social obligations. Here religion is culture and culture is religion. The religious myths and rites thus articulate and empower the techniques, the tasks, and the meanings generating that culture's life. As we have seen, for Tillich the situation does not *fundamentally* change: religion is still the substance *of culture*, culture the form *of religion*. Like Eliade,[6] Tillich precisely reverses the view of most modern social science: namely, that culture establishes religion as a projection of culture's own powers, ideals, customs, and neuroses onto the so-called "gods," so that when culture reaches the autonomous stage (secularity) it can dispense with these projected beginnings.[7]

Tillich's explanation of the phenomenon of a secular modernity is

---

6. Cf., e.g., Mircea Eliade, *Images and Symbols* (New York: Sheed and Ward, 1969), preface; *Myths, Dreams and Mysteries* (New York: Harper and Row, 1957), chaps. 1 and 9.

7. Cf. Ludwig Feuerbach, *The Essence of Religion* (New York: Harper and Row, 1967), and *The Essence of Christianity* (New York: Harper and Row, 1957), chap. 23 and also chap. 4.

different, as is Eliade's. With the development of culture, a diversification and separation of tasks take place: the arts, politics, philosophy, and science of the culture separate off from its explicit religious base. In principle, these now self-generating cultural activities establish their own autonomous self-understanding and praxis, based, to be sure, on the continuing religious substance of the culture's life. But this development of autonomous techniques, norms, and goals for art, knowledge, politics, and morals need not diminish or qualify the need for the *depth* of autonomous reason, nor does it make their own autonomy impossible. For Tillich, theonomy represents both a relation to a divine ground and the fullest freedom for the exercise of autonomous reason or spirit. Theonomy is, therefore, as much dependent on a creative and independent culture as it is on a continuing and strong religious basis. In this sense, let us note, the development of culture in history makes theonomy possible by effecting the autonomous growth of independent and self-governing aspects of cultural life.

As another consequence, the development of cultural diversification effects a corresponding specialization of the religious in culture. Religious institutions become themselves distinguished from their cultural offspring; they develop within, alongside of, and, frequently, against the rest of cultural life. Specialized "religious" priesthoods, rites, myths, theologies, social organizations, and laws appear, and these "religious" institutions relate themselves, in a bewildering variety of stages and arrangements, to the political, economic, and social institutions of the culture. In most so-called archaic or pre-modern cultures, this religious center remains dominant, but a relative autonomy begins, as we have seen, to characterize the political, military, artistic, intellectual, and economic institutions of society.

In modern culture (since roughly 1650), the possibility of a completely *secular* culture, a culture without explicit religious foundations and so established only on "natural" grounds, quite separate from any religious control, has appeared and become the assumed norm for most, if not all, of modern communities, and certainly for the intellectual classes in those communities. As we have seen, Tillich agrees with a part and disputes a part of this interpretation of modern life. Most fundamentally, the ideal of a secular culture represents for him a misunderstanding both of human being and of culture. Even modern secular cultures depend upon and exhibit a "religious substance," a presupposed basis expressed through symbols, myths, and cults. This presupposed basis, or world and self-understanding, grasps the members of that culture as expressive of what is taken to be real, what is taken to be true, and what is taken to be good; therefore, it unites and empowers them and expresses itself through their creative production and achievements. In some of the most virulently secular countries (e.g., fascist and communist), this grasping of each member is assumed to be unconditional for all participants; as a result, unrestricted assent and obedience to the truth about reality and so to the goals of the community are required. Here a secular ideology is functioning in the modern period as an archaic religious culture once functioned, and with the same heteronomous results. In modern diversified cultures, therefore, there remains a religious substance. In liberal cultures this is implicit, as with the Enlightenment faith in reason and progress. In totalitarian cultures, it is explicit in the political, economic, or nationalistic ideology that dominates their life. In such cultures, explicit *religious communities* (e.g., Christian churches) still remain and enjoy a variety of relations (some separated from it, some united to it, some a little bit of both) to the wider secular cultural life. Let us, therefore, now turn to a consideration in Tillich's terms of such explicit religious communities as churches and synagogues.

Religious communities, that is, *explicit* religious communities such as Christian, Jewish, or Buddhist, are thus originally intrinsically related to culture, but in time become differentiated from the other functions of cultural life. These other functions, as we have seen, continue to presuppose the religious substance, and then go on about their work (e.g., science, law, art, and so on). The religious community reverses this. It presupposes and expresses the culture, and concentrates its *life*, its expressions, and its *reflection* on its own religious substance. In cultic and mythic expression, in reflections on its myths and traditions, and in the organization and implementation of moral and ceremonial law, the religious community preserves and makes available its own religious substance. In some cultures (medieval Christian culture or Islamic culture), that same spiritual center represents the religious substance of the culture as a whole; in modern liberal culture or secular cultures it does not. Thus in modern culture church and synagogue—and the corresponding forms of religious institutions elsewhere—perpetuate only aspects of this traditional role: neither dominates the culture yet neither çan, in principle, separate itself from culture and history without self-betrayal. The relations of contemporary religion to the rest of culture, where religion is understood as an *aspect* of culture and not as its dominating and organizing center, represent a very crucial debate in present American political life. These relations also represent, of course, the complex subject of most of Tillich's theology of culture, his social theory, and his philosophy or theology of history; we shall return to all of this frequently.

Now, however, we must proceed to review briefly Tillich's understanding of *revelation* (*ST* I:106–59) in this more restricted context: as the revelation of the divine ground (of "God") establishing or founding the *religious* community as a religious community (for example, the Christian community, the Buddhist community, the Islamic community). In the development of his concept of revelation as representing the foundation of a religious community or tradition, Tillich genuinely felt (as did Van de Leeuw) that he was giving an "objective" and so phenomenological analysis of religions generally, of all religions. If one looks back on this description, however, it seems plain (at least to me) that the Christian example stood clearly central in Tillich's mind and provided the guiding structures and themes of his conception. At least it is relevant that what he says here is very close to what both Barth and Brunner say characterized "biblical" revelation as *unique* from all of the world's other religions. Let us note, as we proceed, that just as in his discussion of reason Tillich has emphasized reason's roots in the religious dimension, so here in his discussion of revelation he gives to it a quasi-philosophical interpretation. Typically, Tillich takes *unambiguously* "religious" categories, categories saturated with "supernatural" and to our culture even "superstitious" connotations (for example, miracle and ecstasy) and proceeds to translate or revise these into the ontological terms he has begun to develop in his interpretation of reason. Thus, Tillich moves these two modes of being, of experiencing and of knowing (I refer to reason and revelation) into enough proximity to one another to make their cooperation in theonomy (their "correlation") possible.

Revelation, says Tillich—the communication that establishes and preserves a religious tradition—is always of what is *essentially* a *mystery*, and both words are emphasized (*ST* I:153–55). Here again he seeks to demarcate, and so to limit, the religious from other modes of knowing, as in his definition of religion as ultimate concern he has distinguished what is religious in our experience from what is not. A revelation thus is not of what one did not yet know in science or in history, nor is it an inspiration or thought as yet unthought, an inspiring idea or a puzzle not yet unravelled. Revelation, then, is not ordinary knowledge, even scientific knowledge, knowledge of other objects, knowledge about our world; it is not a revelation of "facts." Religious knowledge has never been of that sort, despite the usual "modern" view that revelation represents early scientific cosmology combined with intuited moral obligations. What, then, is it? What *other* sort of knowledge (than empirical or moral knowledge) could there be? Revelation, says Tillich, is of the dimension of depth, the depth of reason (*ST* I:79–81), the unconditional mystery of reality, truth, and value. This depth appears in the unconditional *unity* or *power* beyond subject and object on which the permanence of being, the power of life, the order of things, and the possibility of cognition depend;

it appears as the unconditional *norms* that inescapably accompany all our personal and communal existence; and it appears in the promise of *reunion* that heals us in body, in spirit, and in community. It is this manifestation to which religion, in all its infinite varieties, responds; it is *this* dimension that revelation reveals.

This depth of reason (what later he will call the power and ground of being and meaning), is the basis of reason (thinking) and yet itself transcendent to reason or thinking; hence it is essentially *mysterious*. As the unity of subject and object, self and world, this depth is neither a subject nor an object. Hence neither the language, concepts, and modes of inquiry appropriate to objects in the world nor to subjects over against the world are appropriate here. God is not *a* being, and God is, therefore, not to be conceived *as* a being; nor is God a self in polar relation to a world. Since the divine represents the *ground* of reason, and especially the ground of the rational structure of experience, the divine is not totally beyond reason or speech. Yet as the ground of order and not itself a being within order, the divine must be spoken of differently. Thus symbolic language, in effect metaphor, myth, and especially analogical discourse, alone represent appropriate ways of speaking of God. One notes here the philosophical way that the category of mystery in revelation is explicated.

Revelation, says Tillich, always comes through and contains the "shock of nonbeing" (*ST* I:110, 113, 163, 186f.). There is, then, no religious knowing without deep existential involvement. With the shock of nonbeing, *my own being* has here become the question, not an intellectual puzzle as yet theoretically unresolved. Revelation occurs in shattering experiences, in matters of our *being* and our *nonbeing*. Such experiences appear at our limits: at the edges of our finitude, at the crises of our wholeness or unity—when, therefore, a fundamental threat appears, a threat arising out of an essential, not an accidental, aspect of our being. In revelation we cannot—and we know we cannot—provide an answer: for example, to our contingency, to the fertility of our fields or of our tribe, to the benevolence of destiny, to our death, or to our guilt. These "limit situations" are the areas of religious crisis, and so of religious answers. It is in relation to them that revelations occur, and that *we too* receive revelation. Unless we break through the apparently stable and satisfying realm of ordinary experience, of stock problems and of ordinary answers, of subjects and objects, or unless nonbeing breaks into that realm, we are not open to revelation. The experience of the void shattering us precedes the appearance of a solid ground; the "no" precedes the reception of a "yes"; anxiety is the precondition of both courage and faith.

Revelation occurs in a correlation of "ecstasy" on our side and "miracle" on the objective side. It is always the experience of *someone:* revelation is received, received in this historical and personal situation, and received as an experience of shock, of healing, and of reunion. The character of the revelation is thus, in part, determined by the receiver, that is, by the historical, social, and cultural situation of the receiver—otherwise, it could not be received at all. It is received and expressed, therefore, in *their* terms, but for Tillich it is not to be *explained* in their terms. Further, revelation is not "objective," "*there*": a book, a creed, a substance, an entity, even a theology, which in itself is sacred. No finite thing is unconditioned; it can only function as a *medium* of the unconditional *to* someone who receives it as a medium. The revelation is a *correlation*, a uniting, an *event* of healing; revelation is also always salvation (*ST* I:144–47).

This experience of receiving and thus being healed, Tillich calls "ecstasy" (*ST* I:111–14; III:112–20), a word referent to a long tradition of shamans, seers, prophets, and so on whose reception of revelation far exceeded "ordinary" knowing. For Tillich, ecstasy does not represent the irrational, a break into and so a destruction of reason; rather, it represents precisely the transcendence of the subject-object realm we have noted, an awareness of the sacral and unconditional ground of being and of reason (mystery), an "opening up" of that dimension essential to our life but hidden from us, an awareness mediated by the existential shock of our nonbeing and the wonder of healing. It is not ordinary experience, but it is *experience;* it is not ordinary thought but it is thought—it is ecstasy.

Correspondingly, the event to which ecstasy responds is a "miracle" (*ST* I:115–17), again a word with traditional supernatural connotations. Tillich affirms unambiguously that there is an objective side to revelation: a "medium" or an event provides the objective ground for the experience of ecstasy. (The ultimate referent of ecstasy: the unconditional ground of being and meaning—"God"—is also objective, "there," "real," though God is neither unambigously an object nor "there" in the world.)

The referent of revelation is, for Tillich, not an illusion, nor a hallucination, nor a projection; ecstasy is a response to an appearance of the divine ground, a miracle in and through a given, "objective" medium. There is an event of revelation, and it has an external as well as an internal side. On the other hand, a miracle (and there Tillich "demythologizes" the word) does not break the objective order of natural and historical happenings, the process of becoming via regularity and spontaneity, destiny and freedom. As Tillich puts it, the objective *logos* structure of reality is not destroyed in *miracle*, as the subjective *logos* of the mind remains unimpaired in *ecstasy.* Rather, through "a special constellation of elements of reality" (a "shaking event"), a correlation with ecstasy is established, and the uniting ground or depth of both object and subject manifests itself *through* the objective logos structure and *to* the subjective logos structure.[8] Here is the basis in his interpretation of revelation for his category of theonomy: the presence of the ground or depth of reason in and through reason's autonomoous structures. The depth of reason—its essential basis and ultimate condition—appears in revelation: thought is thus grounded in the religious, ontology in the ontic. Or, put in terms of Tillich's later main categories, the depth of reason, and so of culture and of thought, appears in revelation as God: Being-itself appears as God or the divine.

Tillich has here understood in ontological terms, and so of course in modern as well as existential ones, an old theme in religious self-understanding, namely, the foundation of cultural life in and through religion. We shall note this theme throughout his work. Let us also note how much he has "demythologized" religion in the process. In turn, we should note how much that demythologizing process is itself dependent on the development of *modern* culture: its scientific and social understanding, its historical consciousness, and its philosophy. Without these "secular" developments applied critically to religion and its categories, religion would have remained heteronomous: characterized by "supernatural" miracles, ecstasies, interventions, divine beings, and the absolute heteronomy of supernaturally authorized scriptures, dogmas, and priestly hierarchies. It is, therefore, through the steady and profound *historical* and *cultural* criticism of religion, as well as through the powerful yet intermittent *prophetic* criticisms of religion, that this reinterpretation of the religious has been made possible; as, on the other hand, it was through his own *theological* criticism of culture that the grounding of culture in religion became credible. Thus, Tillich's religious reinterpretation of culture, and his cultural reinterpretation of religion, both presuppose a "mutual criticism" as an essential part of his way of doing theology.

As is already evident, revelation always takes place through media or vehicles (these were also Eliade's terms). Actually, the most Tillichean term is "symbol" (*TC*, 53–67; *DF*, 41–54; *ST* I:239–41), a finite entity which in a miracle becomes "transparent" to the divine ground and so communicates the presence of that ground to others in ecstasy. Tillich points out that any finite creature, any being among beings, can become such a medium, since all beings possess an intrinsic and essential relation to the divine ground. As religious history shows, however, certain sorts

---

8. Schleiermacher represents much the same emphasis: the "feeling of absolute dependence" is mediated to us *through* the objective order of the world. Cf. F. E. D. Schleiermacher, *The Christian Faith*, ed. H. R. Macintosh and J. S. Stewart (Edinburgh: T. & T. Clark, 1928), 178–84.

of entities appear and reappear as significant media. For example, natural objects expressive of fundamental characteristics of reality: stones (permanence), sea (infinity and mystery), and seeds (fertility), trees, storms, and so on; the order of nature or the terror (disorder) of nature; significant events or powers in a community's life; words that communicate sacral meanings, and so on, to persons. For Tillich, persons represent the highest medium, that is, those media that contain the most dimensions of being (ST I:118, 143, 150).

As Tillich sagely remarks, to each community that has received revelation through some medium, *that revelation* becomes definitive and final, the criterion of all others. Thus, every religious revelation central to a community functions as its "final" revelation and as its criterion for other revelations and religions. Every "religious substance," therefore, whether it be merely cultural or that of a specific religious tradition, in the end occupies what Tillich terms a "theological circle" (ST I:8–18; II:14–15). This circle represents a framework from which all else is viewed and assessed, a standpoint which is in itself not proved (all proof depending on this framework), but is derived from the ultimate symbolic vision of reality and truth dominating that culture's life.

Modern secular culture, of course, regards this "circle" as the peculiar problem of religion, of faith, of church authority, and so of theology. It likes to contrast this "making a relative standpoint absolute" practiced by religion with its own *universal* position based on common sense, science, and critical reason. If Tillich's analysis of culture is correct, however, then secular culture, too, possesses a presupposed standpoint, namely, the standpoint that the critical and constructive rationality of modern culture reflects in all that it describes and assesses. For Tillich, there is escape neither from the *relativity* implied in this analysis, nor from the need for a *criterion* by which judgments between as well as within cultural viewpoints can be made. Later, we shall see how he seeks to deal with this paradoxical problem of the inescapability of relativity and yet the absolute need for a criterion.

Finally, Tillich distinguishes originating from dependent revelation (ST I:126–28). *Originating revelation* represents the founding event or miracle that establishes and begins the religious community. This event is, as we have seen, received in ecstasy; in that process, witness is given, proclaimed, and recorded of that event, worship and rites are centered around it, and behavior is changed in its light. In this way, a religious community is established: the event represents the miracle; the reception and its consequences represent the ecstasy. These consequences—scriptures, laws, rites, verbal and material symbols (sacraments), institutional hierarchy, doctrines, to name a few Christian examples—then become what Tillich terms *dependent revelation*, media over continuing time that communicate again and again the originating manifestation, the renewing power, the new interpretations of life, and the new laws resulting from the original event. For most of Christianity, word (scripture, creed, or confession) and sacrament have represented these continuing media of revelation, though church (community) and "saints," individuals who communicate grace to others, have also been dependent vehicles. All of these understand themselves as dependent on the original events of the incarnation, atonement, and resurrection; and all (or most) recognize that only if they witness to and communicate "Christ" are they media of *Christian* revelation. For Tillich, this entire discussion represents a phenomenological analysis of religions. As this last distinction between originating and dependent revelation shows, however, it is more accurately (so it seems to me) labelled a reflection by a Christian theologian on the general category of revelation in the light of the way that category has manifested itself in Christian experience; that is, it represents a Christian theological reflection on revelation in general. On the other hand, when one reads an "objective" reductionist account of revelation (e.g., that of Feuerbach, Freud, or Durkheim), one is even more struck with the effect of their "philosophy" on their reflections, that is, of the naturalistic and reductionist standpoint of the interpreters. As Tillich realized, a completely neutral phenomenology, standing "nowhere in particular," is probably only something to be hoped for in heaven!

*   *   *

With this introductory account of Tillich's understanding of reason and of revelation, we are, I think, in a position to understand what he means when he speaks of the unity, within a distinction of roles, of philosophy and of theology. Better put, this unity represents the coming together of the religious dimension of existence (the depth of reason), on the one hand, with thought or philosophy (cognitive reason), on the other, to create, first, theology, and, as we have seen, then to create alongside theology itself all the many varieties of theonomous thinking. We will discuss more fully elsewhere the particular way Tillich puts these two aspects of reason together to form theology in the well-known "method of correlation." Let us now, therefore, turn to the way philosophy and theology, thought and the religious dimension, cooperate or should cooperate in all forms of important thinking.

We have reviewed the dependence of cognitive reason—the power to know, to grasp reality—on a religious dimension. Thought cannot proceed without the awareness of and confidence in the unity of subject and object in the ground of both; without an apprehension of the universal order encompassing both, a religious awareness of the unconditioned as being-itself and as logos; and without an ultimate concern for truth, again a religious awareness of truth itself. The role of cognitive thought as philosophy is the uncovering and the analysis of the *structure of finite being* manifested to our experience, the classical role of metaphysics or ontology. This role ("philosophy examines the structure of being") is not in itself religious (it does not uncover, nor does it seek, the ground of being, God); but as noted it presupposes that ground, and it cannot proceed without that presupposition. Thus philosophy depends on a "mystical a priori," a religious base, a manifestation of revelation, to proceed. Whether the philosopher is aware of this or not, for Tillich all philosophies possess such an initiating and presupposed foundation. Philosophy, he once said, represents the courage to explore all the implications of that foundation, whatever their difficulty or whatever their risks. Generally, for Tillich this "religious" foundation comes from the religious substance of the culture, from the vision of things characteristic of the philosopher's time and place; accordingly, each philosopher expresses in empirical and rational form the implications of that religious substance. Thus is his or her philosophy "Greek" or "modern," depending on the shape of the symbolic basis or religious substance on which it depends. Philosophy has, therefore, a universal urge or goal; but the universality of philosophy is limited by its historical and particular "destiny." In always expressing all things from its own particular standpoint in time, "Logos has a Kairos" (*TPE*, chap. 1).

Correspondingly, religion depends on philosophy for its reflective explication, if it is to be theology. As we have seen, religion for Tillich is ultimate concern; in turn, ultimate concerns, when rightly understood, have to do with our being and our nonbeing. Thus, *reflection* on religion (theology) must understand and interpret the *structure* of our being if it is to understand the religious; theology, as reflection on religion, thus depends on philosophy, as the analysis of our structure, if theology would understand reflectively religious crises and religious answers (*ST* I:22). One of Tillich's favorite examples, taken from Plato, is that while one has no need to be a doctor in order to become diseased or even to enjoy a renewal of health, still if one is to *understand* disease and health, one must understand the structure of our organic bodies, what can threaten and what can heal them. Correspondingly, if we would understand the religious crises of our finite being (the issues of our being and nonbeing), we must first understand the structure *of our being*, and that is the role of philosophy.

Further, if we would understand the religious answer (as well as receive it), we must understand that answer (the religious symbol) as the answer to our diseased structure, that is, again in terms of philosophy. Reflected religion, reflection on religion (theology), is thus ontological and depends upon philosophy. Finally, as our discussion has shown, religious myths and symbols, without scientific, social, and philosophical criticism, become superstitious, incredible, ideological, and heteronomous, "authorities" that oppress our autonomous reason and our autonomous moral judgments instead of grounding them. To bring the symbols and the norms of religion into correlation with our own inner assent, our rational autonomy, and so our moral and spiritual existence, mediation with our own *cultural* situation becomes necessary. Without that correlation with present culture, and especially with its philosophical expressions, religion quickly becomes incredible and irrelevant, or, as in our day, it turns in the direction of the demonic.

Finally, it was, I think, Tillich's judgment that neither philosophy nor religion could in this day fulfill itself alone. Both were deeply problematic. In the face of secular criticism and secular ultimate concerns, religion has increasingly become removed, moribund, irrelevant—an empty form. In its turn philosophy, in the face of scientific knowing, on the one hand, and of anxiety about reason, on the other, has slowly shrunken into skepticism and positivism. Each has thus lost its living touch with its object and with its powerful élan toward its goal, namely (religion), to relate itself in ultimate concern to God, and (philosophy) to fulfill itself in understanding the wholeness of being. Each is at once imperialistic, claiming all of being to the exclusion of the other, and yet noticeably weakened, unable to make good on its own claims. Only in *union* can either one hope to complete itself. This potential "working together" is not, for Tillich, the classical cooperation of orthodoxy, especially Catholic orthodoxy, in which philosophy is a relatively independent but ultimately subservient step based on "nature" towards an "independently" revealed theology. Reason is not the independent and self-standing "ground floor" of theology, nor is theology the higher and "supernatural" culmination of natural philosophy. Each essentially *depends* on the other, as the method of correlation will show, from begining to end; each is fully human and subject to *criticism*, and yet each, in its own way, is related essentially to the divine ground. How that cooperative method works will become clearer as we proceed.

4

The Master of Mediation:
Theology of Culture and Correlation

Reflecting on the impact that Tillich's thought has made on subsequent decades, this chapter is concerned to answer the query: What is it that has proved most important in Tillich's thought since his death over twenty years ago? That his thought has remained influential or significant—read and reread, discussed, criticized, appealed to, and in many cases (certainly my own) followed in whole or in part—seems unquestioned. In theological studies, while many of the once-important systems of the first half of this century are now of more historical than contemporary interest, Tillich's, almost alone, represents *the* theological system with which almost everyone (at least in American theology) must wrestle, discovering themselves in encounter with him, perhaps in differentiation from him, perhaps in agreement with him, or, more usually, in a good measure of both. That this influence also penetrates the many fields associated with or adjacent to philosophy and religion, philosophy of science, of language, of existence, art criticism, psychology and therapy, culture studies, social theory, and so on, seems almost beyond doubt. Yet as many observers have remarked, there is no Tillichean "school," that is, a self-conscious community of thinkers who not only pattern their own thought on that of one great thinker, but who seek in that thought deliberately to extend, make more coherent, and defend the basic categories of his or her system, as there unquestionably is still a Whiteheadian school, a Thomist school, a Lonerganian school, and as there were in Europe once Barthian and Bultmannian schools. Tillich is without such an explicit band of followers, and yet he remains in the forefront of our intellectual scene: a massive and widespread influence pervading and reshaping much of our thinking.

If one asks for the ground of this persistent influence—besides the obvious points that his thought is at once original and provoking and yet (unlike Barth's) available in a reasonably limited corpus—it is, I think,

that the passage of time has shown that Tillich's thought elegantly represents a *mediating* position. Tillich loved polarities and saw almost everything in their terms, in terms, that is, of opposites in deep and precarious
tension and yet potentially (and necessarily) forming a creative unity. It
might please him to hear that rather than providing *one* option in our
present scene (though there are one or two Tillicheans), the main role of
his thought has been to provide a point, on a surprising number of
different axes, where seemingly utterly opposite positions come into a
tense, if still comprehensible, relation, a point in relation to which,
therefore, they cease to be opposites and become polarities. Such is the
scope and tensive unity of his thought, that it has the capacity to make
contact with, to "touch," and so to relate itself to almost every sort of
position in almost every sort of diverse area. In this sense, he continually
mediates in so many areas, and for this reason he interests and stimulates
so many different sorts of thinkers.

Whether one be a philosopher (analytic or speculative) or a biblical
theologian, whether one be an ontologist or an existentialist, interested in
forms of personal angst or social liberation, in public arguments or deep
personal experiences, in cultural analysis or doctrinal issues, in language
analysis or experience, in humanism or the transcendent, in hermeneutics
or speculation, in mysticism or in rationality, in the religions of the world
or in the Christian message—in each of the varied axes (and probably
more), persons involved in one or another of the options on that axis find
Tillich not only and significantly *there* but, so to speak, "next door,"
possibly for many too much with "them over there" rather than "with us
over here," but still the nearest to *us* of all those "them"! To philosophers,
he is the most sensible and bearable of the religious thinkers and certainly
of the biblical theologians, to the latter, the most religious and theological
of the philosophers, to Protestants, the most Catholic of "us," to Catholics, the most nearly Catholic of "them"; to students of religion,
therapeutic theorists, sociologists, and art critics, "the only theologian we
can or wish to read," and so on. He mediates *not* by bringing them all
into his unity, but by standing "next to" or "within sight of" almost
everyone. Thus, even if there are few Tillicheans, his influence is widespread. Whitehead said, "existence never takes a holiday from metaphysical categories."[1] In that sense, Tillich is almost metaphysical! If he
does not appear on almost every bibliography in almost every humanistic

---

1. A. N. Whitehead, *Process and Reality* (New York: Macmillan, 1929), 4. An
intriguingly similar phrase appears in Luther's *Bondage of the Will:* "[We] do not
sufficiently consider how unrestingly active God is in all his creatures, allowing
none of them to take a holiday" (*Luther's Works,* ed. Philip P. Watson [Phila-
delphia: Fortress Press, 1972], 3:178).

field, one feels he ought to have, and that is not true of many other genuinely great and widely influential thinkers.

The reason for this power to mediate between opposing positions in a wide number of areas of interest and of thought lies, of course, in the character as well as the originality and profundity of Tillich's thinking. This is not only because he is a systematic thinker; Barth, who is also a systematic and coherent thinker, hardly appears naturally just to the right or left of anthropologists, philosophers of science, or of language analysts, sociologists, therapists, and so on. Even more, it is because Tillich's thought itself mediates, in the sense that it uncovers massive and significant unities between diverse areas of life, of culture and of history, and so importantly touches all of them. Most great philosophers—and here Tillich is a philosopher to the core—in the classical tradition have done this: Aristotle, Leibnitz, Hegel, Dewey, Whitehead, to name a few. What is unique about Tillich is that he not only mediates *philosophically* (on the basis of culture) the various facets of historical life: science, art, law, government, morals, and religion; he also mediates *between* culture and religion, philosophy and theology. He is not only philosopher but also theologian, and thus he is "on the boundary" between culture and religion, standing in both and viewing each from the center of the other. Thus, unlike the other philosophers—even Hegel—he brings to culture a *religious* or *theological* interpretation of the elements of culture as well as a *philosophical* interpretation of religion and theology. Such mediation has been rare: possibly Augustine, certainly Thomas, Schleiermacher (though in that case more in potentiality than in actuality). As a *theologian*, Tillich has genuine philosophical wisdom on any number of cultural issues, and yet as a *philosopher* he brings to his analysis a "theological" profundity, a religious interpretation of things and events, that few philosophers can manage. It is, I think, this role of mediation, of mediation between almost all facets of cultural life and religion, that gives to his thought its uniqueness, its fascination, its near-universality of relevance, and its unceasing ability to illuminate the obscure corners of our existence. It is, in fact, only those for whom any religious interpretation of anything is anathema (and that is, of course, by no means a small number!), or those on the other side who view any philosophical interpretation of religion as blasphemous, who find Tillich empty of all interest.

The foundation for this unique mediating role in the system itself is, of course, its basic equation: Being-itself equals God. Or, set in less cryptic language, the *ground* of finite being, and so of all ordinary cultural and historical experience (when the latter is truly understood), is the same as the *referent* of religious concern and faith (when truly interpreted), namely, God; the ground of culture and the ground of religion are in the end the same. Moreover, a proper *religious* analysis of culture will uncover that sacral ground of culture (theology of culture), and a proper *cultural* (philosophical) analysis of religion will most truly uncover and manifest that ground or referent of religion (philosophical theology). Thus, not only are cultural and religious institutions (e.g., states, artistic and scientific communities, churches) deeply associated for Tillich; cultural expressions and activities, on the one hand, and religious realities, on the other, are also interrelated. Finally, cultural thought or self-interpretation (science, psychology, social theory, and philosophy) and reflection on religion (theology) are "correlated." Works (literary, artistic, philosophical), acts, propositions, and theories in culture have an essential relation to religion because they depend on and express, for Tillich, a "religious import" or "religious substance." In turn, religious acts, communities, propositions, symbols, and theories have relevance to culture and its modes of discourse because they inevitably are expressed and enacted in particular cultural form. The continuing experience of many students in a diversity of academic fields, that Tillich proves to be the single theologian most relevant and interesting to their own area of concern, is no accident. On their subject matter, and especially on its religious ground and its religious implications, Tillich already had something novel and stimulating to say because of the way he viewed and interpreted the width of common experience, namely, as in the end an expression of the relationship to God, the ground of all being and meaning.

If it is so that the persistent influence of Tillich is related to the mediating character of his thought—and to the *truth* or *insight* that such mediation or interrelating of diverse, opposing polarities brings with it—then perhaps it will be useful in entering the wide realm of Tillich's thought to locate why his thinking has such uncanny relevance to so many areas. To me, there are two major sources or grounds for this mediating role: (1) the close interrelation of culture and religion (the Tillichean theology of culture), and (2) the interrelation, in fact the interdependence, of philosophy and religion, resulting in theology (the method of correlation). This chapter will, therefore, provide an introductory account of Tillich's theology of culture, on the one hand, and his method of correlation, on the other. It is hoped that subsequent chapters will provide ample illustrations of both Tillich's analysis of culture and his method of correlation.

Culture and Religion

As we have noted, Tillich is unique not only in seeking (as a philosopher) to unite in one coherent conceptual analysis all the various aspects of culture (as Whitehead and Dewey did), not merely (even) in seeking that unity in the unconditioned ground of culture (as did Hegel), but in viewing that ground as the object of *religion,* as fully manifest only via religion (in response to revelation), and so as explicable only by means of religious symbols and through reflection on religion (theology). This "correlation," interrelation, or (best) "mode of cooperation" methodologically between culture and religion, on the one hand, and between the substantial analysis, interpretation, and understanding of culture and of religion, on the other, runs through all of Tillich's thought. In each case, the finite represents an essentially real, valuable, and coherent but religiously transcended realm: there is being (finitude) and the infinite ground of being (God); there is reason (the culture-producing power) and the depth of reason (revelation); there is culture and the religious substance of culture. This is, therefore, a *religious* analysis of cultural life, that is, one based on a religious relation to and understanding of what is regarded as the foundational center of culture's life, its religious substance.[2]

The negative theme, moreover, characteristic of most high religions, namely, that a serious derangement, estrangement, or "fall" has taken place, also characterizes Tillich's analysis of culture and all its aspects and differentiates him radically from most philosophers, especially Dewey and Whitehead. In fact, this differentiation from "essentialist" philosophy reaches a climax in his interesting *reversal* of Hegel. Whereas for Hegel, cultural history exhibits the *rationality* of a gradual synthesis of opposites into a higher unity, for Tillich that history exhibits *estrangement* in its inexorable unraveling of an original unity into a self-destructive disunity. It moves from an original creative theonomous synthesis, through the ambiguous thesis of autonomy, to the nemesis and destruction of heteronomous antitheses. (See especially *The World Situation.*) Here we see a religious and theological analysis of culture, based not only on the religious apprehension of the immanent holy and the sacred ground (creation), but also on the religious awareness of our estrangement from that sacred ground, an awareness expressed in this case by the particular symbol or myth of the Fall. Without such a dialectical (positive *and*

---

2. A theological analysis of culture pervades all of Tillich's writings. Specific examples of its theoretical grounds are "Aspects of Religious Analysis of Culture," in *TC,* 40–51; and "Religion and Secular Culture," in *TPE,* 55–65. Cf. also Paul Tillich, *The Meaning of Health,* ed. Perry LeFevre (Chicago: Exploration Press, 1984); Paul Tillich, *On Art and Architecture,* ed. John Dillenberger and Jane Dillenberger (New York: Crossroad, 1987); and J. Mark Thomas, ed., *The Spiritual Situation in Our Technical Society: Paul Tillich* (Macon, GA: Mercer University Press, 1988).

negative) analysis based on the symbols (creation and fall) of a particular religious tradition—a *theology* of culture as opposed to a philosphical analysis of religion—Tillich (after World War I!) believed that the true situation of culture and of reason within it could not be understood. And again, it was on mainly religious grounds that Tillich looked forward, even in the present "void," to a *new kairos,* where a new form of creative theonomy, building on the preceding cultural "time of troubles," would appear.

To most theologians, this analysis is too concerned with culture and too dominated by philosophical procedures and categories to be legitimate. To almost all philosophers, while this analysis is comprehensible philosophically, still it is not quite acceptable: its premises are neither those of cultural common sense nor are they demonstrable; it is far too religious, too dependent on strange religious myths; and it is unquestionably too gloomy. One may remark that the only things in its favor are the clear facts of our historical present. So let us turn to this analysis in more detail; it seems to me that the current situation in Western culture at the end of the century, even more than did his own earlier situation (Germany during and after World War I, in the '20s and '30s) warrants the need for this sort of theoretical mediation between the cultural and the religious, for this theological dialectic of affirmation, negation, and reaffirmation.

Tillich's affirmation of the creativity, value, and integrity of culture is remarkable for a theologian. Here his deep indebtedness to the German *Aufklärung* reveals itself: culture (as culture) is not essentially fallen, a kingdom of Satan, or even a merely "natural" and so preliminary level of value. On the contrary, it is the creation of ontological reason, of reason in touch with its depth; thus, in its own way each culture represents an apprehension of the unconditioned power and meaning that are the divine. He defines culture as that which *reason,* essential reason, produces. (He also defines *reason* as the culture-producing power of human beings, but that is another issue.) Thus, on the one hand, culture, as the product of essential reason, has an unconditioned depth or import and embodies an unconditioned meaning; on the other, as the product of reason, culture has its own autonomous integrity. It sets its own canons, procedures and norms; it produces autonomously its own autonomous criteria. The divine is the *ground,* not the *controller,* of the sublime forms and the infinite variety of human culture; the meaning, quality, and value of culture's works are immanent within them, not extrinsic to them. This is one important meaning of Tillich's category of *theonomy* as descriptive of a creative culture.

This analysis of culture sharply distinguishes itself from many "secular" analyses of culture in two divergent ways. In the first place, it regards *all* of creative culture as rational, as the product of creative reason, and therefore as potentially unified and coherent: art, morals, law, government, economic and social structures, arts of healing, and practices of religion. If reason and the rational are exclusively associated with scientific, technological, or organizational reason (with the laboratory, the academy, the corporation), then correspondingly, much of culture is regarded as the product of instincts, emotions, arbitrary preferences, fantasy, unexamined tradition, habits, chance arrangements—the irrational in all its many forms. As a consequence, reason and rational discourse are excluded from many of the areas essential to culture's actual life, a situation Tillich regarded as arid and dangerous.

On the other hand, this entire rational panorama is, for Tillich, also saturated with the "depth of reason," with what transcends and yet is in union with reason, with an unconditioned import, meaning, and value that provide the eros, purpose, commitment, integrity, and responsibility (in essence, the "vitality") necessary for any form of rational creativity, that is, for any form of creative cultural life (*ST* I:79–81, 83–86). This latter transcendent dimension is even more strange to most contemporary analysis, although, interestingly, a number of sociological interpretations of society and philosophical interpretations of science and of the scientific community have uncovered many of these unexpected aspects of ultimacy (of the "religious"), foundational for the life of wider cultures and of specialized communities alike. For Tillich, culture is essentially separated neither from the rational nor from the religious; it is both humanistic and religiously based. A theonomous culture is created and penetrated not only by human reason but also by the infinite divine ground of reason. Thus, while culture is a rational and so human creation, it is also an aspect of the work of Providence, an effect of "revelation" in its most general sense, and a constituent element in the Kingdom or the final and perfected form of divine creation.

The above extremely positive assessment of culture as the creation of reason offends not a few theologians. Tillich's equally definite assessment of the negativities of culture, of its estrangement, and so its path to injustice and self-destruction, has seemed to others, a goodly number of philosophers and social theorists, far too gloomy, "*typische deutsche Weltschmerz*," or possibly the idiosyncratic consequence of four "upsetting" years as a German army chaplain. In any case, it was typical of Tillich to view history dialectically, as evidencing the career of creative reason inspired by its ground, and thus ever full of new possibilities (*kairoi*), but also evidencing an apparently inexorable process of unraveling, a progressive disunity, separation, and conflict, resulting in the end in catastrophic nemesis, which may then lead to a new *kairos* and so to new possibilities (*IOH*, 123–25; *TPE*, 32–51). Further, he was convinced (against secular analysts) that the basic forces or factors at work in this dialectical process could only be understood by a religious and a theological analysis (theology of culture), and (against the optimistic rationalists among the latter) that actual history—in fact, the history of the culture stemming from the Enlightenment, that is, the career of our own culture—illustrates this dialectical unraveling process. As I remarked, the facts of our present situation seem to bear him out.

For Augustine as for Tillich, the loss of the unifying ground of life results in a disunity, a separation from one another of the interrelated facets and aspects of life. Thus (to use slightly different language) God is the principle of unity and harmony, and separation from God is the cause of disunity, disharmony, and a final consequent loss of being (reality) and meaning (value). As did Augustine, Tillich applies this fundamental principle of interpretation both to individual and to social or historical existence. He sees Enlightenment culture as beginning with a powerful assertion of the *autonomy* of reason against *heteronomy*, the absolute and yet uncreative authority of the now alien and external religious powers of the receding medieval world. This was, however, an autonomy with *theonomous* elements: it assumed the ultimate identity of reason and nature, of the rational, the good, and the beautiful, and so of objective and subjective, of reality and value, of cognition, morals, and art. As a consequence, in the Enlightenment the "rational" stood not only for that which is true (the result of the rational cognitive processes of science) but also for that which is just (the result of rational and radical politics) and that which is beautiful (the harmonious and the orderly). In that theonomous unity (that is, through the exercise of ontological reason) the power and meaning of modern culture were nurtured.

Reason, however, in its self-conscious autonomy, has slowly cut itself off from its theonomous ground, and so it has gradually lost these theonomous elements. As a result, fatal separations in cultural life have taken place. Reason has become "technical reason," solely concerned with cognition, manipulation, and organization (*ST* I: 72–74); it has become divorced from consideration of ends and so from both the good and the aesthetic. Human subjectivity has shrunk to a process of rational calculation, seeking to control and organize unordered and undirected desires; thought has become separated from its objects, and thus is either skeptical or merely manipulative; reality has become mechanical and vacuous, dominated by a meaningless fate; and inner spirit has become irrational and subjective, ultimately empty, determined by outside forces, and so unreal to itself. A technological culture, dominated by a scientific and technological definition of reason, thus objectifies its world and infinitely subjectifies its persons. Communion with nature is only achieved by manipulation and exploitation, communion with one another only by the creation of primitive communities that further submerge persons into a new heteronomy. Thus for Tillich, autonomy in history (in existence) is not self-sustaining. Inexorably it dissolves itself, or it dissolves the hidden unities on which its power is based, then, in order to save itself, it creates against itself a new heteronomy that smothers all autonomy and creativity. The development of bourgeois, scientific, and humanistic German culture into the emptiness of the Weimar and the ideology of the Third Reich provided, of course, Tillich's actual model. But, unfortunately, the problems he discerned there have progressively characterized the whole of the post-Enlightenment West with its manipulation and exploitation of nature, its new sense of industrial fatedness and loss of strong inwardness, and its ever-present and threatening ideologies (compare *WS*; ST I:83–86; *RS*).

Central to Tillich's interpretation of culture is that there are extra-scientific and extra-technological elements of cultural life that are crucial to its existence. These elements are represented by the foundations of its customs, norms, law, institutions, and its values or aims in life, not to mention its religion (its ultimate concerns). These elements are characterized and upheld by deep emotion, commitment, and loyalty (eros); they structure and shape the ends, purposes, meanings, and values (the object of eros) that constitute and direct every culture's life. When reason is seen as merely scientific and technical, these elements in turn become irrational; that is, they are seen as merely emotive, arbitrary "preferences," as merely subjective, or possibly even as only self-interested. In the laboratory and the academic department, such irrational elements are (for the moment) controlled by scientific commitment, by adherence to procedures, and so on; but in society at large, they represent a continuing powerful, in fact, a foundational, presence and so a potential danger. In any case, they do not and will not go away; however, they may be banished from the rationality of the self-interpretation of the culture carried on by the academy. They need to be penetrated by reason (they are its creations); they need to be unified among themselves, unified with scientific cognition and in relation to the depths of reason, that is, in terms of the fundamental mythical and cultic structures of the society's life (for example, such symbols as democracy, freedom, a "free society"). Unless this unifying process in thought, social legislation, political life, education, and common custom takes place, these elements will form themselves irrationally and heteronomously into a new and destructive unity, into a false or demonic substance, also unconditioned, holy, mythical, and cultic.

Tillich himself, therefore, would hardly have been surprised that in our advanced technical society the religious would return in a multitude of unexpected forms. In the isolated, precarious, and vulnerable life of private individuals, fundamentalism and charismatic possession, religious cults, old and new, and even a modern concern for the occult have manifested themselves anew amongst us, not as slowly weakening carry-overs from a dying tradition but as powerful, novel responses to the threatening forces and debilitating emptiness of an industrial and tech-nological culture. Correspondingly, in the public sphere these non-technical and nonscientific elements—participation in community, loyalty and commitment to its myths and cults, ideologies of class, race, and especially nation—reappear in potent forms as bearers of oppressive and dangerous heteronomy. In the most recent years, fundamentalism, grown to new proportions, has begun to seek to control and reshape our public life. The realms of value and of the sacred, even if banished in principle from the academy, are never in fact banished. They return, given new force through the coherence, unity, and ultimacy provided by a unified ideology, to take over the culture and even the rational elements within it. Science, technology, and a rational industrial society, which once saw themselves as conquering and eradicating the religious, at that point become its servants, and in doing so, they, too, become instruments of the demonic. This process has repeated itself with surprising and disturb-ing frequency in the twentieth century and continues to do so: in Shinto Japan, in Nazi Germany, in Stalinist Russia, in Maoist China, and now in Shiite Iran—and, as a mere cloud on the horizon, in a fundamentalist and nationalist America.

The central theme at work in this analysis is the *interdependence* or *interpenetration* of the autonomous elements of culture with the religious elements. As unconditional meanings and commitments make the creative autonomy of a culture possible, so heteronomous meanings and commit-ments can render any culture demonic. More specifically, they can hallow with an unconditioned value the unjust and oppressive economic and political structures of a culture's life, and they can unify the culture around an exclusivist and fanatical mythos. It is the religious substance of the culture, its forms of ultimate concern and of ultimate meaning, that can render dangerous, as well as creative, the existence of cultures in history. Correspondingly, the specifically religious elements, forces, or communities (churches) exhibit the same potential ambiguity; they can become either esoteric and trivial or heteronomous. In either case, they pose a danger, both to their own health and to that of culture. As trivial, the churches merely follow the culture's mythos and concentrate on their own separated sacred realm, when they should be challenging the culture's forms of injustice and its complacent and possibly heteronomous myths (as in the religious socialist protest against capitalism and as in Tillich's resistance to Nazism). As heteronomous, the churches can unite with the national myths to annihilate all autonomously creative cultural life (as in the Moral Majority). The culture desperately needs, therefore, on the one hand, a *political* criticism of its injustice, as Tillich embodied in his early career; on the other hand, culture needs a *rational* and a *religious* criticism of its ultimate presuppositions if it is to be whole and healthy. The first (the rational critique) is to render these mythic elements "rational" and to set these religious dimensions within creative relationships to the autonomous elements of the culture's life; the second (the religious critique) is to criticize the demonic tendencies of that religious substance and to give the latter a firmer and more creative grounding in the depth of reason, in being-itself, or God. (Thus should socialism be *religious* as well as theoretical.) Correspondingly, religion desperately needs (and equally so) the rational and moral critique of culture so that it is neither esoteric, trivial, and irrelevant nor heteronomous. Culture and church depend on each other; they equally need each other and the critique that each gives to the other. In fact, their separation manifests the "fall" of *each* from its true essence; their unity, as our argument shows, manifests the fulfillment of each in theonomy, or, in eschatological terms, in the Kingdom.

Philosophy and Religion

We now turn to a more specialized issue within the general relation of culture and religion, namely, the question of the relation of philosophy to religion and so to reflection on religion, that is, the questions of philosophical and of theological method (*ST* I:18–28; *TPE*, 83–93). Here, too, Tillich is negatively and positively mediating: negatively as disliked by philosophers for seeming, after a lot of rhetoric, to abandon philosophy and to reduce it to a mere instrument of theology; negatively by theologians for abandoning theology by subordinating it to philosophical questions, categories, and norms.[3] Positively I will argue, first, that Tillich, partly because of the way he himself described his famous method of correlation, is, more frequently than not, misunderstood on this issue as giving philosophy only a preliminary, question-asking role in significant truth. Second, when it is sorted out, his position turns out to be a

---

3. "No theologian should be taken seriously as a theologian, even if he is a great Christian and a great scholar, if his works show that he does not take philosophy seriously" (*BR*, 7–8).

genuinely mediating one between philosophical and theological thinking (provided, of course, that the latter is recognized at all), one that recognizes the essential dependence of each upon the other and the role of each *from start to finish*, so to speak, if either one is to complete itself—much as culture and religion need each other to be what they essentially are.[4]

Tillich always regarded himself fully as much a philosopher as a theologian, and he always defended philosophy as an essential, legitimate, and exciting vocation. Probably he was more deeply shocked and offended by any belittling of philosophy than of revelation or theology (he *understood* the "why" of the latter), whether by empiricist and positivist philosophers ("nominalists," he called them), or by religious enthusiasts. He saw himself as representing the classical tradition in philosophy, that is, as one who regarded philosophy as a form of knowing, as a first-order discipline, and not merely as the analyst of the claims to know of other disciplines. The latter represented to him, of course, the reduction of reason to technical reason and so the immediate dissolution of the unity of cultural life (*ST* I:231). Philosophy, then, was an aspect of *cognitive* reason; it represented the ability of mind to "grasp" the structures of given reality, to interpret those structures in terms of universals, and thus to unify the cognitive powers of reason, in the sciences and between science, philosophy, and religion. As the most universal cognitive discipline, philosophy is also able to help to guide and make coherent and unified the other noncognitive aspects of reason, the "shaping" of reality embodied in the practical activities of culture in economics, law, political life, education, literature, the arts, and above all, in the moral dimensions of all of life. Since these latter active, shaping aspects of cultural life are also powers of "reason," they, too, represent principles and structures about which we can and should think. Philosophy, therefore, has the widest possible range, coextensive, so to speak, with the extent of culture itself. It is, on the one hand, cognitive of the structures of given finite reality as the unifying discipline of the cognitive sciences; it is analytical of the structures of cultural activity: morals, law, art, politics, economics, and so on; and it is normative in expressing the obligations and ends inherent in these structures and activities. Unlike the British empirical tradition and Kant, Tillich believed that an ontology, a metaphysical "science" of experienced, finite reality, was possible, and that philosophies of art, law, of society, and of morals were possible and relevant—for the structures of finite being (the objective logos) could be known by philosophical reason (ontological reason or the subjective logos).

---

4. "Both philosophy and theology become poor and distorted when they are separated from each other" (*TPE*, 89).

The philosophical understanding and analysis of the structure of finite being is, for Tillich, not only possible but essential for the health both of culture and of religion. Without such an ontological analysis spanning the separate disciplines of inquiry and the separate aspects or "niches" of culture, no unity either of cultural discourse or of individual life is possible; nor is any understanding of the different modes and perspectives of "knowing" possible, how they differ and how they relate to each other. Further, no rational discussion or discrimination of overarching and uni-fying ends or meanings is possible, and so anxiety, irrationality, and heteronomy hover in the wings. Without understanding of the structures of being (of self, of community, of temporality, and of history), no understanding of the existential anxieties, derangements, possibilities, and so obligations of personal or communal life is possible. We are subject, then, to unknown and arbitrary terrors and have no inward (for Tillich, autonomous) way of dealing with them. Finally, without such analysis, it is not possible to penetrate, disclose, elucidate, and render as coherently as possible the unconditional dimensions of culture: the depth of reason, the unconditional, the sacred, and the holy, the realm of myth and cult—that vision of ultimate being, meaning, and value which pro-vides the import or the religious substance that in turn permeates, ani-mates, and directs all of culture's autonomous life. While in significant ways transcendent to the subject-object realm where cognitive and ana-lytic reason is at home, this realm of the unconditional nevertheless represents, for Tillich, the depths of reason, in union with reason, and so available in its own manner to reason. This penetration of reason into the realm of transcendence is crucial for him: otherwise, there can be no unity of autonomy with its own transcendent elements (there is, therefore, an increasing emptiness), and there can be no rational criticism of the "reli-gious" dimensions of a culture's life (and so an encroaching heteronomy makes its appearance). How Tillich seeks to integrate this religious level with the other "secular" levels of culture we will see soon enough when we discuss his method of correlation; but *that* such interpenetration is necessary, both for the culture and for its religious communities, both for philosophy and for theonomous religion, is by now obvious.

In any case, it is clear that Tillich felt the utmost respect for philosophy. Its aim is to understand the *structures* of being as given in experience (*ST* I:20, 22, 230); it is thus critical of tradition, of authority, of any hetero-nomous claims; and it thrives on distance as well as on commitment and on participation. It pursues its task of understanding, "whatever the consequences," to dearly cherished theories and views, and it represents, I once heard him say, "the infinite courage to carry an interpretation out to the end in the face of *all* the evidence and in the face of all that one might desire not to be the case." It must consistently refuse to introduce alien and heteronomous authorities into its discussion, whether representing traditional political, ethical, or religious interests. Representing autonomous creative reason, philosophy appeals only to its own norms: common experience and rational coherence (*ST* I:23). Tillich always believed (or *believed* he believed) that any argument about the structures of finite being—about reason, human being, nature, society, history, and so on—was a philosophical and not a theological argument, one that could therefore be adjudicated by purely empirical and/or rational warrants.

For Tillich, however, philosophy—and finite reason—is by no means omnicompetent. It is itself dependent, as is all of finite being, on something beyond itself, something that grounds its powers and gives meaning to their exercise, on what Tillich calls the "depth of reason" (*ST* I:79–80). Philosophy thinks *from* this depth, on its basis. From this basis comes reason's apprehension of unity with its world, of unity of subject and object, of subjective and objective logos—and so its confidence in the relevance of thinking. From this "ground" come reason's participation in significant ends or meanings and reason's eros toward the truth, its subservience to autonomously recognized norms, its discernment of possibilities, in short, its courage, its self-confidence, its commitment, and its hope. Without this participation in its unifying ground, as we noted, reason shrinks to technical reason, becomes skeptical and manipulative, uncertain, and rudderless—and so vulnerable to being crushed by the return of this "depth" in its demonic forms. As culture lives *from* its religious substance and expresses it, and cannot itself, therefore, produce it as one of its own artifacts, so philosophy thinks *from* its depth and cannot itself "think" *to* it; without that depth, philosophy becomes technical reason and cannot "think" at all.

This dependence on the depth of reason for reason's own essential exercise or possibility represents, for Tillich, the inescapable *finitude* of reason, its confinement to the subject-object realm, to this given world of nature, history, and the self, to ordinary or common-level experience. It means that a "natural theology," a proving of "God" on the basis of thought about the world, history, or the self, represents, for Tillich, a "category-mistake," a confusion of what is the depth and ground of thought with what is within the subject-object realm of thought and so can be concluded by it—it is to mistake God for "a being," an object of thought, instead of the ground or depth of thought (*ST* I:205). Despite his earlier disagreement with Kant about the general possibility of ontology, therefore, Tillich is in agreement with him at this point on the impossibility of proving God from ordinary experience.

Reason, furthermore, is not only finite and incapable of establishing its own ground; it is also in estrangement (*ST* I:81ff.). Thus its powers are not only transcended by its own depth; they are separated from that depth, and, as a consequence, unable so to unify and order themselves as to establish and heal themselves. Tillich is, in certain significant respects, a humanist, as we have seen. With regard, however, to the capacity of human powers, including that of reason, to overcome their own deepest problems, he is adamant that this is not possible. Human capacities, like human finitude itself, can be rescued only from beyond themselves if they would fulfill or realize themselves. If some new theonomy appears out of the nemesis of autonomy and heteronomy, it is a manifestation of a new *kairos*, a new uncovering of the ground of being and meaning, the appearance of the Eternal Now in the midst of the moments of time (compare *The Religious Situation*, "Introduction"), an historical turn that can only be called "revelation." To be sure, a *kairos* can be expected and anticipated; it appears as a challenge to and a demand on us, a demand for criticism of the present, for assessment of its needs, for creative thought and action into the new. But such creative historical work is a *response* to a *kairos*, not the cause of its appearance. A *kairos* bringing in a new creative theonomy is the *basis* of a new cultural life, not the result or consequence of cultural life.

Tillich is very clear on this point, namely, that reason is fulfilled in revelation, that is to say, that the "answers" to its own antimonies and contradictions are received there. In seeking to become and fulfill itself in the face of its destructive antimonies, reason seeks for its own ground, it "asks for revelation" (*ST* I:93–94, 105). In the reception of revelation, unity with that ground is provided, that is, in cultural and historical life in the appearance of a new theonomy, an historical *kairos*, in which the possibility of ontological reason is once again given to us. Culture lives from its religious substance, from the manifestation *(kairos)* of the ground, power, and meaning of being—of reality, truth, and good—that establishes that culture's life. Correspondingly, philosophy, as the epitome of cultural reason, lives from its relation with its own depth via that cultural *Gestalt* or religious substance. Every great epoch of philosophy (Hellenic philosophy, medieval philosophy, Enlightenment philosophy) expresses and so lives from the religious substance of its culture insofar as it depends as a condition for its own possibility on the unity of thought and being, subject and object, of reality and value, apprehended in that culture's creative life.

It is, therefore, with this understanding of the relation of culture and the religious that Tillich's insistence that "religion provides the answers to philosophy's questions" must be viewed. It is not that Tillich thought that, descriptively speaking, philosophers do not, in fact, provide answers or should not provide them—he loved the pre-Socratics, Plato, Plotinus, and Spinoza, as well as Schelling, Schopenhauer and Nietzsche. Whatever fundamental answers a given philosophy may offer represent theoretical expressions of the most fundamental presuppositions implicit in the religious substance of the philosopher's culture, and function, therefore, as the basis rather than the conclusion of his or her thought. In this he would agree with Hegel, Collingwood, and Whitehead (to name a few), except that he prefers to view that presupposed and given substance which metaphysics expresses as *religious* in character. These presuppositions form the "religious" element in a given philosophy corresponding to the religious substance of the culture, or, as he also put it, "the mystical a priori" (*ST* I:9) at the base of every philosophy. The philosopher is, consequently, a "hidden theologian" (*ST* I:25), not dependent on the particular religious tradition (though he or she may be), but a participant in the culture's ultimate presuppositions, its ultimate concerns, and its establishing and healing answers to those concerns (*ST* I:24–25, 230ff.). Without such participation, Tillich believes, the philosopher could neither be nor think as a philosopher. Thus does logos (the power of thought, especially of philosophical thought) have a "fate" or live from a *kairos* (compare *The Protestant Era*, "Philosophy and Fate"), that is, it is dependent on and relative to the historical culture in which it thrives.

For Tillich, then, both religion (that is, the community explicitly centered about a given religious tradition or revelation) and philosophy (representing the self-interpretation of a culture) are unable to complete themselves alone, without the other. As in the relation of culture and religion, they are mutually dependent from start to finish. Without the help of philosophy, religious *reflection* is unable to proceed, that is, unable to express reflectively the "existential estrangement" of human being and the symbolic answers of the religious tradition. Thus, religious traditions or communities separated from philosophy become esoteric, meaningless, and, in the end, heteronomous. Without religion and reflection on its symbols, on the other hand, philosophy cannot reach or uncover its own ground, or ponder reflectively its own deepest questions. It can merely express the inadequate and frequently demonic "answers" enshrined in its cultural heritage or ideology, and it is continually subject to the destructive dialectic of skepticism and relativism, on the one hand, and of absolutism, on the other.

Correlation is the way Tillich viewed this pattern or career of interdependence and cooperation, the combined and cooperative procedure to which both philosophy and religion are naturally prone. In correlation, we see how each is implied and called for by the needs of the other, and the way in which, therefore, each fulfills itself through its partnership with the other. Correlation is the *methodological expression* of fulfilled ontological reason, of theonomous reason, of thought and eros, rationality and faith, in short, of the *union of reason with its own creative depth and ground*, of "true philosophy." Tillich is *not* saying that philosophers are helplessly bewildered vacuities who go around only asking questions, and that theologians pass out answers to impoverished cultural theorists as John D. Rockefeller passed out dimes to impoverished small boys, though some of his phrasings can sound that way. Systematic theology, whose method is that of "correlation," represents, then, for Tillich, the culmination and fulfillment of philosophy as well as the actualization of reflection on a religious tradition. As culture is completed when its religious substance expresses the central *Kairos* of *kairoi* (in theonomy), so the thought of culture is completed when it is grounded in and informed by "final revelation" (*ST* I:132–33, 147–53), when it transcends itself in becoming "theology." How, then, does this cooperative method proceed?

It begins with philosophy, the analysis of the ontological structure of finitude, an enterprise in which philosophy is at home and of which it clearly is capable (*ST* I:20, 22, 230). The reason for this philosophical beginning for reflection on religion follows from Tillich's most fundamental principles. The first of these is the distinction between religion and *reflection on religion*, between religion and theology. Religion consists negatively of *existential* anxieties, problems, and crises, and positively of *existentially* received "answers" or resolutions; it involves an experienced answer to an ultimate concern, but it does not *necessarily* involve a theoretical understanding of itself. To reflect on religion, however, *does* involve such theory, and this is theology. Now (the second basic principle), since ultimate concerns (religion) relate to our being and our nonbeing, and so to the existential awareness of our being and our nonbeing (our *ultimate* concerns [*ST* I:12–14]), so *reflection* on religion requires reflection on the *structure* of our being and the crises (the shocks of nonbeing) to which that structure is heir. We understand what is going on in "religious" ultimate concern about our being and our nonbeing by understanding, first, the structure of our being, and then, especially, the "meaning" of that structure. The first task, therefore, is to uncover philosophically the structures of finite being: of reason, of finitude, of spirit, of history. This is the task of philosophy; it could, in principle, proceed indefinitely, taking up problem after problem in epistemology, in cosmology, ontology or metaphysics, and so on (as, for example, in Whitehead's *Process and Reality*). In principle, Tillich believed this to be possible and important, important both for cultural and for religious communities. Yet he himself did not carry it out all the way, for he was by vocation a theologian, and, I suspect, this is where his real interests lay.

The theologian, says Tillich, is interested in the *meaning* of being (*ST* I: 20, 22, 230), that is, in its ultimate concerns, its crises and dilemmas, its answers and its resolutions ("theology is soteriology" [*ST* I:24]). Thus at this point we shift gears, so to speak, from the philosophical task of analyzing the structure of finite being to the theological task of investigating the meaning latent in that same structure of finitude, a structure now philosophically discriminated. Our own structure, says Tillich, is that of finite freedom; the *meaning* of that structure ("finitude felt from the inside") is *anxiety* (*ST* I:191–92), or, as he should have said in this connection, "*wonder* and anxiety." Thus, in a "theological analysis of our finitude" we look at the affirmations and the dangers lurking in the self-world correlation (this is the central category); at the affirmations and anxieties implicit in the categories of time, space, causality, and substance; at the antimonies and contradictions possible because of the polarities; and at the crucial issues for our existence implied by the infinite-finite synthesis that is human being. By this philosophical/theological (that is to say, first structure, *then* meaning) analysis, we uncover the "questions" (dilemmas, crises, threats) involved in our being—the negative side of our ultimate concerns—to see reflectively what constitutes the "desperate" situation we experience existentially in being human, and so what constitutes "salvation," that is to say, what the received answers of religion *mean.* Philosophy as such does not "ask the questions"; that is poorly or, better, crudely stated. *Philosophical/theological analysis* uncovers reflectively the ultimate questions that our finitude and existence pose—as, in turn, theology will reflectively express the answers received through participation in the revelation present within a given religious tradition. Theological analysis of meaning in union with philosophical analysis of structure, therefore, asks the question.

"Answers" on the level of our actual existence are received existentially within a community of faith, by participation in its life, and by participation in its symbols, its message; such existential ("religious") answers give us courage, self-acceptance, self-criticism, self-affirmation, serenity, eros and purpose, confidence and love, and are made possible by our being "grasped by the ground of our being," which is most fundamentally what Tillich meant by participation, by faith, and by the experience of grace. This is the "ecstasy" within which dependent revelation is received in a particular religious tradition: it is communicated through the media of dependent revelation, especially word, sacrament, and the "symbolic" character of the transformed lives (saints) in the community (*ST* I:116–17, 126–28). As the *basic* meaning of "question" is *existential* dilemma or impasse, so the *basic* meaning of "answer" is *existential* participation in the New Being received through the medium of tradition.

At this point, however, we are discussing reflection and theory (theology is a theoretical discipline), not actual existence. Thus, just as in our question phase we did not analyze our own personal situation (though preaching and counseling well might do so) but the "cultural self-interpretation of our epoch" (its philosophical understanding of itself [*ST* I:4]), so now we concentrate on the theoretical or reflective component (or bearer) of the answer, of the experience of grace. This reflective component of the answer is constituted by the *symbolic* content of the religious tradition within which this participation occurs, namely, its message, gospel, or teachings. In the answering section of theology, therefore, the religious symbols constituting the "message" or teachings are set anew into *theoretical* form, into the form of philosophical or theological understanding. Theology is the theoretical task of interpreting the symbols of its tradition in the light of the questions of human existence to which these symbols "have been found" existentially to be an answer, or *the* answer—that "finding" or experiencing of participation and healing being presupposed, and not established, through the enterprise of theology (*ST* I:9, 23–24, 117, 129).

Thus the symbol or category of "revelation" is interpreted theologically *as* the answer to the dilemma of reason (which is the way it was experienced and received), namely, as the appearance of the depth of reason. The symbol "God" is interpreted theologically as the answer to the questions or dilemmas of our finitude (of our finite freedom), namely, as the ground and power of being. Jesus as the Christ is understood as the answer to the dilemmas of our estranged existence, namely, as the appearance of the New Being, and so on. Since the dilemmas are the negative meanings *of* our ontological structure, the answers to these dilemmas are understood in terms of the fulfillment of that same ontological structure (they are answers to *its* dilemmas and so are meaningful to us). Thus are the religious symbols, experienced as effective on the existential level of religion, transposed on the theoretical level (theology) into the ontological categories uncovered in the philosophical analysis of our finitude.[5]

There is, however, this substantial difference from the use of those

---

5. Tillich did not credit himself with the "invention" of the method of correlation here described. On the contrary, he said that "as method, it is as old as theology" (*ST* II:16).

categories in philosophical analysis.[6] The answers come *to* finitude, help-less in itself, from beyond itself, from the depths of reason (and so is a mystery to it [*ST* I:108–9]), from the prius of subject and object, from that which transcends the finite realm. Thus when they are applied to the "answers," ontological categories of finitude are used symbolically (ana-logically) and not "properly," "literally," or "univocally" (*ST* I:155–56; II:9–10), as in most contemporary philosophical theologies (for example, in process theology). Tillich is, as we have emphasized, an ontological theologian, and his theology is ontological through and through, based on the correlation he perceives between our ontological structure and our religious dilemmas and answers. When, however, he uses these on-tological categories derived by a philosophical/theological analysis of finitude constructively to speak of God, he uses them *analogically* (sym-bolically); he presupposes revelation and its ecstatic reception as the basis both for that speech and for the symbols that are thus ontologically interpreted. It can be assumed that this form of ontological/analogical ecstatic speech (theology) is as relevant to the analysis of the mythical and cultic elements of culture (its religious substance) as to those symbols or

---

6. There are other differences in linguistic style from purely philosophical discourse in the system as a whole. In the case of the analysis of *existence* (*ST* II, pt. III, sec. I), Tillich does not proceed "philosophically," since estrangement is not an aspect of essential structure and so philosophically uncoverable. Rather, as in the "answers" of the other parts, he proceeds via the help of a religious symbol (the Fall), and he recognizes that he is analyzing a "half-way myth" (*ST* II:29–31). Correspondingly, the *answer* to the estrangement of structure (the New Being and so the Kingdom) is likewise initiated via the help of symbols expressive of a revelational correlation, and so his interpretation here is likewise an ontological interpretation of a "half-way myth," though he does not seem explicitly to have recognized this point. Thus, the role of myth in Tillich's philosophical theology is considerable, as the role of myth in expressing the religious substance of culture had already indicated. Myth, or "half-way myth," explicates both the central dilemmas of estrangement and the received answers to those ultimate dilemmas— in fact, the center of "religion" and so of the Christian religion, its kerygma or "message." Again we see how, despite the philosophical *form* of his theology, Tillich's thought is centered on revelation and so finds its decisive center in the appearance of the New Being. Certainly the central thrust of his interpretation of individual and social-historical existence is as dependent on revelation as it is on the philosophical analysis of finitude. Only the *permanent* and *unchanging* rela-tions of God to the world represent, therefore, purely "symbolic-ontological" discourse; all else (and that is most of the system: estrangement, judgment, revelation, New Being, Christ, *ecclesia*, Spiritual Presence, Kingdom) is actually "mythical-symbolic-ontological."

"message" of an explicitly religious community, since myth and cult (however "distorted") express the depth of reason in all cultural life (*ST* I:80–81). In this sense, "theology" is a cultural, public discipline for him, as well as one designed for a religious community—for culture and religion go together throughout historical life. In any case, let us note that as theological analysis joined with a predominantly philosophical analysis to uncover theoretically the *questions* of our finitude and our existence, so here a philosophical (ontological) analysis joins with a theological (a symbolic understanding of religious symbols) on the *answering* side (e.g., *ST* II:13–16).

A brief final word on symbol (compare *TC*, 53–67). As is evident, this crucial category has very wide use in Tillich's thought: linguistic, philosophical, especially religious, theological, and even ethical. Since he dealt with it cryptically at best in those many contexts, it is not surprising that it should seem unclear and even inconsistent to many commentators, as well as nonsensical to all those for whom there is nothing transcendent to talk about or (even if there were) any possibility of our talking intelligibly about whatever "it" might be. Tillich assumes that there is something transcendent to talk about and that we can and do so (and do so all the time). He uses, in the first instance, the word "symbol" to refer to the verbal medium or vehicle with which such speech, if responsible and intelligible, goes about its task, namely, ordinary language used in a self-transcending way to refer beyond the ordinary (*ST* I:123, 131).

Tillich's usage, however, is much wider than this linguistic/philosophical/theological usage. Symbol (or "medium"), at the most fundamental level, means not just a part of language but rather the finite in its creative relation to its divine ground, as manifesting through itself, in its state of fulfillment and so "transparency," that ground, that is, as the ontic *medium, vehicle,* or *hierophany* of the divine (*ST* I:118ff., 123, 133ff.). Through some aspect (excellence or power) of a particular finite creature, aspects or "sides" of the infinite ground can manifest themselves. Thus are mountains, the sea, sky, lightning, sun, moon, water, trees and plants, animals, heroes, states and rulers (king, father, mother), and, finally, special persons symbols of the divine—as, too, are or can be words and concepts (if they, too, are set in this religious/revelatory/ecstatic context). Thus, as the symbol participates in the ground in order to manifest that ground through itself, so do we who "know" through the symbol in turn participate *through the symbol* in the divine ground. A statue of the Buddha, which may be merely an aesthetic object to me, who thus participates in and through it as beautiful and so only "secularly," can become a *symbol* of the Buddha essence to another who participates religiously in or through it. Participation here means communion or union with the symbol and (more to the point) *union* through the symbol with the transcendent. Examples of "participation" *through* a symbol can be in an aesthetic relationship (as opposed to, say, a mere seller or buyer), with regard to an ethical obligation or an ideal, in a personal relationship between persons, in a political relationship to a group (consider flags, capitols, presidents, leaders), and, most deeply, in a religious relationship. In each, let us note, the unconditioned ground is present through the symbol (as beauty, as good, as value, and so on); in each, our participation through it in turn changes, stabilizes, heals, and recreates us. Most important, the participation by the symbol itself is what enables it to manifest power and grace *outward* to others and to establish communion between these other creatures and their divine ground. Here the symbol becomes a medium, hierophany, or "sacrament," a visible sign of an invisible grace.

Granting this range of meanings for "symbol," it is clear why Tillich says that a symbol is "true" in this religious usage when, and only when, it thus communicates the divine ground in which it participates and communicates it to someone (*ST* I:105, 128). In this sense, too, humans can also become symbols, in fact, the most powerful of all: insofar as they participate in the divine ground, they are, therefore, "transparent to it," and so are empowered to manifest it to others (*ST* I:118, 143, 150). The ultimate criterion for a symbol is given by this, the highest and most decisive instance of it. Such a decisive "symbol" is, therefore, the locus of "final" revelation, that creaturely medium through which the divine decisively manifests itself, its power, and its meaning. This is, of course, for Tillich, Jesus as the Christ: that symbol who, by sacrificing himself and thus by pointing beyond himself to his divine ground, was totally transparent to the divine ground and so unsurpassably communicated it (*ST* I:132–33, 150–52). This final and decisive symbol, therefore, becomes the religious center, the ethical norm, as well as the theological criterion, for all else: for the divine itself, for authentic humanity, for church, for the religious substance of culture, for the process and goal of history (*ST* I:137). When Tillich speaks of symbol, he has all of this in mind, especially these universally relevant religious/ethical implications centering about the Christ figure. With this rich and varied set of references, it is not surprising that his rather brief (though highly original and innovative) allusions to symbols should seem to a later age, itself saturated with technical and specialized discussions about words, their uses, and interrelations, incomplete at best and confused at worst.

As our discussion of Tillich's interpretation of culture and reason (chap. 2), of culture and the religious (chap. 3), philosophy and theology, and finally of symbol, has made plain, Tillich's thought presupposed a principle of unity underlying all the diverse facets of natural, social, and personal life. This principle is, from one point of view, the principle of unity of all facets of being (being-itself), and yet, from another point of view, it is the object and ground of religion, of the experiences of ultimacy, of obligation, and of hope that also permeate all of life. As we have said, for Tillich, being-itself, the ground of all experience, is God, the source and object of religion. Since God, or being-itself, is the principle of unity, the knowledge of this depth or underlying ground is various, even diverse. Each aspect of culture manifests or discloses this ground through its own fundamental symbols; philosophy expresses and calls for it through its most pervasive and universal symbols. Thus, this ground appears through the widely various contours of culture and the diverse traditions of philosophy. But it is in religion, explicitly concerned as it is with the unconditional in existence, that the contours of being-itself appear, and, of course, appear as God. Culture, philosophy, and religion together express the power and meaning of the divine; correspondingly, together they provide the means by which we can understand both the divine ground and ourselves. This unity of infinite ground and unity of all the disciplines expressive of the infinite ground is the reason for the wide, mediating role that Tillich's thought has played and for his continuing fascination and relevance.

In subsequent chapters of this volume (as well as in chapter 1 and 2) this mediating role will be illustrated. The essential relation of the political and social issues of existence could not be correctly interpreted as he showed (chap. 1), unless both the political and the social were seen in relation to their religious depth. Correspondingly, (as in chaps. 2 and 5) the problems of our bodily being, of our "space," of our reality and temporality (our ontological problems) cannot be understood or dealt with unless they are seen as "religious" issues of ultimate concern and of our being and nonbeing. Thus, Tillich's thought mediates, on the one side, between the life sciences and the social sciences (sociology, political theory, and psychology) and the humanities (art, history, languages, and literature) and of both with philosophy; then, on the other side, it mediates between all of these and religion. Other examples of mediation to be noted in this volume are the way his thought can help to reintegrate the split between Catholicism and Protestantism (chap. 6) and, on an even broader scope, to interpret the beginnings of rapproachement, at least of dialogue, between Christianity and other religions.

Part Two

The Mature System

5

The Analysis of Finite Being

One of the most fascinating portions of Tillich's thought is his analysis of finitude. First of all, it is perhaps the clearest model of his correlated method, illustrating how he moves from philosophical questions concerning human being all the way through to symbolic theological affirmations about God. Thus, secondly, it shows the intricate and creative interweaving, characteristic of everything Tillich wrote, of philosophical and ontological analysis, on the one hand, with striking existential insight and profound religious (theological) concerns, on the other. Here he convincingly reveals in terms of experiences familiar to each of us the truth of the point his method had long insisted upon, namely, that often the deepest religious problems are *ontological* in character, or, as he put it formally, issues of our being and nonbeing (*ST* I:14). As a result, on both existential and reflective levels we learn through this analysis what he means by the threats of nonbeing, by anxiety, by courage, by the power of being, and ultimately by God as the ground and power of our being. Finally, as this chapter will argue, this analysis uncovers for us the strange yet unadmitted "center" of Tillich's thought—a center of which he was either unaware or shied away in angst from acknowledging—namely, the unexpected *polarity* of being and nonbeing that characterizes both finitude and God.

The Possibility of Ontology

As he had promised in his discussion of method (*ST* I:59–66, compare also 18–28), Tillich's analysis of finitude begins with a philosophical treatment of the structure of finite being generally and so of our being as humans. As noted, such an ontological analysis is, for Tillich, relevant to theology because issues of religion are issues of "ultimate concern," and the latter represent matters of "our being or not-being" (*ST* I:11–15).

Thus, ontological analysis—analysis of the universal structure of being—is the doorway into the *theoretical* understanding of religion, which is theology, just as experiencing these matters of ultimate concern represents the *personal* or *ontic* doorway into being grasped by religious faith. But how is ontological analysis, the analysis of the most pervasive structures of actuality, possible? In the face of widespread modern criticism of the possibility of metaphysics or ontology, such a question is by no means irrelevant.

Tillich's defense of the possibility of ontology (he prefers this word to "metaphysics" though its meaning is almost identical to metaphysics as, for example, Whitehead understands it [*ST* I:20, 163]) reveals his clear debt to Heidegger. Nevertheless, functioning as it does as one of the theoretical foundations for Tillich's entire *theological* system, this defense is both original and compelling. How, then, can we experience and know the universal "structure of finite being," "the character of everything that is in so far as it is" (*ST* I:163), "those concepts . . . which are presupposed in every actual experience," granting that such an inquiry can hardly be one of the ontic inquiries possible for the empirical sciences? How do we know, how could we know, that the concepts *we* always use in all of our experience represent the "universal structure of being" and not just the usages of our own local equipment? How can we get beyond Hume's or Kant's criticism of the possibility of metaphysics?

Tillich's answer to this Kantian question is, so it seems to me, an *existential* answer. Incidentally, this suggests that it is through existentialist thought that not only the concept of angst (compare *ST* I:191–92; II:34), but also that of being, have been revived in modern reflection. As Tillich notes, "every being participates in the structure of being, but man alone is immediately aware of this structure" (*ST* I:168). "Man . . . [is] that being who asks the ontological question and in whose self-awareness the ontological answer can be found" (*ST* I:168). And "man is able to answer the ontological question himself because he experiences directly and immediately the structure of being and its elements" (*ST* I:169). Here we see a point frequently reiterated in these essays: the existential and, further, the "religious" roots of Tillich's philosophical analyses. Let us now see how his argument runs.

All our knowing and our reflection upon it imply, Tillich argues, a correlation between our "subjective" rational processes (our perceptual experience, our modes of inquiry and deliberation, our rational judgments), on the one hand, and the "objective" structure of being, what is real or actual, on the other. These two poles, whose correlation all knowing and doing presuppose, Tillich terms the subjective and the objective logos (*ST* I:75–79, 168–174). The question that has plagued modern philosophy since its beginnings in Descartes has been how we can be certain of this correlation. How can we know that our thinking about reality, our modes of knowing, give us valid knowledge of actuality itself? Appropriately, Tillich answers: not through technical argument and certainly not through empirical inquiry (both of which presuppose this correlation), but through our own *participation* in both sides. That is to say, as existing beings we participate *through our own being* (and our awareness of that participation) in the same rational structure that our *cognitive and rational powers* also exhibit in knowing the world; as existing selves we participate in the same structure that as knowing selves we impose on the world. In existing within the structures of our finitude, we experience and can delineate those rational (or ontological) structures implicit in all our speaking and knowing. Hence our language and our universals (our general concepts and categories) can be known to be relevant to the investigation of the structures of being generally, to "actuality." As the present analysis makes clear, it is in experiencing the *meaning* of our own being as finite in all its complexity of structure that that complexity of structure manifests itself to us, becomes presupposed by us in all we do, and so becomes explicit in our philosophies.[1] Since the questions of the *meaning* of our being are, for Tillich, religious questions (religion represents issues of "ultimate concern"), in this sense there is a religious root to all philosophy.[2]

For this reason, moreover, "man is the entrance into being" (*ST* I:167). That is to say, human being illustrates, as does all else, the structure common to all finite being; but human being represents that structure in a particularly rich fashion. In addition, humans alone (as far as we know) participate inwardly in that structure and so are "inwardly aware" ("immediately") of it. In human being, the structure of being is felt and is inwardly illuminated; we feel and know our existence and its structure "from the inside."[3] Concretely, in experiencing our "existence," we know

1. For example, Tillich says that the "ontological question" (Why is there something rather than nothing?), which begins philosophy and so thought, is "fundamentally the expression of a state of existence rather than a formulated question" (*ST* I:164). Thus, does the existential experiencing of being (Why and how *are* we, over against our not being?) precipitate, for Tillich, reflection on the structure of being; "theology" begins "philosophy."
2. As Tillich defines these two: "Philosophy deals with the structure of being in itself; theology deals with the meaning of being for us" (*ST* I:22).
3. "He lives in them and acts through them. They are immediately present to him. They are he himself" (*ST* I:169). Cf. Whitehead's interesting parallel justification: "It is the accepted doctrine in physical science that a living body is to be integrated according to what is known of other sections of the physical universe.

ourselves as in space and time, as caused and causing, and as "substances"; hence, these categories of our cognitive experience and scientific thought are validated as "actual" through their correlation with the directly ("inwardly") experienced structure of our existence. Hence for Tillich the subsequent analysis of the forms of our finitude in our inner awareness not only prepares the way for theology. For him, it also makes explicit the primordial bases of cognition generally and of metaphysics or ontology in particular. Our scientific and philosophical knowledge of the world (of all the "beings") is in correlation with, in fact dependent on, our inner awareness and so "knowledge" of ourselves as existing selves in the world.[4]

The Basic Ontological Structure

Thus, we move immediately to the first level of ontological analysis, what Tillich terms the basic ontological structure of all that is: the self-world correlation (compare the reference about the correlation of subjective and objective logos, e.g., *ST* I:171f.). We have seen how, for Tillich, this correlation of experience and thought to actuality, assumed in all cultural activity, is itself the *basis* or *ground* of the possibility of all rational inquiry, including that of ontology.[5] Now, appropriately, we find

---

This is a sound axiom; but it is double-edged. For it carries with it the converse deduction that other sections of the universe are to be interpreted in accordance with what we know of the human body" (*Process and Reality* [New York: Macmillan, 1929], 181–82). Whitehead calls this the "subjective principle," which interprets the rest of the universe in terms of the "experiencing" characteristic of our existence (cf. also *Process and Reality*, 28, 252, 288).

4. The similarity here, quite without mutual influence, to both Santayana's and Whitehead's answer to the "critical" Kantian question is interesting. Santayana, conscious that all thought is in terms of "our essences" and thus a projection, reestablishes his confidence that experience and thought encounter and "give signals" of reality, through our self-consciousness as existing beings, our "animal faith" (cf. George Santayana, *Skepticism and Animal Faith* [New York: Scribner's, 1933]). Whitehead, also conscious that all sensory experience, and so all science, deals with "presentational immediacy," a construction of our perceptual equipment, reestablishes his confidence in our relation to "reality" through "causal efficacy," our experiencing ourselves as constituted by our experiencing of other entities in process (cf. A. N. Whitehead, *Adventures of Ideas* [New York: Macmillan, 1933], chaps. 11 and 12; and *Process and Reality*, 125–26, 184–92).

5. Cf. again the interesting agreement with Whitehead, for whom the metaphysical premises of the interrelatedness of all reality and *the order or harmony*

this same correlation of self to world and world to self as the first assumption or disclosure of ontological analysis. It is also, he says, implied directly in the ontological question with which ontological inquiry begins: As itself in the world, the human being asks the question of his own being and so of being, why is there something rather than nothing? (*ST* I:163–64, 168).

As an ontological category, this self-world correlation is, says Tillich, universal, applicable to all beings everywhere as their most fundamental structure (*ST* I:168–74). Let us begin by seeing what this structure means in *our* experience. Humans always experience themselves in "internal" relation to an environment and a world: the self is empty, says Tillich, without correlation with its world (*ST* I:171), and, as a consequence, every aspect of its being arises from and is shaped by its relations with all else around it. Thus, Tillich recognizes the claims of the natural (chemical, biological, genetic, etc.), the psychological, and the social sciences to interpret human beings in terms of their participation in, dependence on, and conditioning by their natural and social environments and so by the "laws" of those environments.

What is, however, not so widely recognized in Tillich's analysis is his correlative insistence that, as there is no self without a world, so there is no world without a self. The world of experience, and so the "world" understood by science, is itself in part a construction of the self; thus, it is dependent for its character on the character of the knowing self. Furthermore, the self-world correlation and the mutual dependence it implies represent, as we noted, an ontological category applicable universally to all "beings" and not an ontic category relevant only to a particular realm of being.[6] "Self-hood or self-centeredness must be attributed in some measure to all living beings, and in terms of analogy, to all individual *Gestalten* even in the inorganic realm. One can speak of self-centeredness in atoms as well as in animals, wherever the reaction to a stimulus is dependent on a structural whole" (*ST* I:169; see also 184–86, where

---

(the rationality) characterizing these interrelationships, and so the relevance of thought, of inquiry, and of logic to what is actual, provide the ground *not only* of the possibility of speculative philosophy but *even more* of all of cultural activity and so all of the disciplines of the university (*Process and Reality*, 12–16, 20–26; and *Science and the Modern World* [New York: Macmillan, 1925], 122, 197).

6. Again like Whitehead, Tillich maintains that *(a)* internal relations (self and world) characterize all of actuality; and *(b)* these relations are best understood as *analogous* to human experiencing of itself in relation to environment and world. Both thinkers are, therefore, in some disagreement with the habit of scientific cosmologists to speak of the "*world*" without taking account of the "*self*" or the "subjectivity" that knows and in part constructs that world.

"freedom-destiny" in humans is said to be analogous with "spontaneity-law" in the inorganic realm).

Tillich's discussion of finitude is generally regarded as "existential" (as it is, to be sure) and thus relevant only to the problems and issues of being a human being. Here, however, we see Tillich as a philosopher defending not only the possibility of ontology for the sake of theology, but, more to the point, asserting with some authority the logical priority of ontological (metaphysical) categories over those of the ontic sciences, even natural science. The relevance of this to the relations of speculative philosophy to science and so of religion to science is immense; it is, however, questionable whether many of those who do scientific cosmology are either willing to listen or capable of understanding what Tillich (and Whitehead) here have to say.

Cosmology, as presently written, assumes that the "self" and its analogues appear very late in the history of the cosmos as science knows and understands it, "two or three seconds ago" on the universe's time clock. Prior to that, there is only "world," world as described by physics, astrophysics, astronomy, chemistry, and later, geology and biology. This is a world of infinitesimal particles, beginning with the "big bang" and proceeding according to law to organize itself into our universe. As Carl Sagan says: "The Cosmos is all that is, all there ever was, or all there ever will be."[7] The world as described by scientific inquiry is thus simply *there;* it is as it is, and apparently also as it is described by science: its habits and laws intact and in place from the beginning, an objective realm, self-existent, self-sufficient, self-perpetuating, and, in the end, capable of generating the rational selves (scientific cosmologists) who will find all this out. Sagan modestly conceives of the *telos* of the cosmos and the supreme excellence of the humans within it to be his fellow cosmologists, much as priests used to view the highest forms of humanity as their priestly colleagues.[8]

Against this view, Tillich maintains that such a "world of things" subject to laws is always in correlation with an experiencing and knowing self. Thus "world" can hardly be self-existent or self-sufficient. On the contrary, world is always a projection or construct of the self: "Man grasps and shapes his environment into a world," and hence, "world-consciousness is possible only on the basis of a fully developed self-

---

7. Carl Sagan, *Cosmos* (New York: Ballantyne Books, 1980), 4. Tillich frequently reiterated the principle that there can be no knowing except there be an implicit world view, that "every epistemology contains an implicit ontology" (*ST* I:19, 71).

8. Sagan, *Cosmos*, 4–5.

consciousness" (*ST* I:171). As a consequence, behind that "world of things" projected and shaped by a knowing and organizing self lies the *mystery* of finite being, a mystery not directly known to us in scientific inquiry at all because our "world" has been "grasped and shaped" by the power, the capacities, and the intentions of reason (so far, Tillich agrees with Kant).

As we have seen, however (and here Tillich goes beyond Kant), for Tillich the "objective" structure of that world (of being) is known to us *directly* or *immediately* ("subjectively") through our participation in that structure as existing and self-aware examples of being. We are, so to speak, human analogues, exemplars, of the universal structure of being. Ironically, although modern science is now well aware of the ever-present role of the scientific observer in every step of its knowledge, apparently it has not drawn the epistemological conclusions implicit in this realization. Thus, when many modern cosmologists sum up what "science" knows about the cosmos, they speak as if neither critical philosophy nor relativity theory had ever occurred; namely, they speak directly and unambiguously about the "real" external world known by science. Tillich's argument, like Whitehead's, is very relevant at this point.[9]

How is it, then, that for Tillich the self shapes the world known by ordinary experience and (more formally) by science and so is itself an essential ingredient in the construction of that world? Tillich's main point, indebted to both Kant and Heidegger, is that human consciousness and self-consciousness bring the *order* we know in the world *to* the world; or, as he puts it, with human being "environment becomes world." This occurs, furthermore, because humans are "selves," that is to say, have reason or (as he later terms it) have "spirit": self-transcendence, self-consciousness, and thus world-consciousness. These latter three are interdependent: without self-transcendence, there is no separation or "distance" of self from environment that makes possible consciousness of the world, that is, a conscious "looking at" the world. In looking at the world as rational selves, we give to that panorama of experience an

---

9. To those familiar with Whitehead, this discussion of the status of scientific cosmology will sound very familiar. For Whitehead, scientific inquiry is based on "presentational immediacy." Therefore, science deals with a projected world in correlation with our senses and rational forms. Science, therefore, concerns itself with an *abstracted* area of experience and so is itself a useful but definite *abstraction*. Through the metaphysical categories implied in causal efficacy—in our self-experience as entities in process—philosophy can come closer than science to "actuality," and thus can it perform its supreme task of being "the critic of the abstractions of special realms of life and special areas of inquiry" (Whitehead, *Science and the Modern World*, 122).

ordered character, "environment becomes world": on the one hand, a *unified structure*, a whole, and, on the other, a whole qualified by *universals* or *categories/kinds* and by *intelligible relations*, and hence also characterized by "forms of order" whereby repetitive patterns of becoming are established (compare especially *ST* I:169–73; III:11–30).

Later, going further (*ST* I:186–88), Tillich argues that, only when humans participate as self-transcending spirit in their own nonbeing as well as being, can negation become possible; only then can the possibilities, both of the consciousness of difference or distinction and that of negative judgments, appear: "With being alone there would be no world" (*ST* I:187). As Kant insisted, the world of scientific law, a world of entities and particles "obeying" those laws, and so the possibility of inquiry and judgment organizing our experience and our knowledge of that world into "science," all this is as much a construction of reason ("spirit") as it is a response to "objective reality." Self and world (subject and object) together construct the "reality" or "world" science seeks to describe in its cosmologies. As a consequence, there literally is and can be no such world as science pictures it without the correlative work of self or spirit, though this represents, as far as I can see, a thought utterly unknown to and bizarre for most scientific cosmologists. Science is *one* way, and perhaps the most reliable one, of delineating the world prior to the advent of human existence; but it is itself a human construction and so, by implication, it is by no means the only one. Thus, ontological categories as well as scientific ones are necessary if "finite being" is to be described. To fail to recognize this, as much science does, is to separate a construction from the context of its constitution and thus to present to us an abstraction ("world") as if it were the actuality described.[10]

One could wish that Tillich had pursued these philosophical arguments—so relevant to the relations of the humanities and of theology to science—further than he did. As always, he was a philosopher, and, as this has shown, a pretty good one, hurriedly on his way to being a theologian; as we shall see, he quickly moved his analysis of structure along toward his real goal, an analysis of the *meaning* of being for us, namely, the whole of the analysis of *existence* in volume two of his *Systematic Theology*. Let us note, however, that he has now doubly defended, and on philosophical grounds, his ontology against its present most persistent detractors: those who regard scientific knowledge of "objects" as the primordial, definitive, and, in fact, exclusive form of

10. This represents, I take it, precisely what Whitehead complained about in much of the physics of his own time: namely, that it took the necessitated, atomic, and so exhaustively material world of its own inquiries as "actuality." Whitehead called this "the fallacy of misplaced concreteness" (*Science and the Modern World*, 51, 58).

knowledge of reality. He has shown, first, the ground for our confidence in both scientific and philosophical reason as adequate to the description of reality, and now he has shown that the former is subordinate to, an abstraction from, the latter. Unable to include the self or subject in its "world" (even though the cognizing scientist is always a constituent part, in fact, *the* constituting agent, of "world"), scientific cosmology of necessity regards "objects" alone as the "really real"; thus cosmology is embarked on the hopeless task of deriving the subjects essential to the constitution of those objects from the subjectless world of objects, for "whenever the self-world correlation is cut, no reunion is possible" (*ST* I:171; see also 173).

The Ontological Elements

Tillich then moves from the basic ontological structure of self and world to what he terms "the ontological elements," that is, polar traits (polarities) universally characteristic of both selves and world, that is, of all that is. Interestingly, while Tillich insists that self and world are not, even analogically, to be predicated of God, this is not the case with these elements, which represent "symbolically" or "analogically" the most important and revealing characteristics of the divine being (compare *ST* I:244–49). The reason, it seems, for this somewhat unexpected rule of predication is that to Tillich the self-world correlation represents the structure of *essential* finitude, and thus applied to God makes God either "a being" or "the sum of beings," either a self or world. On the other hand, the polarities ("elements") represent the universal structures of being as being pulsates not only in and through us as finite beings, but also as being appears analogically in being-itself as the source and ground of all finite being. In any case, these elements are constituted by the familiar three polarities characteristic of all beings but experienced and known most adequately "from the inside" in human being: individuation and participation, dynamics and form, freedom and destiny (*ST* I:174–86).

There can be no question that these polarities are important for almost every aspect of Tillich's thought. They appear and reappear continually. Typically, he rushes through his philosophical defense of them, as he had that of self and world, only spending enough time to define and briefly to justify their use as "ontological" elements characteristic of all beings everywhere. Where they do appear more significantly is in the "theological" section of his philosophical analysis, namely, when he is describing the *meaning* of our being, that is, the forms of our anxiety, the tensions and disruptions of our existence both individual and social (*ST* I:81–94,

The World Situation, and *The Courage to Be*), and the stages of our self-destruction and despair (volume two as well as volume three of *ST* in his discussion of the forms of life's ambiguities). The forms of our health, power, and activity, on the one hand, and the forms of our anxieties, dilemmas, disruptions, and the structures of our disintegration, on the other, reflect, Tillich maintains, the *ontological structure of our being,* as our physical diseases reflect the organic structure of our bodily selves. It is, then, in terms of these ontological polarities that Tillich analyzes, as we shall see, the ways our anxieties and estrangement appear in experience. As always, it is this philosophical/theological analysis of the *meaning* of our being on which he concentrates, not the philosophical/ontological analysis of the *structure* that the former presupposes.

This is a pity because there are (to me) matters in the philosophical analysis that remain unclear. I suspect (though I do not know) that here Tillich saw new difficulties arising, could not resolve them in terms of his older categories, and so left the matter somewhat cloudy. The first unclear matter has to do with the relation of the polarity of dynamics and form to potentiality. Tillich begins this discussion, one might say, "as Greek": in distinguishing between form and dynamics, he identifies dynamics—the "matter in process," so to speak, that is formed or structured into whatever is—with *potentiality* of being, and so apparently he identifies form with settled *actuality* of being. As a consequence, dynamics is said to be characterized by relative nonbeing *(me on):* that which is in process, coming to be, and passing away, and that which, therefore, cannot be clearly named or thought but still must "be." Correspondingly, form is identified with the defining essence of something, "its definite power of being" (*ST* I:178); and, of course, form represents that which can be named or thought.

But clearly, Tillich is not satisfied thus merely to reproduce the Greek worldview. Tillich is also, as a modern, very conscious of the *creative* role of dynamics, of process, of "life" and, as a consequence, the way process undergirds, overpowers, and even subdues form. Hence, for him vitality, élan, "life," which "is the creative drive of the living substance," represents a drive "towards new forms" (*ST* I:180). As the eros or drive toward the new form, vitality represents, therefore, the secret essence of intentionality or purpose, and it is the latter that propels the living self beyond itself into the next moment, into "transcending itself." Dynamics as vitality is, therefore, the ground for the creation of new forms (*ST* I:181), and thus it is essential for the fulfillment of meaning in being.[11] Finally,

---

11. Again, one is reminded in this concept of the similar role of "creativity" in Whitehead's metaphysics.

therefore, "becoming is just as genuine in the structure of being as is that which remains unchanged" (*ST* I:181). Clearly, Tillich's thought is here itself in process: if new forms arise, then potentiality, and with it relative nonbeing, infect the realm of forms as they do the dynamic principle of becoming. Hence, as Whitehead saw, the more radical ontological contrast lies between settled actuality in the past and possibility or novelty in the future, than it does between changing matter and changeless form. Tillich (so it seems to me) is moving toward this position; we shall note in a moment the same movement away from a classical position, and the same resulting ambiguity, in his discussion of nonbeing and finitude.

Being and Finitude

With the discussion of being and finitude, we reach the center of Tillich's analysis of finitude: the opening up of the *question* (or problematic) of finite being and so the call for being-itself, or God. We are, therefore, now entering explicitly into what can be called a "theological" as well as philosophical mode of analysis, one that is concerned with the *meaning* of our being as well as with its structure, or, as we put it earlier, one exhibiting the *interweaving* of ontological and religious concerns— for ultimate concerns (religion) are matters of the structure of our being and nonbeing. Tillich begins with the interesting point that the consciousness or awareness of our finitude, and so any ontological analysis of it, arises only out of the relations of our finitude to what lies beyond the finite, and, so to speak, in *both* directions. That is, we are conscious of the *meaning* of our finitude through the relation of our finite being to nonbeing, on the one hand, and through the relation of our finite being to infinity, on the other hand. It is, therefore, only in the context of our relation to nonbeing and to infinity that finitude can understand itself.

Nonbeing is, for Tillich, by no means merely negative, though he often seems to imply it is. Without the "shock of nonbeing," an *existential* shock of anxiety before it becomes a *theoretical* shock of puzzlement, there is no awareness of finitude as finite. Without the consciousness of nonbeing, moreover, there cannot be the "separation" from our own being that leads to self-awareness, and so no possibility of the negative judgments (*A* is not *B*) that make discrimination of a world possible: "There can be no world unless there is a dialectical participation of nonbeing in being" (*ST* I:187). Thus humans, in realizing their humanity, participate positively in nonbeing as well as being: in vitality and life, in movement into the future, in self-transcendence, in negative judgments, and so in rational judgments. Nonbeing is a positive and creative part of our own being as we experience the latter; being is thus in us "becoming," partly being and partly nonbeing. Hence, conversely, an aspect of nonbeing is "dialectical nonbeing," *me on*, an ingredient in finite being and even in God (*ST* I:188–89; *CB*, 178–81); "finitude unites being with dialectical nonbeing" (*ST* I:189).

For Tillich, on the other hand, nonbeing is also the *opposite* of being, "the undialectical negation of being." Nonbeing, in this aspect, is *ouk on*, "the 'nothing' out of which God creates and so which has no relation (except opposition) at all to being" (*ST* I:188). Here the relation of being to nonbeing defines finitude *over against* God; therefore, this aspect of nonbeing is by definition separated from God: "Being, limited by nonbeing, is finitude" (*ST* I:189). *Me on* is in us in such a way that we share *me on* with God; *ouk on* is related to us in such a way that in no way is it shared with God. Again, one feels two polar streams at work in Tillich's thought. One, the classical stream (both Greek and Patristic), stresses the clear opposition of being and nonbeing. The other (the more modern stream of nineteenth-century *Lebensphilosophie*, of modern dynamic ontologies, of existentialism, possibly of Buddhism, and even of some of the implications of the New Testament), seems to see being, whether in finitude or in God, as a polarity of being and of nonbeing.

The other relation, which helps to constitute our awareness of our finitude, is our relation to infinity, or, in Tillich's more precise phrasing, infinity as the "dynamic and free self-transcendence of finite being" (*ST* I:190). Tillich is wary of naming infinity as "*the* infinite," as if it represented an objective infinite and so absolute being. Such a concept would sanction the kind of objective metaphysics based on speculation which, with Kant, he repudiates, and it would represent for Tillich the chilling possibility of a heteronomous absolute over against us. Rather, infinity points to our relation, an experienced relation, beyond ourselves to our ground. Thus as so experienced and so named, infinity refers to the infinite self-transcendence of spirit: "Infinitude is finitude transcending itself without any a priori limit"; it is "an expression of man's belonging to that which is beyond nonbeing, namely, to being-itself" (*ST* I:191).

This relation of self-transcendence to infinity appears, for Tillich, continuously in experience. As the ground of reason and spirit, this relation to infinity manifests itself as the condition of self-awareness and of awareness of world. It is present in our consciousness of "distance" from objects that makes possible the correlation with them implied by universals, by language, and by technology, in fact, in all of cultural life. Finally, as we shall see, it reveals itself also in anxiety. As in classical doctrines of the *imago Dei*, the infinite dimension of finitude, its infinite self-transcendence, is thus at once the seed of the "essential humanity" of the human (compare "essential God-manhood," *ST* II:124–27) and the manifestation in us of the dependence of all creatureliness on its divine ground. As far as our present discussion goes, therefore, it is this "infinite dimension" of the human spirit, its interrelatedness to its divine ground, that again makes consciousness or awareness of our finitude *as* finitude possible: our consciousness of ourselves *as selves in a world*, as "finite freedom" or finite spirit, thus as qualified by anxiety and so as calling for our ground, for God. Nonbeing on the one side, and infinity on the other, constitute us as finite creatures and so as grounded in the divine.

Tillich ends this section with the phrases that reverberate throughout his work: "Finitude in awareness is anxiety" and "Anxiety is the self-awareness of the finite self [from the "inside"] as finite" (*ST* I:191–92). Anxiety arises, on the one hand, from the presence, as threat, of nonbeing to finitude, and, on the other, from the constitution of finitude as spirit, as grounded in infinity and so in self-consciousness. This dual characteristic of finitude as *ex nihilo* and *finite freedom* is essential and ineradicable, to all intents and purposes an aspect of the *definition* of finitude. Anxiety as the *meaning* of our finite being is thus intrinsic to, even identical with, the essential structure of our being as finite. Anxiety is an ontological concept with vast religious and theological overtones.

Clearly, we have now moved into "theological" analysis, if theology deals with "the meaning of being for us" (*ST* I:22). Yet equally we are still deeply involved with the *structures* of finitude, as the subsequent section on the categories of finitude will show. Hence, it should be noted that here theology joins philosophy to raise the "question" of finite being: it is the *anxiety* latent in finitude that raises the question of God. Conversely, at a further stage of the method, philosophy joins with theology to delineate in ontological terms the religious symbols that bear "the answer," in this case, the symbol of God which is the answer to the question of finitude. So, with the recognition that anxiety is essential to finitude, "finitude felt from the inside," let us move into the crucial analysis of the categories where this claim is spelled out in more detail. Let us note, too, how Tillich unites in this discussion his ontological (philosophical) analysis of the categories of finitude with his existential (theological) analysis of the *meaning* of these categories for us as finite.

Finitude and the Categories

In Tillich's analysis of them, the categories vividly unite structure and meaning, and so Tillich's treatment of them combines philosophical analysis and theological disclosure. They also exhibit the interwoven, and

polar, presence of being and nonbeing in our existence. The categories—
time, space, causality, and substance—represent, says Tillich, our most
pervasive "ways of speaking" (ST I:192–98). They structure, organize,
and so shape all our experience; they are "forms of our consciousness,"
present in every aspect of experience and dominant in all our ways of
thinking, even the religious (ST I:192). Thus have they been the subject of
endless philosophical analysis and debate. Yet they are also and at the
same time "forms of being," ways our being and nonbeing, as we are
aware of them, are present in and to us. What interested Tillich the most is
the way we experience our finitude "from the inside" via these categories,
the way the meanings of our being and nonbeing come to us via the
categorical structure of our finitude.

They are, then, the universal forms of finitude. The defense of this
proposition, and the elaboration of it, represent, of course, the task of
philosophy, of ontological analysis. But for Tillich, they are even more
portals to the meaning of our being, ways our finitude experiences itself
as a union of being and nonbeing and so as a mixture of anxiety and
courage, as matters of religion and issues of ultimate concern, which raise
the question of God. We shall comment on Tillich's discussion of the
categories only in terms of the first two categories, time and space. The
same issues of method and substance—the interweaving in each category
of philosophy and theology, of structure and meaning, and the way our
self-experience of embodying each category "raises the question of
God"—are present in the other two, causality and substance.

Time is "the central category of finitude" for Tillich. He was continually conscious of our temporality, our being in time, as posing both
philosophical problems and existential dilemmas. I remember that it was
in his lectures on this section of systematic theology that I awoke for the
first time to what he was about. First, he read us a few passages from
Augustine in which the sense of the nonbeing of the time becomes almost
tangible: You are only in the present; but what is the present except a
vanishing "almost nothing," when last year, last month, yesterday, even
today, in fact, each past moment and second, is now gone and yet the next
moment, day, month, year are not yet here?[12] Then—all of us staring at
him—he put the book down, looked directly at us, and said, "You are too
young to know ze anxiety of having no more time, but remember ze term
paper and its meaning for your time. In October zere is plenty of time, a
seeming infinity of time; in November zere is now only a finite time, a
measurable time, and so you begin to worry. By December zere is no time

---

12. The references in Augustine can be found in Erich Przywara, S.J., An
Augustine Synthesis (London: Sheed and Ward, 1945), 90–97.

left, you *have* no time, and you are in ze panic!" He did not need to say a word more, but he did: "Ze anxiety of time is that having no time grasps your *life,* your being—not just your paper."

For the first time I understood the religious issue involved in structural nonbeing, in contingency "felt from the inside," in the panic such an experience of nonbeing causes, and, as a consequence of that near panic, the futile efforts to escape it. Then, he went on to show the *positive* character of time, the "being" manifested through temporal sequence: the possibility of creative change from the old that now slips away, the "chance," therefore, for new potentialities, for improvement and advance—of graduating, of a profession, of marriage and a family (compare *ST* I:193). The ambiguities of time on the existential level, as well as the paradoxes on the philosophical level, were now clear to us; but what was clearest of all was the nonbeing he had described to us, permeating the interstices of our own being!

The next day he said: "And now ve shall explore ze nonbeing in space." I must admit I was all attention. "Space too unites being with nonbeing, anxiety with courage. . . . We are in space. . . . Not to have space is not to be. . . . But no finite being possesses space of its own. . . . Finitude means having no definite place; it means the always danger of losing your place, finally *having* to lose every place and, with that loss, to lose being-itself" (see *ST* I:194–95).

These were heavy words once one saw what they meant. With them, as I now recall, some of the deepest anxieties and terrors of earth rose before my eyes. I saw again the Jewish family huddled in a dingy restaurant in Yokohama in 1940. Having come eastward all the way from Europe to escape Hitler, they were sitting there silent at that chrome table in the restaurant in Yokohama, white and weightless with anxiety, now that Japan had become Hitler's ally—and they had no more space to go to except the wide Pacific! I recall people in my internment camp secretly moving neighbors' beds *inches* further away so as to have just a trace more space, as one woman put it, "for me to *be* in."[13] I saw the ultimacy and passion surrounding a *border,* whether of my own yard or of my nation, protecting the sacred space within which my community, large or small, can be—and all the conflict that this ultimate concern about space had generated in history.

Tillich's analysis had widened immensely the scope of the religious far beyond the limited confines of our relation to the moral law. Now to me every facet of our being bespoke our finitude, our need, and so our

---

13. Cf. Langdon Gilkey, *Shantung Compound* (New York: Harper and Row, 1966), chap. 5.

vulnerability to destructive anxiety; in a way unknown to me before, every aspect of our being now cried out for the divine. For without the *courage* to affirm the vulnerable present and the precarious space—and yet to recognize their vulnerability and their precariousness—no woman or man can *be* creatively. This universal courage—else how is creative life in time and space possible?—bespeaks the presence of that which transcends finitude, namely, being-itself. For anything *finite* would itself be in the grip of the categories of finitude and so itself subject to nonbeing; as a consequence, it would be unable to provide for us this conquest of anxiety. For Tillich, nothing is divine that cannot provide that conquest; nothing is, therefore, divine that does not transcend the categories of finitude. Tillich's definition of God as the divine power of being conquering in our existence the nonbeing in that existence is thus no "ontological abstraction," once one sees what he is about. Rather, it is a direct transcription into theological/philosophical discourse of what Tillich took to be one of the most important religious *experiences* of our finitude, namely, the experiences of the anxiety of time and of space *conquered* by the divine courage to be.[14] Like Thomas, Tillich used *contingency* to raise the mind to God; but it was contingency "felt from the inside" as anxiety, not contingency objectively contemplated as non-self-sufficiency. It was contingency as an *existential* problem, a "question" answered by the universal divine presence, not contingency as an *intellectual* puzzle logically requiring the inference of God.

That Tillich did not think too highly of the proofs of God comes, therefore, as no surprise (*ST* I:204–10). For him, the mind simply cannot climb up there beyond its creatureliness by itself; it is too finite, not to mention too much in "existence" or estrangement. It is too suffused with nonbeing to experience the power of being "naturally" and so to represent that experience reflectively in a rational proof. To Tillich, unlike Schleiermacher, examining the "depths" of our natural life is to encounter not absolute causality but the abyss of nonbeing. It is, then, only by passing *in our existence* through that abyss and finding given to us *there,* "over that abyss," the courage to affirm our fleeting present and our precarious space—and our contingency as a whole—that we "know" the ground and power of being (God) in and through our being, that is, in and through the courage with which we affirm our being. The proofs point to that existential awareness "representing the question," that is, to

---

14. "The Divine Life is the eternal conquest of the negative; this is its blessedness. Eternal blessedness is not a state of immovable perfection—the philosophers of becoming are right in rejecting such a concept. But the Divine Life is blameless through fight and victory" (*ST* III:405).

the infinite dimension of our finitude which is the possibility of the relation to God but also the possibility of an overwhelming anxiety. Hence, on the one hand, the effectiveness of these proofs to believers is explained, but, on the other hand, their ineffectiveness to those untouched by the experience either of the abyss or of courage.

To me, Tillich's skepticism about proofs of God always made good sense in the context of his deep awareness of the precariousness of finitude and the depth of our estrangement. Yet it is also well to recognize, as noted in chapter 3, that he had, surreptitiously, his own "proof" implicit throughout this section: Courage is, he reiterated, universal; courage cannot stem from finitude; therefore, universal courage has its ground in what transcends finitude. Surely this is a "proof" or at least an argument. Nevertheless, for Tillich being always precedes consciousness. The awareness of the presence of God precedes affirmative language about God; thus, only when the power of being appears in our existence through courage, do symbolic language about God and certainty of the divine reality and presence, appear.

The Character of Finitude

Tillich has, for most of us, a strange view of the creature, of the finite human being both as an individual and collectively as participants in cultural activities: artistic, political, philosophical, and so on. To most of us, humans—and analogously all other creatures—have their powers so to speak from themselves, even if their "natures" have been created by God. To Tillich on the other hand, the life, vitality, and creativity in us are not essentially *from us*. Rather, these powers surge upwards in and through us from an infinite source; they rush and push *through* us, and they culminate in our creative and expressive being, our behavior, our powers, our acts, and our ability to be. The creature *is* in and through the infinite power, order, and meaning of being that rush through her or him, and the possibilities that lure and impel him or her into active being. In all of our aspects we *are* through our intimate relation to the infinite power of being and meaning which is being-itself, or God (*ST* I:156, 235–37, 261–63). Correspondingly, when that infinite power is shut off, the creativity, vitality, power, and being of the creature slowly wither and die. This view is genuinely Augustinian, and in back of that Platonic and neo-platonic: the creature *is* through the presence in power of the infinite—in being, in thought, in love.

This divine power is experienced inwardly in the power and courage with which each creature is, if it is at all in the continual face of nonbeing.

This ground also manifests itself in the presence of the divine energy and order in and through each active being. This unconditional presence is manifest in the necessary presence of *depth* or *import* in all creative cultural work, in the *ultimate concern* essential for any creaturely being, in the eros that makes it possible for the creature to will at all, and which gives it vitality, intention, and so being. Thus, the creature is never really *autonomously* creative, in and through powers already present in the creature for herself or himself; nor is it autonomously powerful. Each of these positive aspects of creaturely existence bespeaks the active presence of the unconditional. As we shall see in a further chapter, it is even the case that only through the presence of the unconditional can the creature elevate himself or herself to the level of hubris and embody the demonic; the creature is not even capable *autonomously* to "sin," to defy God.

This view of the immanence of the divine in and through the creature, if the creature is to be or to do, is very different from the understanding of the creature in most "biblical theologies," and also, of course, in the Calvinist tradition. There the creature has, so to speak, creative equipment of its own, given it, to be sure, by God at creation but present now in the creature as its own capacities. The creature is thus seen as relatively capable of standing on its own, even over against God. It can obey God or defy God; it can cleave to God in faith or turn away—and if it does the latter, its *own power* does this turning—though the divine will has permitted or even willed it.

In Tillich's understanding, however, as God is experienced, known, and spoken of through the divine presence in the creature as the power of its being, the presence to it of ultimate meaning, and the promise of its fulfillment (as being, logos, and love), so correspondingly, the creature *is*, that is, it lives, it knows, it acts, and it loves—even sins—only through the presence of the divine power and meaning in and through its total being. As we shall see, this understanding of the finite creature, of its ontological structure, and of its powers as well as its vulnerabilities, prepares the way both for the development of the symbol of God—as the answer to the question of finitude—and to the interpretation of "existence," the "fallen" actuality of the creature so understood.

6
The Symbol of God

The subject of this chapter is Tillich's understanding of God. This topic is addressed because it is absolutely central and because it has recently been neglected. For example, in Adams's, Pauck's, and Shinn's excellent volume, there is no article on this subject.[1] Apparently, to our generation it seems more real and so more relevant, or more real because more relevant, to speak of theology of culture, or correlation, of the uneasy marriage with philosophy, and so on. There are, however, in Tillich literally no such subjects to speak about without the symbol of God; it provides the unifying ground of everything he says, as it does of the being of all that is: "For theology is first of all doctrine of God" (*ST* I:67).

I shall try to discuss Tillich's God in a Tillichean way, that is, in terms of *polarities*. He did this, concentrating on the polarity of the absolute and the concrete. I shall pick three others that interest me and that are, I think, more revealing of this symbol's contours than even his own favorite. Tillich loved polarities; they expressed unity amid apparent opposition, which delighted his fondness for system and yet for struggle. To him they combined the coherence of internal relations, of mutual interconnectedness and dependence, with the rough shock of paradox, all expressed in his favorite historical reference, Nicholas Cusanus's *coincidentia oppositorum*.

These polarities represent opposing contrasts that still depend upon one another, that, so to speak, rise and fall together; such harmony amidst strife was to him fundamental to the structure of whatever is. Reality, intensity of being, is not for Tillich "laid on," standard equipment; it arises in the victory of harmony over opposition, of unity amidst straining opposites. He constantly reiterated this theme. The more individu-

---

1. James Luther Adams, Wilhelm Pauck, Roger L. Shinn, eds., *The Thought of Paul Tillich* (New York: Harper and Row, 1985).

ality there is, the more, nonetheless, community (and participation in community); the richer the destiny that one acknowledges and appropriates, the more free one is; even the more nonbeing a person is capable of taking into oneself, the more power of being he or she enjoys and manifests. Correspondingly, the less of one pole is present, the less of its opposite will be there; these oppositions rise and fall, flourish and die, *together.* As Whitehead's metaphysical factors are internally related and so imply one another *logically* and relate to one another smoothly in coherence,[2] so Tillich's polarities are contrasts in tensile, dynamic, and yet potentially explosive interrelation to one another.

The three polarities I shall discuss are, first, God is being-itself: a polarity between God, the object of religion, and being-itself, the goal of philosophy, which represents the fundamental equation presupposed in all Tillich says. The second is God as being-itself and God as living, the next fundamental *coincidentia oppositorum.* The final and most mysterious and intriguing of all is God as the power of being and as nonbeing. All these polarities *themselves* appear in brilliant and polar interpenetration throughout his writings. Their opposition provides the inclusive richness and the dynamic tension characteristic of his thought as a whole, and their mutual dependence represents the equally strong pull (polarity!) toward unity and system that is also one of its overriding characters. Furthermore, Tillich emphasized the *unity* of these three sets of polarities: they, too, mutually interpenetrate or rise and fall together, or, to use his phrase, they "drive towards" each other. Being as God is the *power* of being that realizes itself in the dynamics of *life* and that *becomes itself* in its resistance and overcoming of *nonbeing* (compare especially *LPJ*, 37–41; and *CB*, 79–81, 155). Being, life, and nonbeing are interrelated concepts essential for Tillich's analysis of finitude; as we shall argue, taken symbolically they are crucial also for Tillich's notion of God. These three concepts can be understood only as embodying tensile polarities more fundamental, I believe, than his own, the polarity of absoluteness and concreteness.

God as Being-Itself, or God as the Ground and Power of Being

This equation, or as I am calling it, this polarity, is central to all of Tillich's thought: the object of religion, of ultimate concern, is identical to the goal of the philosophical analysis of being: God is being-itself (*ST*

---

2. Cf. A. N. Whitehead, *Process and Reality* (New York: Macmillan, 1929), 5, 9.

I:235–38, 270–71, 279; II:10–11). It is, first, the presupposition of the religious dimension of culture. The object of religion is not apart from cultural life but the central reality on which all culture is established. This equation is thus the premise for the whole range of Tillich's theology of culture, including his political writings and his analyses of art, of health, and of common life. It is also the premise for his interpretation of the being and the anxieties of finitude as *religious* issues, and so for the systematic theological concept of God as the power of being conquering the nonbeing of finitude. Without an analysis of finitude and its problems in *ontological* categories, that is, in terms of being, any understanding of religion for Tillich becomes an analysis in terms merely of moralistic law and ultimately results in heteronomous myth. Correspondingly, without the *religious* dimension represented by "God as being-itself," or by what he terms elsewhere "the ground of reason" (*ST* I:120), the whole range of cultural life, namely, art, law, science, social thought, and philosophy becomes empty, skeptical, undirected, and trivial. The well-known formula that religion is the substance of culture, and culture the form or expression of religion, represents the hither side of this more fundamental polarity: God, the object of religion, is being-itself, the depth of creative reason, and so the ground of cultural life.

The mutual dependence of these two fundamental categories: God and being-itself, reappears everywhere, as in any primal set of internal or polar relations. First, the ground of our being, of reason, and of cultural creativity is experienced and known only in religious ecstasy, that is, through the shock of nonbeing, on the one hand, and through the media of revelation, on the other hand. The ground of culture is not known by cultural means: via a scientific or philosophical argument, or analyzed out of a moral or legal obligation. It is known in cultural experience when a finite medium—a piece of art, a scientific inquiry, a social cause—becomes transparent to its unconditional ground, when the ultimacy and sacrality latent within our cultural life and in its special activities shine through that life, grasp us, and draw out our ultimate concern, when, in other words, a culture is, or nearly is, "theonomous." Interestingly, the goal of *ontological* inquiry, of philosophy, appears in an example of universal revelation, *ontically*, through the ontic media of cultural life. Thus, in the end philosophy is dependent on religion, for example, the religious substance of its culture, for its own basis, for its logical presuppositions, and its eros toward truth. Without the "religious" vision of the unity of thought and of being, of subjective and objective logos, and without final commitment to truth, value, and beauty, culture as a whole could never be.

Second, religion—and so the object of religion, the symbol, God—is in turn dependent upon its polar opposite, philosophy, and upon the results of philosophy's labors, ontology. Religion manifests itself in us in our ultimate concerns; these represent those aspects of our experience that Tillich terms "religious." But ultimate concerns are those that have to do with our being and nonbeing; otherwise, they are only preliminary in character and not "religious." If made ultimate, these proximate interests then become demonic. As a consequence, the religious is intertwined with, even a function of, the structure of our being. A religious issue is one where that structure is itself essentially threatened; thus, a religious issue is to be understood *reflectively* (and that is theology) by understanding the structure of our being (*ST* I:11–15; also compare *DF*). As ill health is a fault in or a wound to the structure of our organic life and is to be understood by the science that discloses that structure, so religious questions are to be understood *ontologically*, in terms of the understanding of the structure of our finite being. Religion is as fundamentally ontological as ontology was itself fundamentally religious. Thus God, the answer to our religious crises, appears as the power of being, as the answer to the question of our being, as the unconditional power that conquers the nonbeing that threatens us by threatening the structure of our finitude (*ST* I:189, 196, 203, 230–37, 251, 272–73; *LPJ*, 35–40). As religion is an expression of God as being, so culture is an expression of being as God.

Third, let us look finally at Tillich's most important argument, the theological issue he was most intensely concerned with: God, to be God, cannot be *a* being but must be being-itself (*ST* I:235). This represents an intensification of the mutual dependence just described: God is being-itself. For God to be *God* (a favorite phrase in those "neo-orthodox" days: "Let God be God"), God must, Tillich argued, be being-itself; otherwise, God is not of religious relevance, an ultimate concern; nor can God save. A finite God has, for Tillich, little or no religious value, whatever his or her metaphysical credentials—and Tillich would not have thought too much of them!" A conditioned God is no God" (*ST* I:248). Despite the presence of a number of philosophical arguments on this point,[3] the argument that Tillich presents here is *religious,* that is, it concerns the necessities of religion. This means—so I am suggesting—that the fundamental ontological attributes of God are, for Tillich, primarily *religious* attributes. Although they are also aspects of God essential for being-itself, they are even more essential for the object of religion as he understands the latter, and they are aspects derived "religiously," in religious ecstasy.

---

3. E.g., the infinite prius to the correlation of subject and object, of self and world, can neither be an object nor a self within the world; the source of the being of beings cannot be itself an example of the structure that "binds" and "limits" those beings.

To state that God cannot be *a* being but is being-itself is an *ontological* statement; but its force for Tillich comes from its necessity as a *religious* statement. That is to say, only the God who is the ground of being and not *a* being can be God *religiously*, the answer to the religious problems, the deep anxieties, of finitude. Any entity among entities or being among beings, however global in scope, is subject to the categories of finitude and so oppressed by the anxieties and the vulnerability—and the possible plunge into "existence"—characteristic of our finitude. If such a being "over against us" were to become ultimate, it would, for Tillich, immediately become heteronomous and so demonic. Like the demi-god of Arius, such a finite god cannot save but is himself in need of salvation, as we are. God is being-itself or else God is not God.[4]

The primary experience of God as being or the power of being is itself an example of religious ecstasy, of the experience of the power of being conquering nonbeing—religious because this is an issue of ultimate concern and because it involves an ecstatic awareness of the transcendent. This primary experience Tillich labels *courage*, the self-affirmation of a finite being over against the resistance of the nonbeing surrounding and permeating it (compare especially *CB*, and *ST* I:193–98, 206–9, 272, 276; II:12, 116; III:226, 228). This self-affirmation in courage is the primal mode of what we might call *spiritual participation* in the ground of being; self-affirmation is, in a sense, self-constitution, and thus it represents the *prius* of all that the finite creature is and does. Courage is at once the beginning of persons and of their creativity, of culture, *and* of the apprehension of the divine.[5] The other manifestation of the divine "secularly," that is, in cultural life—the apprehension we have mentioned of the unconditional import or meaning within every creative cultural activity—

---

4. For Tillich, whatever is ontologically ultimate is always *religiously* "God." Thus, if god be finite, the metaphysical structure that rules over god becomes the ultimate and is then the dubious and ambivalent object of ultimate concern. In Hellenic polytheism, this absolute beyond the gods became Fate, Tyche, and was thoroughly feared. In modern forms of finite theism, now that in a Christian culture "Being *qua* being is good," this ultimate beyond god (the God beyond god) is "process itself," which quite unwarrantably is regarded not as Fate but precisely as the ground of benevolent progress. This, Tillich once remarked, is *because* of the very doctrine of *creatio ex nihilo*, which a finite theism rigorously denies.

5. Of course, along with the self-affirmation and courage basic for finite life in the world and so for community, there are always manifestations of the ground *externally* to persons and communities: through objects in nature, the order of nature, the powers of nature, the power and value of the tribe, of the *polis*, and so on. Here the ground of life manifests itself "externally," ontically, in revelation through media; thus, explicit "religion" begins. There is an internal,

presupposes this courage that founds the self, its activities, and so its creative participation in the community.

Two consequences follow from this priority of courage. First, methodologically it means that the theology of culture is based on the systematically prior philosophical analysis of finitude and the "answer" in courage to the ambiguities of finitude. Secondly, since courage is the self-affirmation of the self as creature and of the community as its locus, and since it is in courage that the apprehension of the divine appears in finite life, courage represents the inward point where the beginnings of life, of culture, and of religion coalesce. To be sure, the self both is created and creates itself in coming into existence—when it not only receives its being from God but also actualizes or chooses itself and falls. In courage its creation is, so to speak, fulfilled as a self with the first beginning of its redemption, when it participates in its ground and affirms itself. Here, then, its ground, being-itself, is experienced as the *power of being*, the power to conquer the nonbeing permeating the self. Though power of being is an ontological concept or metaphor, this "name" is *religious*, referring to a participation in the divine that both rescues and creates the self and enables it to be itself. It is, therefore, consistent for Tillich to prefer this "name," the ground and power of being, to other names. It is, he says, the "direct" symbol for being-itself, "more direct" and "more accurate" than cause or substance. I take it "direct" here refers to the "whence" of courage, the basic religious apprehension of the divine, as the power of being, the primal answer to our ultimate concern.

One final point on this polarity. The experience of courage is, I think, the experience that functions in Tillich as the basis for all religious speech. Hence God equals *power* of *being*. Here the divine ground is apprehended as beyond subject and object, self and world, and yet fully and actively within each of them. It is here, then, in the experience of courage that symbolic speech is born; it is in this religious context that it is

---

"secular" manifestation of the ground in courage and an external, "religious" manifestation in the world through appropriate media in the world, both expressing the dependence of the finite on its ground—the ultimate concerns of dependence for its life, for its powers and gifts, and for its "protection" against the terrors of nonbeing. The "correlation" of the internal, "secular" manifestation in courage and the external, "religious" manifestation illustrates again the close interweaving of culture and religion which is of the essence of Tillich's thought. The *existential* presence of the divine and its *"religious"* presence in "hierophanies" or "revelations" are neither separated nor opposed; they are correlated in the life of any community and culture, the existential giving felt and ultimate relevancy to the hierophanies, and the latter defining, limiting, and explicating through images, myths, and rites, the more inchoate but urgent presence of the former.

primarily used; and it is in its terms that such speech can be legitimated and assessed. Courage is, in other words, the existential or religious "anchor" of Tillich's system of symbolism or analogy—not the philosophical/theological statement that God is being-itself, as he at first proposed (*ST* I:238; for the retraction of this proposal, see *ST* II:9–10). Since, as we have seen, God is first experienced and known *religiously* and not philosophically—in fact, God cannot be known at all philosophically except in the context of courage—such a logical or linguistic base for symbolism was inconsistent with the main characteristics of Tillich's thought.

Tillich, however, is full of surprises. Having denied that an argument for the transcendent power and ground of being was possible (*ST* I:204–10), nevertheless (so it seems to me) he frequently presented one to us, and right at this central point! At each stage of his discussion of the categorical structure of finitude and of its deep anxieties, he makes clear that what he calls the annihilating power of nonbeing *should* conquer the being in the creature and leave it helpless in a frenzy of anxiety. Left to itself, no creature, no embodiment of finitude, can "make it"; the anxieties of time, of space, of causality, and of death, coupled with the loss of ultimacy, will drown out the possibility of self-affirmation, unless a power transcendent to the finite and to the nonbeing permeating the finite manifests itself to us. Without God, the human is inevitably lost; here is Tillich's major, but not his only, argument against humanism. But paradoxically (against the *doxa*), life *does* affirm itself; courage *is* present; and what is more, courage is *universal*, despite the depth and omnipresence of this threat. (For examples of this argument, compare *ST* I:192–98; *CB*). Officially, Tillich leaves this as a "question," an inescapable question, but his repeated assertion about the universality of courage entails that there is, in fact, an answer and a universal one. Thus logically, there being an answer underivable from finitude, this represents an argument, an argument that the presence of the power of being may be "deduced" from the universal presence of courage. Ironically, Tillich wanted a linguistic/logical basis for symbolic speech in the proposition "God is being-itself"—and could not find it. At the same time, he denied there could be any argument for God—and produced a number of persuasive ones based on the experiences lying behind that proposition!

God as Being and God as Life

As is already clear, God as the power of being drives toward God as life, or the living God, just as it is life in its dynamic movement that raises the questions of courage and of ultimate reunion (*LPJ*, 37, 41). Tillich states this relation of being to life repeatedly: "Every being affirms its own being. Its life is its self-affirmation. . . . [Life is] the self-affirmation of a being . . . correlate to the power of being it embodies" (*LPJ*, 39–40). The symbol power of being has, therefore, a dynamic, moving, impelling nuance quite lacking in the concept of being-itself. From this lack in the symbol being-itself has stemmed a great deal—though not all—of the misinterpretation or misunderstanding of Tillich as an "absolutist" and therefore a static thinker. If, so this argument has run, being-itself is the prius of subject-object, and of self-world, beyond potentiality and actuality and the finite categories of space and time, does it not resemble, if not duplicate, the classical absolute, especially when Tillich centers his cultural analysis on the concept of the unconditional and his theological system on the denial that God is *a* being? As a result, those who could only conceive of dynamic process in terms of some form of metaphysical limitation on God, welcomed these intimations of sheer absoluteness contained in being-itself. Here, so many said, is evidence that Tillich's God represents a modern clone of the neo-platonic absolute.

That this is a misinterpretation of Tillich's philosophical theology, the concept of God as power of being has, as we have shown, already indicated. The point, however, becomes clear in the prominence that he gives to the symbol of life in his notion of God. For life is, for Tillich, the name for dynamic and meaningful change, better, as he remarks, than process which also refers to corpses (*ST* III:11). In his frequent definitions of life, he stresses that it represents the move from potential to actual being, the actualization of the elements of being in their move *through* tension to unity, or, in another set of images, as their separation or divergence in creative self-actualization and their reunion in a richer synthesis (*ST* I:235, 241–43, 252; *LPJ*, 38–41; *CB*, 78–85). Clearly, all of this implies that reality is dynamic, in process, moving from one state to another. Insofar as these concepts are applied to God, they entail dynamics, change, process over time (as does power of being), even if they are applied "symbolically" and not literally, as they are to any finite creature. As Tillich admits (*ST* I:248), a fundamental decision was made in modern thought in favor of the dynamic element, a decision he clearly shares by associating his own view with the "philosophies of life." As Hegel and Schleiermacher had already shown (not to mention certain biblical theologians), it is evident that many philosophers and theologians who reject the concept of a finite God, or one enjoying clear metaphysical limitations, espouse, nevertheless, a dynamic or "process" view of God.

This point is crucial for any understanding of Tillich's God (as crucial as is its opposite number, namely, that Whitehead's God is *also* "infinite," "changeless," and "eternal" or "everlasting," for an adequate interpretation of Whitehead).[6] God is, therefore, for Tillich, life as well as being-itself (*ST* I:241–49); or, as we are suggesting, the two represent a *polarity* in Tillich's concept of God. In Tillich, God relates positively and so dynamically to the development of nature and to the process of history as *creative providence*, that is, not only as originating but also sustaining and directing each creature toward its fulfillment (*ST* I:252–64). Thus, history and communal life are potentially filled with meaning and so provide a creative arena for our active and hopeful participation. Here arises, in fact, the other major evidence of the divine in ordinary experience, namely, the presence of the *unconditional* in the import of every cultural activity, the import that can make it a medium of general revelation, on the one hand, and an enterprise of ultimate concern, on the other, all of which makes culture possible by providing it with its religious substance.

As we have seen, the presence of God in ongoing cultural life is represented initially by the courage to be, by self-affirmation both as individuals and as participants. *Import*, however, as the presence of the ultimate in each creative act, makes this immanent, dynamic participation of God in culture and history also utterly necessary, as in the end does the New Being. The Eternal Now (to use another of Tillich's images) is incarnate, as possibility and demand, in the moments of time driving them to their fulfillment and so filling them with meaning and we who live in them with vitality. As Tillich's analysis of culture is impossible without the category of being-itself, so his theology of culture has no content without the dynamic presence of the living God as unconditional import, and as the possibility of reunion. It is, then, in terms of the Divine Life that the moving dialectic of that life is articulated, that the infinite and absolute Abyss unfolds itself creatively in the "many" that represent the world, the concreteness of nature and history (*ST* I:234–35, 252)—and is completed in the Spirit. "The divine life and the divine creativity are not different. God is creative because he is God" (*ST* I:252). God as being-itself is thus both more precisely defined and radically qualified by God as life.

These two are, however, *polar* and so the Divine Life is itself qualified in turn by the necessities of being-itself. As life appears in God, life is, says Tillich, to be understood "symbolically" (analogically), not directly. Thus many of what may be called life's more "temporalistic" qualities are negated, as many are in Whitehead's God. This is not to deny the dynamic element; without it, says Tillich, God would be a "fixed result," *actus purus*, pure actuality devoid of potentiality, and thus not the living God (*ST* I:286). The dynamic element appears symbolically, however, and thus

---

6. Cf. *Process and Reality*, 521–24.

qualified by it opposite, the formal, changeless element. In God, for example, there is no sharp separation of potentiality and actuality, of destiny and freedom, as with us; there is no real or absolute "not yet" that is not balanced by an "already" (*ST* I:246, 276). Both the modal distinction of actual and possible, and the temporal distinction of present and future, characterize us as finite; they represent an aspect of the nonbeing of finitude, of its contingency and temporality. God, therefore, says Tillich, transcends those *negative* characteristics of the finite without sacrificing the dynamic: God is *symbolically* (analogically) life, beyond the distinction of potentiality and actuality, of present and future, yet without annulling that distinction. For God is not timeless nor changeless but the "moving-permanent," the "changeless-changing" ground of change. This is, I suggest, what from the opposite pole Whitehead seeks to say about God in his own categories of becoming, which categories when applied to God he also has to stretch and pull out of their univocal shape as they are applied to ordinary entities. Tillich does this stretching and pulling (1) by recognizing openly the polarity, the tension, between God as being-itself and God as life; (2) by understanding his own speech about God as symbolic; and (3) by admitting in the end that God remains a "mystery for finite understanding" (*ST* I:280).

God as the Power of Being and Nonbeing

We now come to the most mysterious and intriguing polarity of all: God and nonbeing, or the power of being and nonbeing. These are, let me suggest, to be understood not merely as *opposites*, as Tillich is inclined to encourage us at first to take them. Rather, being and nonbeing are, I think, to be taken as Tillich's major polarity, not only in relation to the finite but even more in relation to God. For being and nonbeing, affirmation and negation, are inextricably and surprisingly interwoven in the whole texture of Tillich's thought so that it cannot be understood without grasping this fundamental pattern. Tillich, as we have seen, defines a polarity as mutually related contrasts, a coincidence of opposites such that they depend on each other and rise and fall together: the more there is of one, the more possibility there is of the other. As we shall see, this is precisely the case with God as the power of being and nonbeing. Strangely, these two form a mutually dependent polarity rather than the radical opposition that seems at first to be the case.[7]

---

7. Tillich often cited the influence on his thought of two thinkers for whom this "polarity" represented the center of their thought: Jacob Boehme and Friedrich Schelling.

Let us, however, begin with the initial opposition. This opposition, as we are first introduced to Tillich, seems almost to be an absolute one. As he always does, Tillich starts with our experience of ourselves and of our world, of our finite being and its participation in others. This experience is filled with negativity, trivial and fundamental, temporary and essential; we experience ourselves as deeply and continually threatened, and we are aware of the need to affirm ourselves, our relations, our tasks over against these threats. At the deepest level these threats appear as *essential*, essential to all we are, to our finitude itself. These are felt inside as anxiety, a deep and potentially shattering panic, and yet quite without any specifiable object. The reason for the depth of this panic is that these threats are so bound up with *us*—with our temporality, spatiality, causality, and limited substance—that we have in ourselves no leverage against them. They are what we are, the nonbeing essential to and so permeating our own finitude; they are aspects of our *essential* structure (*ST* I:163–71; 186–98). For we are "being bounded by nonbeing," Tillich says; our power of being, such as it is, finds itself in opposition to the overwhelming power of our nonbeing. In this situation, the courage to affirm our limited being comes to us (as we have noted) from the unconditioned power of being in which we are and through which we continue to be: from God. God is the *answer* to the anxiety of finitude, the power of being that "conquers" nonbeing; thus God is experienced and defined *as* the answer, as that which *resists* and *overcomes* nonbeing (compare *ST* I:235–41; *LPJ*, 36–41). As we have seen, for Tillich a god who cannot thus conquer nonbeing is not God. Thus God does not, as does *a* being, participate in nonbeing or share the essential boundedness brought into the picture by nonbeing. God is, therefore, infinite being, "the abysmal ground of being"; in contrast, we are being limited by nonbeing (compare *ST* I:235–38). At this point the opposition between God and nonbeing seems absolute, for that very opposition appears to represent the *godness* of God on the one hand, and, on the other, that same opposition specifies the crucial distinction between ourselves as the "question" and the divine as the "answer." When we see all of this, we are sure we now "have" Tillich; in the contrast of being with nonbeing, and especially of God and nonbeing, the character and problem of finitude, the role of God, and the meaning of being as the resistance to and victory over nonbeing appear satisfactorily and finally nailed down.

Life and certainly Tillich are not, however, that simple. There is always a dialectic, or, as we have put it, a polarity. And soon enough this one begins to appear. As we move through the system further, the relation between being and nonbeing ceases to be one of stark opposition and becomes one of interdependent, mutual interweaving. Let us now explore this puzzling point.

First of all, it becomes apparent that, as in Nietzsche, being arises only in opposition to nonbeing. It is not that our being is already "there," so to speak, and then resists, as perhaps we first thought. Rather, being as it manifests itself in us comes to be in the struggle with nonbeing. As a result, the more nonbeing there is, that is, the more nonbeing the creature faces and must overcome, the more being it possesses and reveals. Clearly, both of these two represent ingredients necessary for the fullness of finitude. A self-affirming creature (a creature embodying courage) is not *just* the result of finite being and so of the positive power of being; it also arises out of the polar nonbeing that limits it and permeates it (*LPJ*, 40).

If we pursue this theme of the polar interdependence of being and nonbeing through different corridors and rooms of the Tillichean mansion, we are surprised at its continual reappearance and at the importance, even the increasing importance, of this theme. As the power of a finite being comes to be in correlation with the threat of nonbeing, over against it, so the apprehension or awareness of the infinite ground, and thus the possibility of finite courage, appears only through the shock of nonbeing, especially in relation to the nonbeing within the categories of our own finitude. There we encounter the direct and explicit onslaught of the anxiety of finitude, an anxiety arising from the nonbeing (as well as the being) of space, time, causality, and substance (*ST* I:192–98). Courage is thus as dependent on nonbeing as it is on being. Again, the ontological elements, the structures of finitude in its dynamic life, are inconceivable without nonbeing in many varied forms: the potentiality of the dynamic pole is saturated with the not-yet; freedom necessitates not only that same not-yet but the presence of alternatives; and individuation and participation both require separation from what is, from oneself and one's world, "going out," and so precarious risk, if either a creative individual or a participating community are to be possible (*ST* I:174–86; 198–202). Life, therefore, presupposes relative nonbeing, the principle of nonidentity, of not-yet, of here and not there—of "room," of "play," of "cracks" or "gaps," if any dialectical transformation is to be at all, whether we speak of finitude or of God. Thus Tillich insists, and has to insist, that there is *me on*, relative nonbeing, in both finitude and God as the basis of life (*ST* I:188–89).

This principle of relative or dialectical nonbeing is, however, relevant not only for the understanding of change but even more for the interpretation of the spiritual dimension within human being and within culture. Unless humans were "finite freedom" (*ST* II:31–35) and thus in some sense separate from as well as identical with their being, humans could not be "spirit." There would not be the distance from their environment that creates a world out of the latter; no disengagement from culture that allows criticism of it, intentional participation in it, and reshaping of it; no self transcendence that generates the possibility of anxiety and courage—and so no religious questions that lay the groundwork for the answers of faith (see the explicit statement of this, *ST* I:187). Finally, as the most fundamental ontological assumption in the system, nonbeing in the divine creative life is necessary if there is to be ontological "room"—"room" for finitude at all. If the divine creativity is to go out from itself into the manifold of a *real* and *autonomous* particularity, self-limitation in God must appear, a "self-negation" of the divine infinity. The polarity of being and nonbeing in God, the self-negation as well as the self-affirmation of God, is the presupposition for the polarity of the divine absoluteness and concreteness, of divine ground and plural world, and so for the *theonomy* of ultimate ground and autonomous creature that centers all of Tillich's thought. The relation of Tillich's God to the world is more dialectical and even more paradoxical than perhaps even he thought. Nonbeing is necessary not only for life but for self and world as well, and for the relation of the creatureliness of both self and world to the divine ground. Again, both finitude and God participate in these elements of *me on*, of relative or dialectical nonbeing (compare *ST* I:189).

We cannot here pursue this theme more deeply into the symbol of the divine Spirit, though we shall do this in a subsequent chapter. In connection with our present argument, however, it is important to look further at the vital role of nonbeing in Tillich's understanding of revelation and redemption. In these two areas this theme, which began as a minor motif offstage or in the background, now assumes a predominant role at stage center. The New Being is the fulfillment of the Divine Life; in effect, it is the movement toward the reunion of what has become separated and estranged, the pouring, so to speak, of redemptive power and meaning anew into a world separated from God. It represents, therefore, the culminating realization of the power and meaning of being which is God. At the same time, however, it is the apex of the dialectic of being and nonbeing to which we have referred. For the criterion of the New Being, as of all revelatory manifestations of the divine ground, is the medium that negates itself in affirming itself, and thus the medium that is able to point beyond itself (*ST* I:135–37, II:158–59). Here nonbeing becomes not only a polar element in all that is; even more, nonbeing is the overriding condition for the fulfillment of all that is: the true medium sacrifices itself in order to be what it really is, a true symbol transparent to the divine.

Paradoxically, then, the abnegation of power that culminates in the acceptance of the cross becomes for Tillich the true symbol for the reality, power, and meaning of the creature. Nonattachment more than balances attachment, and self-sacrifice becomes at least polar to self-affirmation;

the self-creativity of life, when it fully realizes itself, becomes as well the self-giving of life. The reason is that only the symbol that is willing to negate itself is able to remain in unbroken unity with its ground and so able to point beyond itself. Through death, or at least only through the willingness to die, is there life. In the end, the power of being is more than *only* the power of finite being "conquering" nonbeing. Such an undialectical affirmation of being leads quickly enough to the demonic, as when Christian soldiers and saints alike conquer the world for Christ. Rather, here the power of being is dialectically also the power of *nonbeing* in the finite, that it may represent the divine ground as (one now presumes) both being and nonbeing.

Tillich, moreover, refuses to restrict this powerful theme of negation to the creature, to the finite in relation to the divine (as did the tradition), and thus to exclude God from its implications. Clearly, he insists that in the event of the New Being, God "takes the suffering of the world upon himself by participating in existential estrangement"; and "this element of non-being, seen from the inside, is the suffering that God takes upon himself. . . . Here the doctrine of the living God and the doctrine of atonement coincide" (*ST* II:174). The participation of God in the *nonbeing* of the finite, now the estranged finite, has here enlarged to the point where it more than balances the affirmation of God as pure being with which we began; thus, it radically qualifies the original separation of God from all aspects of the nonbeing of finitude. It seems inescapable that God is here to be termed, in a symbolic and not a literal sense, to be sure, being *and* nonbeing. As each of us has felt baffled and frustrated to find in the Mahayana of the Buddhist tradition that nirvana and samsara are now one and not distinct, as we once thought we had been told, so it is with Tillich: God is apparently both being and nonbeing, the power of being united with the strange and paradoxical "power of nonbeing."

Systematically, as Tillicheans know well, the question in all of this concerns the relations of *me on*, which Tillich says is in God, though symbolically, to *ouk on*, which he maintains is in opposition to God (*ST* I:188–253). The present analysis reflects a slight dissatisfaction with that sharp distinction between the two "types." Are they "types" of nonbeing, and so species in a common genus? Can they be in such stark opposition if the role of nonbeing in its many and varied forms is as determinative as we have shown? Can one of them be such a significant, essential aspect of God and the other the absolute opposite of the divine? As Tillich has left it, *me on* and *ouk on* appear to be starkly opposite and just as starkly unrelated. I suggest an amendment; namely, since nonbeing as a whole seems polar to being, *me on* and *ouk on* might be related as are the two levels of being, that is, *analogously*, as finite nonbeing and nonbeing itself.

The shock of nonbeing and the potential sacrifice of one's own being are thus for finitude the *entrance*, not just to the ground and power of being, but much more to the dialectical mystery of being and nonbeing, which is God. I am here—as many will recognize—reminded of Nishitani's view of nonbeing as at first starkly negative nihility, until (with courage and nonattachment) we pass through nihility by appropriating it, and then it is transformed and becomes redemptive and healing Nothingness.[8] This is, to be sure, hardly Tillich. But if I am right, it is not so far from Tillich, the theologian of being, as we at first presumed.

* * *

We all have questions which we wish we could ask Tillich about his system and about the reality he so creatively there disclosed to us. My first one is: What is it you wished you might have done, had you been able to live further, with the problem of the plurality of religions, the relation of Christianity to other religions as "one among the many"? The second is: What did you mean by nonbeing, by the two "cousins" named *me on* and *ouk on;* how *were* they related to one another, to being itself, and to our own being? The full answers to these two questions, like the verification of the truth of their answers, are "eschatological" in the sense that we will only know all of that later. But these two questions are strangely related; each one presents to us a continuing and fascinating puzzle, a puzzle replete at once with the shock of the nonbeing of plurality and the promise of a New Being of unity.

---

8. Keiji Nishitani, *Religion and Nothingness* (Berkeley: University of California Press, 1982), chaps. 3 and 4.

7

The Character of Existence

There has been no more controversial area of Tillich's thought than his interpretation of what in theology is called "the Fall"[1]—the sources of moral, social, and personal evil that suffuse human existence, what Tillich, as we shall see, chose to name "existence." To his many "biblical" theological colleagues—notably Reinhold Niebuhr—he was, especially on this issue, too "ontological," and for that reason they thought he committed one of the cardinal sins of an unbiblical theology, namely, to identify creation with the Fall and so "to make sin necessary." On the other hand, any careful analysis of his "doctrine" of the Fall reveals Tillich, precisely *because* of this doctrine, to belong among the same "*Krisis*" or "neo-orthodox" theologians as, so to speak, one of their "charter" members. The reason is that, despite the unconventionality of his method with regard to the Fall, Tillich's emphasis on the universality and weight of sin is unqualified; his sense of its utter inescapability and oppressive burden is unmatched; and his picture of the despairing suffering resulting from sin rivals that of even the most realistic of his theological colleagues, and almost any contemporary piece of existentialist literature. As in his emphasis on the necessity of revelation, so in the depth and pervasiveness of "estrangement" or "alienation" in his system, Tillich can hardly be described as a "liberal," however much his thinking on other grounds is correlated throughout with cultural experiences and

---

1. Tillich is very careful, in fact precise, about the language he uses in this connection: about how and when he wishes to employ the symbols of "Fall," sin, evil, and so on. Until we get into the substance of his discussion, however, we cannot use the precise words he uses or make clear his interpretation of them without confusing or misleading the reader. Hence we will, in this introductory section, employ conventional symbols that will become more accurately defined as we go along. Tillich's most complete discussion of the Fall (or existence) is found in *ST* II:1–96.

categories. On the contrary, as he always claimed, his theology belongs, and here especially, strictly in the Pauline, Augustinian, and Reformation line of theologians of "sin and grace," rather than among the liberal theologians of continuity (*ST* II:48–49). Let us, therefore, begin with the issue of his method of approaching the subject, since this is perhaps the point of heaviest criticism.

Ontology and Myth

Like his colleague Niebuhr, Tillich was fascinated by the puzzling complexity of speaking reflectively about human evil: about the Fall, sin, and the suffering that was their consequence. Whatever one thinks of *what* he said about these, there can be little disagreement that his discussion helped clarify why it is so difficult to say anything directly about them. As Tillich makes clear, there are two sides to the experience of human evil. First, on the one hand, it reveals itself as a *universal situation*, as something "already there" as we begin to make our ordinary decisions, and already there for *everyone*, including ourselves. Hence sin cannot be conceived as an ordinary personal act for whose consequences we are in the ordinary way responsible. When did any of us "decide" against God, or determine to "rebel"? Even if we did, how would such a particular, historical act infect *everyone*? Thus is the language of decision, act, rebellion, that is to say personal, historical language, slightly off the target. Sin and participation in evil appear to be universal, and so they seem to represent a necessary condition for all of us. Second, on the other hand, we are not only the conditioned victims of estrangement; we are also participants in it and so perpetuators of it. We *do* it, and we do it as free, self-constituting persons. Thus we are in some strange way responsible for it. It is our clear experience of *responsibility* for the situation of alienation in which we find ourselves that is the clearest and most unambiguous sign of its *non-necessity* and so of the effective involvement in it of our *freedom* (*ST* II:30, 44, 46).

Human evil is, therefore, bafflingly both *situation and act*, and neither one can be construed "literally" (*ST* II:55–58). Our universal perversity cannot simply be understood ontologically; it is not a *necessary* condition of our finitude (a part of the structure of finite being). Nor is it to be explained by a merely contingent historical act or series of acts done by us in our experienced past. As a universal "situation" it seems "ontological"; but as an act of our own freedom in which we ourselves participate, it seems also personal, an act (or better, an event) to be described by a story, a story that is either historical or "mythical." The problem for the

modern theologian is to find some common language with which to unite
these two seemingly contradictory aspects of the experience of sin.

It was, of course, in terms entirely of a "historical story" that previous
theology had interpreted sin. The story of Adam and Eve was taken to be,
as it at first seems to be, like other stories, a straightforward historical
account of an event in the past. Nevertheless, it was always a *special* story,
one with universal, even "ontological" consequences: the concupiscence
that drives all of us, the loss of the likeness of God or the ability to be pure
and holy, and most evident of all, mortality. We note that one other
biblical story has the same form of effecting a lasting and universal
change: the history of the life, death, and resurrection of Jesus the Christ.
The first story could have these universal and "ontological" consequences
because it told of the acts of the first pair who, therefore, "stood for us
all" and because God willed those consequences; the story of Christ had
such universal and essential consequences because it was also the story of
the Incarnate One who united himself to us and our humanity.

Now that the acts of Adam and Eve are no longer viewed as credible
history (*ST* I:252; II:29), the viability of the adamic story as the *historical
explanation* of universal sin has been denied, and so the usefulness of the
literal story language of traditional theology has been questioned. Nevertheless, most "biblical theologians" vastly prefer story or narrative modes
of speech: that is, speech about personal acts, particular events, and
personal responsibility, now interpreted as "mythical" or "symbolic"
speech concerning the situation in which we all find ourselves. For Tillich
such theologians have, through these forms of speech, overemphasized
the personal and responsible side of sin and have overlooked, even
obscured, the universal situational side (except for Origen). For example,
for all his profundity on this issue, Niebuhr's interpretation of the myth of
the Fall hardly explicates satisfactorily the universality and "thrownness"
of the situation of sin. What makes Tillich so helpful, therefore, is not
only his clear interest in method, but also the fact that his ontological
approach to theology helps to bring to consciousness, even prominence,
the universality and the "already there" character of the experience of
human evil.

Tillich always offers multiple reasons for his ontological approach.
First, we have reviewed an important one in the case of this doctrine:
namely, the fact that estrangement is universal, a situation in which, prior
to any conscious act, we all already find ourselves, and thus *like* an
ontological condition of our being. Second, for Tillich religion has to do
with our ultimate concerns and thus with our being and nonbeing.
Reflection on religion, therefore, requires reflection on the *structure* of
our being (ontology) if we would understand what it is that affects our

being and nonbeing. Specifically (as Augustine expressed it[2]), the *disease* of an organism can only be understood in terms of the structure of *health* of the organism, the Fall in terms of the essential structure of our created nature or human nature. Hence, that warping or distortion of human beings which represents alienation or sin must be reflectively interpreted in relation to the structure of human beings. Tillich terms that structure the ontological "essence" or essential nature of humanity as finite. A *theological* diagnosis of our ills requires a *philosophical* understanding of our structure; we can only understand sin by means of a prior ontological analysis of our "nature" as humans. As we shall see, at each step Tillich interprets alienation and its consequences as the self-destruction of the essential structure of our finite being. Part of the power and the credibility of his analysis comes from the clarity with which it shows how sin literally dismantles and so destroys that structure and how, therefore, suffering inevitably results (compare *ST* II:29–78).

Third, like most of his philosophical and theological contemporaries (e.g., Niebuhr), Tillich was fiercely antidualistic. He was convinced that alienation was not originally *bodily*, an issue of fleshly lust or sensual desire; rather, it is fundamentally "spiritual," an act of the centered self in its freedom. Nevertheless, more than those contemporaries, he felt the involvement of our organic desires and lusts in every aspect of our spirit and the effect of this spiritual dislocation on our sensuality. Thus, he needed the language inclusive of both aspects of our nature, of our organic drives and sensuous desires, on the one hand, and our spiritual and moral powers, on the other. To him, only ontological language could be descriptive of our whole being ("being" included the physical, psychological, mental, and spiritual), and thus an ontological description was necessary.

Fourth, Tillich agreed thoroughly with Kierkegaard (and Niebuhr) that the old "story" of Adam's fall from created perfection, if made the *cause* of sin, represented poor theology. If Adam's disastrous decision preceded the Fall as its cause, then Adam's original situation, being without alienation, was quite different from ours. Hence, his sin becomes utterly irrelevant for us and for our problems; the symbolic character of the story as *our* story, and so it's power to "open up" *our* situation, is sacrificed (*ST* II:34, 37, especially 56 and 57).[3]

Finally, Tillich made quite explicit, more than did the biblical theologians, the consequences for theology of our new understanding of the

2. Augustine, *The City of God*, trans. Marcus Dods (New York: Random House, 1950), bk. 11, chap. 17; bk. 12, chap. 1.

3. Cf. Sören Kierkegaard, *The Concept of Dread*, trans. Walter Lowrie (Princeton: Princeton University Press, 1946), chap. 1, secs. 2–4.

early history of the cosmos and especially of humankind. There was, he knew, no "time" in which the "good" creation of world and of selves subsisted, as there was no "moment" when the Fall took place (*ST* II:36, 40–44). The difference between good creation and the Fall cannot, therefore, be conceived as a *temporal* difference: *first* creation and *then* the Fall, as the history of Adam and the myth of Adam alike put it. We cannot distinguish creation and the Fall by saying, as even contemporary biblical theologians were apt to say, "first God created and then humans fell." As a consequence, on the temporal level, creation and the Fall must be identified: as finitude comes to be, so then does it also fall. There is no escape from this sort of identity, however much the biblical theologian might decry this "pantheism." Thus, a temporal (a historical or phenomenal) distinction between creation and the Fall being ruled out, some mode of ontological distinction becomes necessary.

On the other hand, as noted, Tillich is clear that the Fall, however we understand it, cannot be interpreted simply metaphysically or ontologically. Ontology deals with the structure of our being; the consequences of that structure (for example, that we are free as well as determined, mortal as well as living), are inescapable, and an acquiescence to them is therefore necessary. We are not responsible for being either finite or mortal; no use of our freedom can avoid or eradicate either one. Thus, to make estrangement ontological without remainder is to make it necessary, and that contradicts our clear experience of our responsibility for it and so the participation of our freedom in it. As Augustine argued, to give sin a cause is to relieve our freedom of its responsibility for sin, prematurely to pardon our will.[4] In some strange way the Fall is, therefore, an event, a non-necessary moment; it contains a kind of *temporal* element (*ST* II:29). Myth, therefore, is also necessary, for myth tells a story, an event that is related to our ontological structure but not a necessity of that structure. Some combination of ontology and myth, therefore, is called for, what Tillich calls a "half-way myth" (*ST* II:29).

In fact Augustine, whose understanding of the origin of sin as a historical act is now being revised, was right on one point: any "explanation" of sin is impossible. An ontological or metaphysical explanation makes sin intelligible, but by the same token it makes sin necessary. Moreover, a "historical" explanation (in terms of an event in the past)—and here Tillich disputes Augustine—or a sociological one (in terms of social customs), prove alike to be no explanation at all, for the question arises: Whence comes that first evil event or form of human evil? What an interpretation of evil can do is to "disclose" our situation, to uncover "depths" in our experience of which we were unconscious or which we

---

4. Augustine, *Confessions*, bk. 7.

have ignored, and so to bring to consciousness the complex forces at work on us and in us. In this way, we may become in new ways "open" for the counter forces of healing. Through the disclosive symbol we are moved to "ask the question," and thus are enabled for perhaps the first time to hear an answer.[5] Such a symbol, combining ontology and myth, is precisely what Tillich seeks to present to us.

Essence and Existence, Destiny and Freedom, Self-Constitution

Tillich combines ontology and myth, first of all, by means of his distinction between *essence* and *existence*. Essence ("essential humanity") here stands for the ontological structure of human being: its structure as finite, as self and world, as composed of the polarities, and as uniting inorganic, organic, psychological, and "spiritual" being in a unity of dimensions. It is this essential structure that makes a human *human*, that "form" which, as with the Greeks, represents, therefore, the "reality" or identity of a human as human and provides the clue to his or her fulfillment and value—to human *good*. But, and here Tillich appears modern and "naturalistic," essence represents possibility, not yet concrete or real, and so essence is also "potentiality," what might be. From this perspective, therefore, an essence is only potential until it becomes actual, until it "exists" or "stands out of nothingness into being" (*ST* II:20), until it becomes the structure of a concrete, historical, actual human being. Part of the confusion in Tillich with regard to the distinction between essence and existence is this apparent vacillation he exhibits between "essence," which as structure represents the basic *reality* of something, on the one hand, and "essence," which as structure is merely a *potentiality* about to become actual, on the other—between, so to speak, his Greek side and his modern, naturalistic, factual, temporal, and even historical side.

Correspondingly, for Tillich one large part of the validity of these two contrasting categories (essence and existence) was that they represented in modern form the Platonism that he always regarded as true philosophy. This contrast between the unambiguous essential form and the ambiguous existing actuality was, moreover, confirmed for him by two events in the history of modern philosophy. The first was the continual breakdown of "essentialist" speculative philosophies which sought to understand reality solely in terms of its ontological structure (especially Hegel, but one could well add Whitehead). These represented for him "essentialist"

---

5. Cf. *TC*, 56–58, for a discussion of the disclosive power of a symbol.

philosophies that overlooked the estrangement of existence. The second was the rise of existentialism (and also of Expressionist art), a philosophy that to him reaffirmed the estranged character of all that exists (compare *ST* II:19–29).

In any case, for Tillich any actuality, especially human actuality, can only be understood in terms of this dual analysis: an analysis of its *essential structure*, and an analysis of its modes of *actual existence*. This dual approach appeared to him to represent a mode of inquiry that had been shown (by the above) to be both legitimate philosophy and also appropriately "biblical," since it corresponds in ontological reflection to the "myths" of creation and the Fall. While most of Tillich's admirers share his insistence on clarifying through ontology the essential structure in order to understand the distortion of that structure (compare the way the philosophical analysis of finite being prepares the way for the present analysis of existence), many have not been so happy with his use of the category of "existence" to describe "fallen actuality." The reason is that this usage of existence seems merely to add fuel to the already heated criticism that "Tillich identifies creation and the Fall."

The key points where ontology and myth unite, where in Tillich's thought the essential structure of finite being "prepares for" the move into existing actuality, are, so it seems to me, first, the polarity of destiny and freedom characteristic of all being but fulfilled in human being, and the notion, again central to human being, of "self-constitution." These two together express ontologically the fact that human being becomes actual only through the intervention of finite freedom. In fact, as in Kierkegaard, the central act of freedom is the act of self-constitution, the "choosing" or establishing of the self through itself and its decision. We *are* when we actualize ourselves by choosing ourselves, that is, by accepting our destiny as "ours," our projects as our future, and our actions as our responsibility. As Kierkegaard had said, spirit *is* only when it constitutes itself as a synthesis[6]—which meant for Tillich a synthesis of destiny and possibility, of past and future, of the eternal ground and the concrete, a synthesis enacted by finite freedom. Thus, the movement into actuality is already a movement of creaturely freedom as well as of destiny: this is the crucial point.[7] Our freedom does not become active only when we are, so to speak, already here, created and active in our environment; on the contrary, it is our freedom, which, together with our destiny, in fact in *choosing* our destiny, ushers us *into* full existence.

---

6. Sören Kierkegaard, *Sickness Unto Death*, trans. Walter Lowrie (Princeton: Princeton University Press, 1941), First Part, I.

7. "Creaturely freedom is the point at which creation and fall coincide" (*ST* I:256; cf. also *ST* II:42–43).

Hence, the work of freedom is very much a creative part of our coming to be, even a part of our "creation" (*ST* I:259; II:35).

This is a very deep root of almost everything Tillich says, especially the autonomous element within his category of theonomy: the self is genuinely created *only* when it also creates itself. Spirit is self-constituting, or it is not spirit at all; it does not exist as spirit until it creates itself. Tillich explicates this through his own interpretation of Kierkegaard's analysis of the anxiety, dizziness, and "fall" that characterizes the spirit's plunge into actuality: that is, Tillich's designation of spirit's movement out of "dreaming innocence" and its passage through its own act into an ambiguous and guilty actuality represent an attempt to portray "psychologically" the coming to be of freedom through freedom (*ST* II:33–36). If, I think, we understand this Kierkegaardian role of freedom and of self-constitution, then in the coming to be of the self, we can understand what Tillich is about in his explication of the Fall.

It is, then, the categories of freedom and self-constitution that mediate between the ontological analysis of the structure of essential humanity and the understanding of the Fall represented by actual existence. For the movement or passage which these two analyses portray is a move from *potential* essence into *actual* existence, and it is a movement made possible by the intervention of freedom, an act of self-constitution. It is, therefore, intelligible for Tillich to maintain, as he does, that ontology has here been united to myth. Ontology uncovers the essential structure of human being as one structurally and so necessarily qualified by freedom and self-constitution; but ontology can go no further, for if that structure of "finite freedom" be the case, finite human being appears only through the act of freedom. Yet freedom is an event. It is not necessary, and its consequences happen but are not determined; novelty, the unexpected, even the unpredictable enter here. Above all, what constitutes freedom and so the self is the centered self, the self itself, not any necessary chain of causation. Finite actuality, therefore, comes to be in part through a principle of non-necessity: freedom in union with destiny and self-constitution of the self which is also a "choosing" of the destined self, its past and its relevant environment. Thus, the description of that process is inescapably "myth": a story of a contingent or free fall into actuality rather than the description of a process enacting a metaphysical necessity. Since this description points to an "event" prior to the becoming of every actuality, it is not the story of an event among other events in the past, even the first event, as in orthodoxy. It is, therefore, "a half-way myth" pointing to the temporal and the non-necessary element in all becoming, especially in all events of human becoming, the participation of freedom in all being and of self-constitution in human being, but an event without a date (compare especially *ST* II:29–44).

By this means, moreover, Tillich explains how he can without contradiction say, as he does, that creation and the Fall "coincide" (*ST* II:44, 41) and yet affirm what he holds to be the biblical emphasis: (*a*) that the Fall is not a necessary consequence of the structure of finite reality (so that creation is good); and (*b*) that redemption is possible, that is to say, a *New Being*, a restoration of creation, represents the real meaning of redemption. If the Fall were a necessary part of the structure of being human, no escape from the Fall or its consequences would be possible without the loss of humanity. The possibility of a New Being for humanity, therefore, promised in the gospel, rejects the necessity of the Fall.

As we have seen, each finite being comes to be through the power of being which is God; in that coming to be the creature is given its essential structure, its form, and the dynamic vitality through which it is. There is and can be for Tillich no creation without the infinite power and universal order that God alone provides; in this sense, everything that is is created *ab alio*, not by itself or even by other beings, but by God. Nevertheless, as we have just learned, the structure of finite being is such that it becomes only through the participation of its own finite freedom; in this sense, it also *creates* itself. Insofar as beings are *created*, they are created by God and are (as structures or potentialities) "good"; insofar as they create themselves, they become ambiguous, that is, they are in estrangement and are fallen. Thus creation and the Fall coincide and yet are not identical, the one being the work of God, the ground and power of being, and the other, the work of finite freedom in constituting itself (compare *ST* II:44). So interpreted, Tillich is not pantheistic; nor is estrangement necessary. On the contrary, his doctrine here is very close to that of the early Augustine. The final proof that this is neither pantheistic nor necessitarian—that evil is not structurally identical with the becoming of finitude—is his category of the New Being, in which finite being appears in one actual life in undisturbed harmony with its ground and so in fulfillment of its essential structure. Or, as Tillich defines the New Being as it appears in Jesus as the Christ: essential humanity now under the conditions of existence (*ST* II:94). At this point existence as actuality separates itself, at least in principle, from existence as a sign of the Fall. Surprisingly, Tillich, like Barth, will not without qualification call existence "good" except on the ground of the appearance of Jesus as the Christ.

Estrangement and Sin

Existence, then, is both creation and fall, a mixture of a structure which is potentially good and an actuality that is a distorted realization of that structure. How, then, is this distortion to be understood? We cannot at this point just look to philosophy or even science, for they present us all over again with the potential structure of our existence (as rational, as moral, etc.), and we are looking for its distortion, its element of unhealth, not its structure of health. Our actuality, so Tillich holds, represents as much unhealth as it does health. As a consequence, we can only look to witness or witnesses to our actuality: to experience, to literature, to some elements of science and philosophy (for example Freud and Marx), and to religious myths. (Note the similarity to what Paul Ricoeur later makes more precise in 1970.)[8] For this reason, Tillich begins this part, not as in parts one and two with a philosohpical analysis of the structure of reason and of finite being, but with the "myth" of the Fall, which presents us with the story of the passage from essence to existence. Tillich then analyzes this myth (a "half-way myth") in terms of the ontology he uncovered in part two. This is, therefore, a theological/philosophical analysis, an analysis of myth derivative from revelation in terms of the philosophical ontology relevant to the myth. We shall note that throughout this analysis, Tillich chooses *traditional* theological catego-ries, terms and symbols (unbelief, pride, concupiscence, etc.) and seeks to give them "revised"[9] and so relevant meanings, meanings in terms of his modern existential ontology.

Tillich begins with his own most fundamental category in interpreting existence as fallen, namely, "estrangement." "The state of existence is a state of estrangement." We are "estranged from the ground of our being, from other beings, and from ourselves" (*ST* II:44). This is, as he says, a "state," a condition in which we find ourselves, a condition (like an ontological structure) which lies in back of and influences, even deter-mines, all we feel, think, and do—our whole being. Estrangement, there-fore, expresses four aspects of existence which Tillich wishes to emphasize: (1) the "already there" character of dislocated existence as our situation; (2) the universality of it as a condition of all beings; (3) its effect on our *whole* being: body, mind, spirit—and the community, race, and history.

(4) Finally, estrangement especially indicates that this predicament is "unnatural": it is not our essential structure, who we really are. It is,

---

8. Paul Ricoeur, *The Symbolism of Evil*, trans. E. Buchanan (New York: Harper and Row, 1967), especially pt. I, intro., chap. II; pt. II, intro., chap. III, and conclusion.

9. This is a clear example of Tillich's thorough revision of *both* sides of the correlation: the theological "answers" are as thoroughly reconceived in terms of the ontological "question" as the latter is transformed by the former. In this sense, modernity *and* the tradition are both criticized in being correlated.

therefore, *un*health, even disease, not nature. To be estranged entails that "we *belong essentially* to that from which we are now estranged: to our ground, to one another, to our real selves" (*ST* II:45). The Fall is neither nature nor essence; it contradicts the structure of our being. It is, therefore, not good, good being the fulfillment of nature. On the contrary, it is precisely "estrangement"; it is the distortion of our nature, the separation from that to which we belong: God, one another, our real self. Although estrangement and its consequences are universal—and empirical—they can never be taken either as normative or even as signs of what our real possibilities are. Despite the use of this seemingly untraditional word, therefore, Tillich interprets estrangement in a genuinely Augustinian way; in both Augustine's use and in Tillich's, (1) the distinction between creation and the Fall is made clear, and yet (2) the dependence of the Fall on creation—of disease on health and of estrangement on essential nature—is also made clear.

"Man's predicament is estrangement, but his estrangement is sin" (*ST* II:47). Here again the category of freedom enters. This distortion from what we really are is experienced by us not only as *unnatural*, it is experienced even more as an act of *ours*, as a *personal* responsibility, as guilt. This is an act both of our freedom and of our whole being, that is, a "personal act." We are willing participants in estrangement as well as unwilling victims of it. Estrangement as sin as well as alienation illustrates, for Tillich, the universal interweaving of destiny and of freedom: freedom represents freedom only if we choose our destiny (otherwise, it is arbitrariness); destiny is actualized only through freedom (otherwise, it is fate [*ST* II:36–39]). In this case, the destiny participated in by freedom is the universal destiny of estrangement we all both inherit *and* create anew: "In each the work of all, in all the work of each."[10] While *estrangement* bore for Tillich the connotation of universality, situation, and "already-thereness," nevertheless, it equally bears the connotation of *sin*, that is, of unnaturalness, of personal choice, personal participation, and so of responsibility, hence of being wrong or guilty.

As we have noted, however, both estrangement as situation and sin as choice are *analogical* concepts, metaphors in which *in each case* the usual connotations are qualified. Tillich is here, like Niebuhr, pointing to a level that lies *behind* or *below* the objects and subjects of ordinary life and so behind and below the deliberations, decisions, commitments, and actions of our personal histories. As a consequence, no form of language,

---

10. Friedrich Schleiermacher, *The Christian Faith*, ed. H. R. Macintosh and J. S. Stewart (Edinburgh: T. & T. Clark, 1928), Sec. 71/2, 288.

whether of necessitating conditions or of personal decisions, quite fits this case. We are estranged here, but not quite as in the case where we come to be estranged by a word or act from a lover or an old friend. For here we *find* ourselves estranged; we are estranged from *everything*, and *all* of us are estranged. Correspondingly, it is also true that we have "freely chosen" this, and that we are "personally responsible" for it, but not quite as it is when we chose to do a specific and concrete historical act about which we had deliberated and for whose consequences we are thus responsible. In speaking of both estrangement and sin we are pointing below the surface of events, choices, acts, and consequences to a "deeper level," a level below consciousness and so below the manifold of experience, a level which for Tillich in large part affects, in fact almost determines, the events, choices, and acts on the ordinary historical surface of life. It is his view, as it was Niebuhr's, that "there is less necessity at this level and more personal responsibility than most views assume"[11]—that is, that the category of freedom is relevant at this deeper level as well as the category of destiny.

It may seem strange, even irrational, to point in this way to a level below the surface of ordinary experience as the key to understanding the events on that surface. This is not, however, in itself unintelligible to modern culture, as the examples of Marx and Freud as well as Kierkegaard show. Marx pointed to the "unconscious" level of class participation to explain the thoughts, viewpoints, standards, beliefs, choices, and actions on the conscious and "public" levels of bourgeois experience. Freud pointed to the level of the unconscious and its "neuroses" to explain the anxieties that appear in conscious experience and in our objective, ordinary patterns of behavior. For Tillich, this deeper level involves our most fundamental relations: to our divine ground, to others, and to ourselves, and it is actualized in part through our self-constitution, our freedom—for it is thus that "spirit" comes to be. In the sense that estrangement represents a level of our actuality *behind* all our acts, it is "original" or "primordial," and so we may speak of "original estrangement" or sin as involved here. Insofar as this original estrangement affects our conscious, historical, and public acts, it can be said to be the "cause" of our "sins," those thoughtless, selfish, cruel, and self-destructive acts which clutter up our lives. Tillich has here (as Niebuhr did in a different way) thoroughly revised the ancient doctrine of Adam's Fall and our inheritance of the Fall's consequences into a symbol "disclosive" of our situation, a symbol according to which a primordial estrangement in

---

11. Reinhold Niebuhr, *The Nature and Destiny of Man*, vol. 1 (New York: Scribner's, 1941), chap. 7.

which we participate distorts our being, its loves, thoughts, and acts. In effecting this revision, Tillich has achieved a remarkable union of ontology and myth.

The Three Faces of Estrangement: Unbelief, Hubris, and Concupiscence

Tillich proceeds to analyze estrangement/sin further and so to display the entire tragic scene in ourselves and in our world which this symbol "discloses" to us. Several aspects of this analysis are worth emphasis: (1) Each aspect Tillich will now name *presupposes* estrangement; each is thus a consequence or effect of estrangement as much as one element within it. As a result, all the language here is very analogical: what have been traditionally termed *causes* of estrangement (e.g., unbelief) are in Tillich's analysis more clearly viewed as its *effects* or symptoms. (2) Each aspect represents a traditional symbol or doctrine once taken to represent the cause or center of "sin." As in other parts of his system, Tillich deliberately chooses to use these traditional terms, however seemingly inappropriate they may be, and to reinterpret them to fit the modern situation and so to communicate the relevant modern "message." Thus do situation and message, modernity and tradition, transform each other in this discussion. (3) Each aspect or face is directly dependent for its importance and the content of its meaning on the ontological structure of essential humanity. In that sense, each points to a significant *distortion* of that structure, and so to one form of estrangement from that essential structure.

1) Estrangement as unbelief and/or disobedience

This traditional symbol, taken by the entire tradition as the "cause" of sin, refers to the "turning away from God," either by lack of trust or by disobedience, in either case representing a clear instance of spiritual rebellion. For Tillich, such concepts, taken literally, presuppose a conscious decision against God and/or a deliberate act of disobedience on the phenomenal surface of experience and so of history. Thus, such a literal (univocal and not analogical or metaphysical) interpretation carries us back to a "story" of an actual historical event either in our own history or in that of the race. And this, we have agreed, cannot in this instance be the interpretation of the theological category of unbelief as the "cause" of sin. On the contrary, our concrete acts of distrust and disobedience, real enough to be sure, are themselves symptoms of a deeper, analogical "turning away," expressed metaphorically by the categories of "unbelief" or "disobedience," but for Tillich better expressed by estrangement.

In any case, this face of estrangement expresses the contradiction of the most important element of our essential structure, our grounding in God, the divine power of being and meaning through which we are what we are. As a result of this separation, as we shall see, the balance of being and nonbeing in our existence is upset; we are "left alone in our finitude," and absolute nonbeing inexorably overcomes us. As Tillich always insists, creatures *are* through the divine power; thus, in estrangement from God they can barely be at all.[12]

2) *Estrangement as hubris or self-elevation*

This symbol has been traditional in the form of "pride," inordinate self-love, the effort to replace God with the self, and so the worship of the self or its works as "divine." It has, therefore, been called "idolatry," "making the self God" or, as Tilich prefers to express it, the "self-elevation of man into the sphere of the divine" (*ST* II:50). With hubris or pride the power, creativity, glory, and goodness of the human creature are made ultimate; the cultural creations of men and women, and the egos that accomplished that creation, are, although finite and transient, given infinite significance, made into idols and elevated to matters of ultimate concern (*ST* II:51). The notion of hubris in Greek tragedy reflects (for Tillich as for Niebuhr) this biblical motif of "pride," of raising the self to the level of God. For Tillich, however, self-elevation contains a slightly different nuance than pride and rebellion do in the Reformation tradition. "Self-elevation" is not so much a rebellion *against* God and so *pride* in the self as God's equal, each expressing an antagonistic relation established through the self's own power. On the contrary, in Tillich self-elevation represents the *misappropriation* for itself of the divine power surging in and through the creature and the *misappropriation* for itself of the divine meaning intrinsic

---

12. One of the most interesting and helpful points that Tillich makes in this connection is the near identity he sees between the central Catholic category of *caritas* (unrestricted love of God) and faith, an ultimate commitment or trust in God, the central Protestant category. These two ancient rivals, Tillich maintains, are really two ways of talking about the same thing: the *spiritual grounding* of the self in God, the one speaking of this through *love*, the other through *commitment* and *trust*. Both affirm the centrality of the relation to God and the supreme character of that relation, though they describe that relation in the different psychological categories of love and trust. Once seen, this part of Tillich is so obvious as to be unforgettable; one can only wonder that the differences of language and emphasis should have caused such a long and bitter warfare (*ST* II:48–49).

to the creature's life. In self-elevation, the creature takes this immanent divine power and meaning to be "its own" and claims credit and glory for it (compare *ST* II:66–67, 69). It is the immanent power and meaning of the divine, not autonomous rebellion over against them, that make hubris possible, as it is the immanent divine power and meaning that make all creaturely creativity possible (compare *ST* II:48–51). In all of this, the creature remains a *medium* of the divine power; in the case of hubris, the creature appropriates that power and meaning to itself, pointing to *itself* rather than beyond itself to God. Thus, "sin" represents not so much a semidualistic confrontation with God as the claim to possess and control for oneself the divine power present in all things and so in the sinner himself or herself. To Tillich, therefore, sin reflects the continuing belonging to God as well as the sudden or contingent separation or estrangement from God.

Nevertheless, the reality of hubris does signal "an over-againstness" of creature and God, though surely muted when compared with Reinhold Niebuhr and the biblical theologians. For Tillich in sin the "separation" of creature from creator becomes actual; it is, as we have seen, real estrangement, estrangement as self-elevation and, therefore, separation from the ground of its being. As a result of this estrangement from its ground, the self loses itself. Self is incurably finite, in correlation with a world, and dependent in order to be itself on that world, as it is on others. Consequently, in seeking to make this finite self not only autonomous but infinite, the self distorts its finite structure and, as a result, loses itself, the other, and its world, and that represents the next step in the process of its self destruction.

3) Estrangement as concupiscence

The most important face of estrangement, the one Tillich emphasizes over and over, is also an ancient symbol but one frequently discarded in the modern period: *concupiscence* (*ST* II:51–55). Traditionally identified almost entirely with sexual lust, this word in most twentieth-century theology has hardly appeared. Tillich gives it a new and surprisingly relevant meaning, with the help, as is often the case, of motifs drawn from Augustine. In estrangement from its ultimate ground, human being still participates in infinity; thus it longs for and desperately needs infinity. But now finite being is "left alone among the finite." As a consequence, he or she, or they, must seek the infinite *in and through the world*, that is to say, in infinite desire.[13] As Tillich defines it, concupiscence is "the

---

13. References in Augustine are, for example, *The City of God*, bk. 11, chap.

unlimited desire to draw the whole of reality into one's self" (*ST* II:52) or, as he put it verbally, "the attempt to cram the whole world into one's own mouth," to "attain and devour unlimited abundance." Thus, the particular seeks the universal by stuffing the latter into its own particularity by owning, possessing, and enjoying *everything*. The finite desires the universal through the enlargement of the finite to encompass infinity rather than through the sacrifice of the finite. Concupiscence, therefore, represents a distorted form of reunion with the whole; as such, it is a "spiritual" sickness wedded to the sensual and the bodily. This drive to universality and wholeness *through* the expansion of the finite is, therefore, both concupiscence and hubris, and it is directly the consequence of estrangement from the infinite ground.

Concupiscence represents an unlimited, heedless, even ruthless striving. Like the passion of Don Juan, the endless grasping of Doctor Faustus, the libido of Freud, or the "desire" of the Buddhist tradition, it represents a multifaceted, irresistible, uncontrollable, and unstoppable drive: for sex, for goods, for controlling power, for knowledge—even for status, fame, significance, and endlessness. It is, paradoxically, both unlimited and self-oriented, a self-love grasping for the entire world. Thus it possesses neither limits nor real or proper objects. Each object or person encountered is merely used, enjoyed, "swallowed up," and discarded. As a consequence, there is and can be no stopping place, no possible satisfaction—infinite desire drives on over the latest victim and on to the next object or person to be used. Thus the self here ceases to be a real self, a self in an encounter with another real self, a self, therefore, participating in real relations and real obligations. It experiences no eros (or ultimate concern) toward activities of genuine importance in themselves, and it has no genuine *philia* or eros toward particular persons in their individuality. The self, therefore, has no "world," no ordered environment with meaningful projects to call out and discipline its vitality, and no real persons to center and hold its affections and obligations, its inner participation. Since its world is a limitless plain with only scattered, meaningless, haphazard objects, the self becomes empty of guiding purposes and real emotions, and it finds itself driven only by momentary and arbitrary desires or whims. An objectless and purposeless world creates an empty and driven self. (When I read Tillich's analysis, I am reminded of the terrors of Dali's limitless and bizarre landscapes.) Concupiscence thus resembles libido or desire, an endless and heedless striving for pleasure; these categories represent for Tillich an *estranged* condition. Such a

28; and "The Trinity," in *Augustine: Later Works*, trans. John Burnaby (Philadelphia: Westminster, 1955), bk. 10, 5–9.

condition is, to be sure, everywhere actual, as Freud and Buddhists have noted. But though it be universal, and so universally empirical, it is not *necessary*. In essential humanity, libido is focused, controlled, and directed by eros toward value, by *philia* toward the uniqueness of another person, and by *agape* as acceptance of them despite their faults (compare *LPJ*, 115–25). In union with these, concupiscence can be transformed (or restored) into a creative sensuality, a source of joy, meaning, creativity, and, above all, of intimate community.

Like other aspects of estrangement, concupiscence is not only an individual phenomenon. It can also characterize a social world. For Tillich, the analysis of both essential humanity and "existence" as estrangement is as relevant to an interpretation of society and history as it is to an understanding of personal existence. The turning of the self toward itself (hubris or self-elevation) and concupiscence dominate cultural and historical existence, and these account for the latter's disastrous process of self-destruction as they do in individual lives. As *The World Situation* makes clear (see also *ST* I:83–86, 147–50), in history (in this case modern history) an epoch of *theonomy* unravels, so to speak, into a period of autonomy, which in turn ushers in a destructive heteronomy; much as in personal existence there is a process of self-destruction that existence characteristically exhibits. In both cases, estrangement as unbelief, as hubris, and as concupiscence represent the main "faces" of our distorted existence.

In any case, concupiscence is for Tillich the main face of estrangement for a consumerist goods-society, scrambling for money, for place, for possessions. It is the estranged root of such a culture's materialism, that is, its concentration on the possession and use of "things," of wealth, and of mindless sensuality. It is also the deepest drive behind the infinite expansion of its industrial processes, an expansion that can despoil and ultimately destroy the earth. Tillich has here provided a set of categories extremely relevant to the personal vices as well as the spiritual, moral, and economic problems of a commercial society, as the categories of pride and hubris have previously illumined the political sins of our epoch.

Estrangement as the "Structure of Self-Destruction"

For Tillich, estrangement initiates and carries through a process of self-destruction. The estranged self or community slowly destroys itself, dissolves the meanings and relations that give its life vitality and joy, dismantles the structures of its being, and so descends into nonbeing. Put another way, it loses its being and so is inexorably overcome by nonbeing. As is evident, Tillich's main emphasis is on the self-destruction and consequent suffering resulting from being evil; he does not stress, as many do, the destruction of the *other* as a consequence of evil. He is deeply aware of injustice and of the call to rectify it; nevertheless, his theological concentration is on the way an unjust culture dismantles *itself* or a sinner destroys himself or herself. Here the sinner is both perpetuator and victim of sin, whereas in the Social Gospel, in Reinhold Niebuhr, and in liberation theology the sinner is almost without exception the *perpetuator*, and it is the oppressed who are the victims of sin. In these more "moral" and "political" interpretations of sin—largely as injustice—sinner as perpetuator and oppressed as victim are sharply differentiated, although Niebuhr will always remind us that even the oppressed are and surely can also become sinners.

Nevertheless, Tillich's analysis is powerful and so heavy, not unlike much modern drama (e.g., Tennessee Williams, Eugene O'Neill, and Arthur Miller) in its depiction of the inexorable and painful process of self-destruction. Self-destruction is experienced as suffering, the suffering of the gradual dissolution of the structure of one's being: isolation, loneliness, fatedness, meaningless sensuality, emptiness, despair. Experience as suffering, as the process of self-destruction, is understood *reflectively* (as theology) in terms of the destruction of the ontological structure of essential humanity, the dissolution of the being of the finite creature. Hence, Tillich's analysis follows the structure uncovered in his philosophical analysis of finite being, but we note that here (as above) the ontological analysis is *guided by* the relevant religious symbols of estrangement, judgment, and condemnation.

The basic ontological structure is the correlation of self and world; consequently, in estrangement both are lost, and they are lost together. Since freedom is the power to transcend and so to create or constitute both self and world (*ST* III:38–39, 303), it is also the power to lose both (*ST* II:31–32, 42–43). Subject to concupiscence (infinity of desire and so desire for the whole world), the self loses itself. The self is unified and so established by meaningful purposes, by self-discipline, and by its powers of decision and commitment—an eros toward value, a sense of definite meaning, and a commitment to that meaning. Above all, the self is established or constituted by its real relations with, and its participation in, *other persons* in community (*ST* III:40; *LPJ*, 78). Without such meaningful purposes and relations in community, subject now to an infinite desire, the self has no center around which to organize its many drives. Thus it is unable to constitute itself and to direct itself as a self; it is subject to arbitrary desires and whims or to the infinite, endless pursuit of pleasure, power, eminence. The centering, shaping, and directing of the self—the self-constitution of the self—depend on real relations to others, participation inwardly through commitment in those relations, and real but limited projects in the world. These give "meaning" and so definition and discipline to existence, and meaning gives the self order, vitality, and purpose. To desire the whole world is to have neither project nor meaning, and so no definition to the self or limit to its projects. The self is thus empty, except for the chaos of its infinity of desires.

Correspondingly, the world is lost. it is filled only with flat, empty objects, objects there "for me" and for my use. Consequently, the world is latent with no real projects that *draw* me out, lure my eros, shape my commitment, and make possible my self-discipline. The forces that move the world—and they remain—are unrelated to the projects, opportunities, or "tasks" that lure and motivate me; unrelated to my eros, these external forces become arbitrary, irrational, external, "fate." Thus inner arbitrariness and emptiness, "drivenness," are complemented by outer fatedness and isolation. There are here no real people, no real relations, no tasks, no communion with others. Humans here lose a "world" and have only an environment: a meaningless place full of infinite possibilities for desire but ruled by alien forces; they lose community and have only isolated emptiness. This picture reflectively analyzes the "self" and the "world" of innumerable contemporary films and novels. This is the picture of an empty and lonely self in a structureless world, both dominated by a demonic infinity, and both characterized by an encroaching nonbeing. Tillich is well aware that this represents both a cultural description and a portrait of individuals participating in that culture.

Tillich's analysis continues through the polarities: as self and world dissolve, the polarities separate and come into conflict with one another. Individuals lose all participation, and, as we have seen, wither in emptiness as individuals; the dynamic élan of life loses its guiding purposes and forms and dissolves into arbitrariness; without destiny and genuine potentiality, freedom becomes directionless whim.

Perhaps what is most interesting, and chilling, is the way Tillich returns to the categories of finitude (space, time, causality, and substance) and shows how estrangement accelerates and increases the anxiety latent within these structures of finitude until that anxiety becomes unbearable. Each category expresses both being and possibility, on the one hand, and nonbeing and so dissolution, on the other; in estrangement, the affirmative being, the possibility of courage and of self-affirmation, recede, and as a consequence, the negative possibilities of finitude increase and become dominant.

Temporal passage, for example, is the potentiality of creativity and the new; it is also the inexorable source of loss and ultimately of "having to die." In estrangement from the eternal ground, human being, says Tillich, is left alone to its finitude and so in effect abandoned to nonbeing, to an accelerating loss of meaningful moments of life and ultimately to the onrush of death from which eternity alone can rescue finitude. The essential anxiety about nonbeing has been transformed here into the emptiness of a meaningless life rushing toward nonbeing and death, what Tillich calls "the horror of death" (*ST* II:67). There is, moreover, the realization of our responsibility for this ultimate predicament, the "pain of a lost eternity" (*ST* II:68). Essential finitude, at this point, becomes the experience of existential evil. This pattern of the conquest of finite being by an unobstructed nonbeing repeats itself with the horror of "having no space," of lostness or placelessness, of "being totally determined or caused"; that is to say, of fatedness, and of being without substance, of emptiness and unreality. The results are intense suffering and loneliness accompanied by doubt, uncertainty, and final meaninglessness. For Tillich, estrangement from the infinite ground signals the victory of nonbeing in finitude over the positive portion of being there; and unbearable emptiness, an unreality, and a meaninglessness suffused with guilt and regret result. Again this description appears and reappears in contemporary art and literature (compare *ST* II:65–75, and *CB*, 142–48).

The finite, however, is essentially related to the infinite ground. Hence, even at the onslaught of nonbeing there is resistance. Humans resist the loss of time, the vanishing of their space, the appearance of fatedness, the onslaught of unreality. The vast and frantic efforts of humans and of their culture to stop time, to prolong their brief time, to fence off, protect, and so to guarantee their small space, to amass and control their meager power, to grasp and to hold on to their vanishing reality—these efforts are repeated over and over again in personal lives and in social history, and yet none succeed.

It is, says Tillich, awareness of the breakdown of these efforts of resistance that is the initial element in *despair.* "It is not the experience of time as such which produces despair; rather it is defeat in the resistance against time" (*ST* II:69). Here one finds one's self caught in an unbearable and terrifying situation, a menacing slide into nothingness. One resists, and then one realizes that that resistance is utterly futile and that, in fact, the terrifying slide *cannot* be stopped. Despair is the awareness of this uselessness, of this futility; it is not despair at life or even at its negativities so much as it is despair about the futility of the *attempt* to rescue life from negativity and death. The deeper pain is that it is the self which has brought this on itself; one is oneself its responsible cause as well as its passive victim. "One is shut up in one's self and in conflict with one's self. One cannot escape, because one cannot escape from one's self" (*ST* II:75). Despair is the realization of our destruction by the nonbeing that suffuses our own reality and that of our world, combined with the sharp awareness that our destruction has been a self-destruction, a union of tragic destiny and bound freedom from which there is neither respite nor escape. Few reflective writings have communicated a heavier message of negation than this. Tillich's sensitivity, empathy, and pity for the varied and deep modes of human suffering manifest themselves in each line of these passages.

*   *   *

Anyone who has read with care Tillich's description of the self-destruction, suffering, and despair of estrangement recognizes its validity, that it uncovers and illumines very real characteristics of human existence, both individual and social. Artists and especially writers have felt this and expressed it, but few theologians. To most of the theological tradition, it has been the *moral* outrage of sin that appears as the predominant evil: the selfish perversity of depravity, the self-love and cold cruelty of oppressive injustice, the heartless egocentricity of imperial ambitions, the immorality and "badness" of vice—and thus the *guilt* before God for all of these. In these descriptions, on the one hand, the *wrongness* and guilt of the sinner are emphasized and, on the other, the devastating *damage* wrought on the victim. After the symbol of sin in the twentieth century lost the traditional connotation of vice, this symbol came—much more legitimately—to point to the moral fault, the self-centeredness, and the selfish cruelty in the sinner and to the terrible exploitation and suffering in those sinned against. Idolatry, said Niebuhr, issues into injustice, and it is clear that for him it is mainly the injustice that makes the idolatry wrong, wrong to God and to humans alike. There is no question that Tillich is quite aware of all this; his social writings glow with indignation at the selfish cruelty of bourgeois oppressors and with rage at the suffering forced upon the oppressed proletariat. After all, it was because of moral *injustice* (in fact, it was the cruel exclusion of the Jews from German university life and their continuous persecution by the reigning Nazi government) that he himself protested publicly and was forced to leave Germany.

A new note, however, appears in these later writings: the sense of the destruction wrought on the sinner himself and herself, the suffering involved in the process of self-destruction, and the sharp pain that the consciousness of responsibility for that process brings. Here there is less a sense of the intrinsic *wrongness* of inordinate self-love—that it is *immoral*—or of the cruelty to the other that sin involves. And because these represent the main modern connotations of sin, many theological readers fault Tillich for this omission. To put it sharply, he does not seem outraged by sin or angry at the sinner. On the contrary, he seems mainly to pity him or her as the primary victim of his or her own waywardness.

There is, let me suggest, still another element in Tillich's account that adds to the impression that, for him, sin is hardly "immoral" or "outrageous." This is the consequence of the way Tillich views the problem of estrangement or sin in its present context, and the method and language he uses to resolve the problem. Tillich is deeply aware that sin begins below the level of ordinary consciousness, of ordinary deliberations and decisions, and so of ordinary acts on, so to speak, the surface of life; that each of us "sins" or "has sinned" is not a matter of a particular decision or act, a so-called "immoral" act at some point in time. Rather, sin as estrangement subsists *back of, under,* or *behind* these ordinary decisions and acts as their major determinant. We may not even be conscious of it, and we certainly have not simply willed or decided to turn from God, to elevate ourselves to the center of things, or to devote our lives to concupiscence. Yet, says Tillich, it is we who have done these things, we are "slyly" aware of this, and we know we are responsible for them. So far he agrees with his colleague Niebuhr.

Whereas Niebuhr, however, at this point speaks of that deeper level of our existence—where sin or idolatry replaces trust—in the language of the "surface," namely, in the personal and historical language of decisions and acts (as self-love, pride, "making oneself the center," defiance of God, idolatry—all words implying selfish choice and so permeated with moral outrage), Tillich eschews this language. He speaks, on the contrary, of the coming to be of the self out of "dreaming innocence" into actuality, of dizziness and anxiety and then the plunge into concreteness and into self-centered actuality, as if the self, in coming to be, closed its eyes, leaped, and *only then* awoke as conscious, on the one hand, and guilty, on the other. The moral vibrations here are very different: this seems to be destiny and not freedom, a process and not a decision, a becoming and not an act. Since the self is in that process *coming to be* and is *not yet there*, it appears unintelligible and misguided to speak scoldingly of selfishness, cruelty, cold indifference, and self-glorification—all the outrageous, immoral ingredients of sin. Tillich is, to be sure, surely right, as was Kierkegaard, to seek to illumine the obscured depths in which the self through itself becomes a self and to point out the relevance of this process to our estrangement and sin. Even Niebuhr has briefly to explore these depths represented by "the moment before the act."[14] The problem is that

---

14. Reinhold Niebuhr, *Nature and Destiny of Man*, vol. 1 (New York: Charles Scribner's Sons, 1941), 276–80.

locating sin *here* tends to minimize or downplay the ethical, to ignore the relevance of sin to the outraged neighbor, and thus to obscure the social and so the moral *wrongness* of sin.

If, then, Tillich lacks emphasis on some elements of the problem of existence, nevertheless, he uncovers many more areas of negativity in life than he obscures. The moral interpretation of sin we have here described has, for all its validity, ignored areas of suffering that are genuinely regions of "evil," which are pervasive and very real, and not least which initiate, encourage, and drive forward the immoral consequences of estrangement. These are the *ontological* aspects of estrangement: transience and loss, having no space, vulnerability, fatedness, emptiness or unreality, isolation and loneliness, loss of self and the self's freedom, loss of world and of a meaningful vocation in it, and, finally, "having to die." Tillich is surely right that most of the immoral things we do are done to *resist* these ontological terrors of sin; correspondingly, most of the sufferings we undergo are due to the way estrangement twists and tortures these possibilities of our finitude. Here Tillich is very helpful and perceptive, and theology is infinitely richer because he held up before us these *ontological* consequences of our separation from God.

Finally, let us note that this analysis of existence has a dialectical relation to Buddhism, at least to that of Professor Nishitani.[15] In both Tillich and Nishitani, the weight of negativity is heavy indeed, driving those who experience it into terror and despair; in both, this experience leads, or can lead, to an openness to healing. In Tillich, as we know, it is consciousness of our helplessness under the conditions of existence that "raises the question" of redemption, of the New Being; by that he means we are, by the "shock of non-being," opened to receiving a new divine initiative toward reunion and restoration from our estrangement.

It is also the case, however, that in relation to negativity we can see how differently the two traditions view what Tillich calls *the structure of finite being*, our essential humanity, namely, the polar structure of self and world and the polar elements. In Nishitani it is *that* structure, generated out of attachment and desire, that constitutes the *problem* of existence; in redemption (nirvana), it is precisely this structure that is negated and transcended, in fact dissolved. Nonattachment brings to a halt our participation in and commitment to "world," and with that the self as a self participating in and correlated to the world itself dissolves. World is transformed into nothingness and self becomes *no self*, and with that identity of *no self* with nothingness, then suchness is realized.

---

15. Keiji Nishitani, *Religion and Nothingness* (Berkeley: University of California Press, 1982), esp. chaps. 3 and 4.

In Tillich, a very different process takes place. The essential structure of self and world, with its polarities and categories—finite being centered in finite freedom—is "good" and hence potentially creative. In estrangement from that real nature, the structure goes awry; existence is a *distortion* of that structure of finitude (it is *"unnatural"*), not its essential and so inescapable consequence. As a result, redemption, the work of the New Being, restores the structure of finitude and renews self and world together in both power and meaning; in that sense, grace *restores* nature. This is a very different interpretation of finitude and its problems. Meanwhile, let us now with Tillich turn from the "question" raised by the terror of existence to the "answer" appearing with the New Being.

8

The New Being and Christology

There can be little question that the New Being represents the central category or symbol for Tillich's theology. Let us, therefore, begin our discussion with a brief look at the significance of the New Being for Tillich's thought as a whole: for his understanding of Christology, of Christianity, of religion, of God, finitude, church, and culture. As disciplined reflection on the self-interpretation of the Christian community (*ST* I:15, 28), theology for Tillich puts into intelligible, and thus for him into contemporary philosophical (ontological) discourse, the message that is constitutive of that community. In the case of the Christian community, that message is the message of the appearance in history of the New Being, the "new state of things," the "new reality," in Jesus who is therefore the Christ (*ST* II:97). The New Being is thus, first of all, the fundamental principle explanatory of Tillich's Christology and so represents the determinative "Christian" aspect of his system.

That is to say, when one asks, "What does the Christ represent, do, or bring?" or alternatively, "How does he save, if at all?" Tillich's answer is: in him the New Being makes its appearance in historical existence; Jesus is said to be the Christ because he brings in the New Being, in "time and space" (*ST* II:98–99). For Tillich, the central problem of life as modern persons experience it is the self-destruction and despair of estranged existence. Correspondingly, for him the central reality to which all religions (including Christianity) dimly and often misguidedly witness, and the real center of the Christian good news, is the appearance of a healing reality, the reality of reconciliation and reunion, that "in which the self-estrangement of our existence is overcome" (*ST* II:49). As Tillich repeatedly reminded us, *salvation* derives from the Latin *salvus*, which meant "healing" (e.g., *ST* I:146, II:166; III:277, 282). All religions presuppose the presence of this healing, redemptive reality (*ST* II:80–86; III:138–41, 147). Christianity is based on witness to its *explicit* and *definitive* appearance in a personal life, in Jesus who is therefore affirmed to be the

Christ, the bearer of this new reality. Thus, for Tillich the New Being as it is manifested in Jesus represents the decisive criterion for all *religions* (especially *ST* I:137), "that revelation is final if it has the power of negating itself without losing itself" (*ST* I:133; see also II:150ff.). The New Being represents, amid the variety of Christian documents, theories, and themes, the "norm" for *present* Christian self-understanding, for a modern, relevant interpretation alike of Scripture and tradition with regard to their most fundamental message (*ST* I:47–52). Since the New Being is the creative principle for religions generally and for the Christian religion among the religions, the decisive manifestation of the New Being in Jesus—the description of which is the task of Christology—provides for Tillich the basis for the most fundamental interpretation of religions and of Christianity.

This message of the appearance of the New Being works its way, so to speak, "backwards" in the system as a whole to give definitive shape to Tillich's most fundamental conceptualizing of God, of the nature and purposes of being-itself. Being-itself is known in experiencing the victory of being over nonbeing through the presence of courage; this "conquest," creative of culture and religions alike, in turn is the work of the creative, reuniting work of God as Spirit; finally, the divine Spirit is *itself* known as such (as *divine*) in the universal appearance of the New Being, the creative principle in all religions. Thus as the universal principle of religion, the New Being provides the entrance into the knowledge of Spirit, and through Spirit of God, the knowledge of being-itself; it is, as Tillich insists, in *religion* that reason finds its own ground.

It is characteristic of Tillich's thought that the positive is always experienced "over against" the negative, being "over against" some form of the "shock of nonbeing."[1] Thus the constitutive principle of actuality (being-itself) is experienced in and through a redemptive principle of actuality, that which manifests itself in overcoming separation, alienation, and the threat of the conquest by nonbeing.

Being for Tillich is always existentially encountered; that is, it is known and so defined within the context of the experienced conquest or victory of being via *courage* over the nonbeing inherent in *finitude*. In turn, the New Being is existentially known when the divine power and meaning are experienced as conquering the *estrangement* characteristic of existence.

---

1. Note that while Tillich always holds that "the negative lives from the distortion of the positive" (*ST* II:86), still for him, as for Kierkegaard, the positive is *experienced* and *known* only through the experiencing of the negative, e.g., *ST* I:110. The negative depends *ontologically* on the positive; the positive epistemologically on the negative.

Now, as finitude and estrangement are in our experience inextricably mixed, so is the experience of their conquest, that is, the experience of the ontological *courage* resulting from being-itself and the experience of the salvific, unifying *healing* resulting from New Being. For both experiences presuppose and manifest the reuniting activity of God, the ground of being and meaning. The experience of the ground of being presupposes (1) the shock of nonbeing, and (2) the "religious" experience of reunion with the ground through the universal reuniting work of God. That reuniting and so redemptive principle within the divine is, of course, God as Spirit: "the most embracing, direct, and unrestricted symbol for the divine life" (*ST* I:249), and so "the ultimate unity of both power and meaning" (*ST* I:250). It is, therefore, through the work of the Spirit as the constitutive principle of the Divine Life that the uniting and reuniting of finitude with God in all aspects take place: in the actualizing of creatures, in the appearance of courage throughout finite existence, and in culminating fashion in the New Being.

To repeat, the category of the Spirit is the symbol for the divine forces of redemption and healing (*ST* I:251); correspondingly, the category of the New Being represents the *way* in which the creative and redemptive work of God is experienced in human history, that is, in religion generally, and especially in the Christian community. In this sense the long, detailed description of the Spiritual Presence in volume three of *Systematic Theology* represents the effects in continuing history of the New Being, as Tillich's Christology in volume two represents the definitive manifestation of the redemptive Spirit of God in history. Even the content of volume one on finitude and being-itself is, as Tillich says, *known* through "revelation" and not autonomous reason, that is, through the appearance of the New Being as the reuniting, reconciling work of the Spirit.

As the understanding of God moves *from* the knowledge of God as Spirit (via some form of the New Being) *to* the knowledge of God as being-itself (*from* religious experience *to* philosophical theology), so the true understanding of *finitude* as real and good is made possible by the appearance of the New Being, by the experience of essential humanity under the conditions of existence. Tillich is convinced that the power of estrangement is such that in *estranged* finitude, the nonbeing inherent in all finitude in the end always conquers, smothers, and dissolves the being also inherent in finitude. This is his continual and omnipresent polemic against secular humanism: without the divine ground, finitude in every one of its aspects is unable to *be*, or better, to maintain its being, over against nonbeing (*ST* I:192–201; II:66–75). Thus the universal presence of the courage to be reflects or manifests the universal reuniting and reconciling work of God as the transcendent ground of that courage.

Without that reuniting work, therefore, finitude would not experience itself as "real" or as "good." The possibility of a creative finitude, in fact, the possibility even of a *theory* of creative finitude, is thus dependent on the presence of the New Being. Without that, finitude would be experienced, as it is in the depths of despair, as unreal and vacant of possibility, as "illusion," and as "evil." Correspondingly, for Tillich pantheism, as reflecting the experience *alone* of the divine ground, an experience without the courage of self-affirmation, and so an experiencing of finitude as *maya*, represents a relatively imperfect apprehension of the New Being. In contrast, in the *full* appearance of the New Being, estranged existence is united with essence, essential humanity with our alienated condition. Here the destructive effects of nonbeing and the marks of estrangement are overcome. In the New Being, finitude as *essential* and yet *actual* (actual and yet unestranged) manifests itself; thus it is possible to speak of a real and good finitude (and so to affirm *creatio ex nihilo*). Systematically, the anthropological and cosmological implications of the symbol of creation, as is the knowledge of God as being-itself, are dependent on the experience of the New Being in Jesus as the Christ.[2] Incidentally, it is here that, despite his well-known identification of creation and the Fall, Tillich presents a *fundamental* defense against the accusation of pantheism: finitude, seen through the experience of the New Being, represents neither an essentially fallen humanity nor an unreal *maya* in the Hindu tradition, nor is its reality identical with that of the divine ground; on the contrary, it is "finite freedom," a real, a good, and a potentially creative and self-creative finitude, if also absolutely dependent.

The concept of the New Being, defined through its definitive appearance in Jesus as the Christ, likewise represents the central symbolic source for Tillich's view of religious symbols, for his ecclesiology, and for

---

2. Despite their many and important differences, Tillich and Barth (and also Brunner) reveal here some unexpected similarities, namely, that all knowledge of God and of the *true* status of the self, its problems, and possibilities, and especially of history, come via revelation and thus under the criterion of special revelation in Jesus as the Christ. Of course, for Tillich there is, despite this, an "anthropological starting point" and thus a correlation with general experience, with culture, and with philosophy; our existence, and a philosophical analysis of our existence, can raise the question and hence interpret the answer. I would prefer to label this common *ultimate* dependence on revelation as characteristic of "neo-orthodox" or "dialectical/*Krisis*" theology rather than as "Barthian." This, along with the correlated emphasis on estrangement/sin, was what united that epoch of theology despite their real differences, with Barth on the far right, Tillich (and Bultmann) on the left, and Brunner, Aulen, and Nygren somewhere in the middle.

his interpretation of culture. The fundamental character of the New Being in Jesus (of essential humanity under the conditions of finite existence) is that here a finite actuality "negates itself without losing itself," that is, on the one hand, it points beyond itself by self-criticism and ultimately by its sacrifice of itself ("by surrendering its finitude"), and yet, on the other hand, in so doing, that finite actuality "becomes completely transparent to the mystery he reveals" (*ST* I:133, 147). In this, Jesus represents (1) the perfect medium or symbol of the unconditional, of the divine, of God, and so the paradigm for all other religious symbols as that finite actuality through which the infinite is fully *communicated* to others; (2) the conquest at once of unbelief, of "hubris," and of self-destructive concupiscence and, as a consequence, the religious-ethical model for all other individual finite entities (each of *us* is also called to become just such a "symbol"); and (3) the source of the picture of a *creative community* as well as of a creative individual and so for the definition of creative hope in historical life.

Spelled out in this fashion, it is evident that the New Being in Jesus is the ground in Tillich's system for his well-known, and ecumenically helpful, ecclesiology: the church is "a true church" when it embodies both the Protestant principle (the principle of self-criticism and so of "pointing beyond itself" to the divine source of its grace and power) and the Catholic substance (the principle of the presence through the media of dependent revelation of divine power, divine truth, and divine grace). As in the paradigm of the Incarnation itself, these two principles are polar, mutually dependent: without Catholic substance (the presence of the divine in the church's symbols of word, sacraments, and "saints") the Protestant principle is empty, unredeemed, and unredeeming, and the church becomes vulnerable to other, alien "spirits." Without the Protestant principle, the Catholic substance can become demonic, a medium that claims ultimacy for itself and thus becomes heteronomous and destructive to cultural life. The church is the church, therefore, when it "continues the Incarnation" (to use an old, orthodox phrase), when, that is, it points (1) beyond itself to its message of judgment on itself and its world and of grace to that world, that is, the message about the appearance of the New Being in Jesus, and *through* that message to God as Spirit, as power united to meaning; and (2) when *through* this self-negation and through this affirmation of grace it communicates the divine creative power to the world, to culture in all its phases. The church thus points beyond itself to God as ground and to the Kingdom as end; essentially, if latently, it represents, on the pattern of its Lord, the communal "symbol" communicating the Divine Life to culture, and the potential center for a "religious substance" of culture that could be creative and not demonic, that is, a theonomous culture.

As these last remarks indicate, for Tillich ecclesiology, interpreted through the category of the New Being, shades quickly into a theological understanding of culture. As he notes, church and cultural world are separated only in estrangement (for him, the doctrine of the two kingdoms is an *error* resulting from the Fall, not a *truth* illuminating the Fall's consequences). Eschatologically, they *both* are fulfilled in becoming one in the Kingdom. "One could rightly say that the existence of religion as a special realm is the most conspicuous proof of man's fallen state" (*TC*, 42). More specifically, as the category of real and good finitude (a finitude united to the divine ground and yet creative rather than destructive in and through its own finite powers) resulted from the experience of the New Being, so the concept of a "theonomous culture" has its origin there as well. A developed autonomous culture is a culture cut off from participating in its ground; like the "Protestant" church without Catholic substance, culture is then empty and subject to other, alien, destroying spirits. As autonomous, such a culture has ceased to be a "symbol" of the divine ground, of unconditional meaning, and thus will it die. A heteronomous culture is one where the necessary unconditional base of the culture, its "religious substance," has *itself* become absolute and beyond criticism (a *cultural* "Catholic substance" without Protestant principle). In other words, in a heteronomous culture the religious substance of the cultural community has refused to "negate its finitude," to sacrifice itself, to point beyond itself. As a consequence, it has made that substance *absolute*, an alien and unconditional authority over all else.

Such an authoritarian, absolutist, and yet partial culture also will die ultimately of internal or external conflict. As finite beings cannot without the divine ground escape estrangement and be at all, so cultures (and history with them) teeter between demonic hubris and destructive emptiness and vacillate between autonomy and heteronomy; in the end, all long for "theonomy." Theonomy, therefore, as the "answer" to the "question" of history, represents a culture at once autonomously creative and yet dependent upon and so affirmative of its unconditional ground, its religious substance: "autonomous reason united with its own depth" (*ST* I:89). Here, as Tillich notes (*ST* I:147–48), a culture in touch with and expressive of the divine ground possesses "a spiritual substance to all forms of its rational creativity" (*ST* I:147). But equally, a theonomous culture, through "the self-sacrifice of the finite medium, keeps heteronomous reason from establishing itself against rational autonomy" (*ST* I:148). Thus, as the church *qua* Catholic substance and Protestant principle represents the latent center for the new theonomy (*ST* I:148), so a *culture* expressive of its religious substance and yet prophetically self-critical of its own absolutes represents the cultural environment appropriate for theonomy and for a creative church. Both together culminate in the Kingdom, the symbol of historical fulfillment, of a "complete theonomy" (*ST* I:54).

The purpose of this section has been to indicate the centrality of the concept of the New Being for the entire scope of Tillich's theology. We have sought to show that not only his views of estrangement and Christology are derived from this category, but also that the particular shape of his conceptions of being-itself and so of God, of finitude and so of human being, of religions generally, and, finally, of ecclesiology, culture, and history and its hopes are formed by this category as it is defined in and through his Christology. Several important implications follow if this presentation is correct.

First, Tillich's is a *christomorphic* theology.[3] While by no means does awareness or cognizance of God stem for Tillich from Christian revelation alone (revelation and the presence of the New Being are *universal*), nevertheless, for his theology the revelation of God in Christ gives to every significant theological symbol its final shape and definition. To be sure, the whole, from the beginning to end, is set within philosophical/ontological categories; nevertheless, knowledge of God and *all* theological symbolism, as Tillich repeatedly insists, come through revelation, and so, for the Christian community and theologian, through the decisive revelatory appearance of the New Being in Jesus who is the Christ. (Many have wrongly concluded that *because* his is a philosophical theology, *therefore* revelation is deemphasized, if not negated.)

Second, as the answer to estrangement—estrangement in turn being expressed in the language of "half-way myth"—the New Being is itself to be spoken of in "mythical" rather than in strictly ontological terms, though its categories (as with estrangement) are ontological. Although Christology, says Tillich, must be "deliteralized," it cannot be "demythologized" (*ST* II:29, 152). For the appearance of the New Being cannot, anymore than can the Fall, be deduced from the universal structures of being as these are experienced in ordinary existence. Thus is the appearance of the New Being "paradoxical" (against all opinions); thus is it a subject of reception, faith, and believing witness; thus do we speak (as does Tillich himself) "mythologically" of "event," of "bringing," of

---

3. For the development of this helpful descriptive category, I am indebted to Richard R. Niebuhr's book, *Schleiermacher on Christ and Religion* (New York: Scribner's, 1964), esp. chap. 5.

"appearance," of the "coming of the new reality" (as well as his use of the traditional "mythological" symbols of the Messiah, Son of Man, Mediator, Logos, etc.). Let us note that if correct, this point, coupled with the central significance for the whole system of this category of the New Being, implies that there is much more mythical as well as ontological symbolic language in Tillich than is usually recognized. In fact, one might argue that the fundamental theological symbols (Fall and New Being, estrangement and grace, and "event" of actual revelation) are linguistically "half-way myths" or "mythological symbols," which are in turn interpreted *symbolically* by means of the epistemologically secondary categories of ontology, those of being, of the categories of finitude, and of the polarities. After all, for Tillich, all fundamental ontology is begun and completed via some form of religious ecstasy, when reason comes in touch negatively and then positively with its own ground.

Third, it has for some time been recognized that Tillich's theological system represents a "dynamic" ontology, an ontology in which process and becoming are the central aspects of being, and so in which historical passage rather than timeless forms or static being constitutes the most fundamental notion. This point can be argued in a number of ways: dynamic life and not rest are the basic symbols for God; the Spirit is in turn more fundamental than is Logos, and so on. If correct, our present interpretation of the New Being makes much the same point. As "mythical," the categories of estrangement and New Being are *historical* as well as ontological; neither one is an aspect of the timeless (logos) structure of things; rather, they "happen," although universally, and thus they include a temporal element as well as form or structure, human and divine, the one being an "irrational" fall, the other an "event," "against all historical opinions." It is *from* these fundamental events that for Tillich the ontological knowledge and so use of the timeless structures of being can be derived. As he repeatedly insists, and as we have argued, *valid* or *fulfilled* ontology or philosophy is derivative from religious apprehension, cultural or theological (though ontology is necessary to deliteralize the latter). Logos, therefore, has a *kairos* dependent on (universal) revelation. The structures of finitude, of existence, of authentic humanity and community, of history and of God have their origin in some aspect of universal revelation and achieve their most valid form in an ontological theology based thereon.

Every student of Tillich is aware that his earlier political works were centered on history and the relation of religion to history, and that his earliest interpretation of Christianity viewed Jesus as "the center of history" (see chapter 1). The above remarks should remind us that, despite the implications of much of his thought that seem to carry us beyond the finite to its timeless and infinite ground, the corpus of his theology taken as a whole points to an understanding of truth and of being alike as *historical*, to a consequent interpretation of being as dynamic and in process (life), and to a view of a completed philosophical ontology as existentially and religiously grounded (philosophical analysis plus religious answers) through participation in revelatory events as well as in the rigors of the philosophical analysis of structures. Theological reason is philosophical and religious at once; it is *reason in touch with its own ground*, "theonomous" reason or "ontological" reason. Thus, it is an ontological reason that combines reflection and participation, analysis and ecstasy. And our present point is that this religious element relates itself to religious events and uses the language of myth to interpret what is there uncovered. Theological or ontological reason (and they are one and the same, i.e., reason in touch with its own ground) uncovers the universal structures of finite actuality *because* it also witnesses to events revelatory of the ground and meanings of those structures. It is at once *historical*, and so as Christian christomorphic, and *ontological*, and so as cultural philosophical.

* * *

It is now time to discuss Tillich's Christology explicitly. I shall deal only with three somewhat puzzling and controversial issues: (1) his reinterpretation of the Incarnation, (2) the question of the historical Jesus, and (3) the relation, for Tillich, between the particularity of the christological event and the claim—necessary for any Christian theology and especially for any philosophical theology (*ST* I:137)—to universal relevance or significance (i.e., the question of universality), a question that concerns at once the relation of theology to philosophy and of Christian witness to other religions.

The Incarnation

As he was well aware, Tillich offers a radical reinterpretation of the Incarnation. That this interpretation is *not* a humanistic one is beyond question. Human powers are for him helpless, caught in estrangement, condemned to self-destruction and despair. It is through the divine "activity" alone, the appearance of the New Being, that rescue appears, that an answer—existential or religious in life, theoretical in philosophy or theology—to the question of existence (estrangement) appears, and, as we have pointed out, that insight into the essential nature of finitude itself becomes possible. For Tillich, therefore, the appearance of the New

Being, the new reality of salvation, the "incarnation" in that sense, is not at all to be interpreted as an achievement of human powers or of history, or even as representing merely a new presentation or uncovering of ever-present human possibilities. Rather, the central message is that *God* has "acted" for human salvation, has established a new reality in which we may now participate, and that on the basis alone of that divine act, new possibilities for us and for our powers are opened up. Thus, Tillich's reinterpretation of the Incarnation represents a reinterpretation of *how* God saves, not a denial *that* it is God who saves. In that sense the "myth" of the divine "descent" to earth and the philosophical category of the divine nature united with our nature, both of which must, to be sure, be deliteralized for Tillich, are by no means rejected, denied, or even removed from his theology. Rather, they are *reinterpreted* by the central assertions (1) of the divine event on which and through which the New Being appears ("God is the subject, not the object, of mediation and salvation" [*ST* II:93]), and (2) by the presence of the divine Spirit as constitutive of the New Being definitively present in Jesus as the Christ (*ST* III:144ff.).

Tillich begins his reinterpretation by a criticism of the classical theology of Incarnation.[4] In that traditional theology, Tillich argues, Incarnation has been understood, or misunderstood, as the juxtaposition in Jesus the Christ of two contrary, even contradictory, opposites: eternity and the temporal, the changeless and the changing, the immortal and the mortal, God and the human. Tillich regards this interpretation, if taken literally, as "pagan" (*ST* II:109–10, 149–50): (1) the conception of God "becoming" human is an inheritance from pagan mythology, and (2) the conception of a divine "nature" uniting with a human "nature" is an inheritance from pagan philosophy. Both presuppose polytheism, the assumption of the finitude of God, for only a finite entity can "become" something else or have "a nature" that belongs to it. Thus both are nonsensical if God is, as in Christian thought, the source and ground of finitude; God cannot will to become a human being without ceasing to be God (for Barth, of course, this is precisely the wonder of the divine freedom). The "paradox" of Christology is, therefore, not the paradox of God becoming a human being, or of the divine and the human united in one. Rather, it is the paradox of the unexpected, of the seemingly impossible, granted the universal experience of human estrangement; it is the paradox of the radically new in the alienated history of human existence. This is, therefore, as noted, a *historical* paradox, contrary to historical

---

4. Cf. Paul Tillich, "A Reinterpretation of the Doctrine of the Incarnation," *Church Quarterly Review* 147, no. 294 (1942).

experience and to our own existential situation, not an *ontological* or *metaphysical* paradox, contrary to the logic of philosophical reasoning.

This unexpected, paradoxical reality, this radically new, is thus an "event," an occurrence. In that event essential humanity, what we really are, the structure of authentic humanity, and so what we ought to be ("human possibility"), has (in Jesus) appeared in actuality, in a historical life, and so (most important of all) under the conditions of finitude and under the conditions of the estrangement of finitude ("existence"). This is the New Being, the new creature: essential humanity not, as hitherto, merely as an unreachable, impossible (and yet demanded) possibility, but as actuality, as a historical person, "under the conditions of existence." Here, therefore, the powers of existence—of bondage, of the structures of destruction, of the old age—are broken. Essential humanity and, thus, humanity in unbroken relation to God has appeared as actuality and, therefore, for us as actual, though fragmentary, possibility: "The paradox of the Christian message is that in *one* personal life essential manhood has appeared under the conditions of existence without being conquered by them" (*ST* II:94). Tillich interprets the most important christological symbols of the New Testament—Son of Man, Son of God, Messiah, and Logos—in the light of this reconception. For him, each points to the appearance in historical actuality of the new and yet essential humanity, or humanity in intrinsic relation to God, a humanity, therefore, that ushers in the new age of salvation (*ST* II:107–13).

As we have noted, this unique, transformative, and decisive event, the appearance in fullness of the New Being, is for Tillich the work alone of God: it is a divine event, whose subject is God as Spirit (*ST* III:144ff.). This unprecedented unity with God that establishes the New Being is for him, therefore, not the work of a person called Jesus; no human, however good, could for Tillich break the power of existence and establish this new reality: *essential* humanity *within* existence. For this reason, despite the fact that seemingly the "divine nature" (God) of orthodox Christology has been replaced by "essential humanity" in Tillich's formula (a "monophysite" Christology in which Jesus the Christ is essential humanity within existence, not a divine nature united to a human nature), in this view the "divine nature" is replaced by the category of the reconciling and reuniting redemptive *activity* of God that establishes the New Being through the presence of the divine spirit, uniting in one person essential humanity with the conditions of existence. Jesus, of course, as finite freedom, must accept this, his unique destiny, and through his own act of self-constitution embody and re-embody the New Being: in his person, his lifestyle, his teachings, his deeds, his passion, and his death.

Nevertheless, the whole event of his appearance, life, death, and resurrection is primarily the work of God as Spirit. The similarity in structure, though not in language or category, to Schleiermacher's Christology, is apparent: perfect God-consciousness is here replaced by New Being and "unbroken unity with God." Nevertheless, in both cases there is no supernatural, transhuman nature present in Jesus; instead, it is through the work and presence of the divine Spirit that the perfection of the human appears in history (*ST* II:150).

As the historical person who brings in the new reality, essential humanity within existence, Jesus is for Tillich wholly or entirely human. Since there is no supernatural "nature," there is here no qualification of his humanity: he is simply and solely a human being ("Jesus") but one in this unique role, embodying throughout his being this new redemptive reality. One notes the modern emphasis on the humanity of Jesus and the Protestant emphasis (perhaps the one consistent note in all Protestantism) that redemption (even in the case of Jesus) represents the *fulfillment* and not the *transcendence* of the human. Tillich underlines both of these points through his critique of the usual designation: Jesus Christ. This usual "name," he says, sounds like a proper name. It functions like the name of a person with a *human* given or first name and a *divine* family or surname (*ST* II:97–98). Thus, "Jesus Christ" expresses and implies not only a two-natures theology; it tends to compromise the reality of the human, for inevitably the divine, as constituting the person, overshadows and smothers the human. Preferable for Tillich is the title: "Jesus *who is* the Christ," that is, the human person who has this role or function, namely, to bring in the new reality, the one therefore who is the Messiah, or "Jesus *as* the Christ."

The Historical Jesus

As the implications of our remarks to date indicate, the *actuality* of the historical person ("Jesus") is crucial to Tillich. To deny that actuality, to deny that essential humanity entered existence and submitted to its conditions (e.g., finitude; the categories of finitude such as space, time, substance, and causality; the polarities; and all the anxiety, suffering, doubt, and weakness implied in them), is to deny Tillich's whole point, the crux of the Gospel message. If this paradox is not real, if no essential humanity actually entered existence, then nothing ultimately significant or new has happened, the New Being remains merely a hope, religion merely a quest—and there *is* no message, no faith, and no hope (*ST* II:98). The validity of the message (that the New Being has appeared in history), therefore, implies, on the one hand, a divine event in which essential humanity *entered* historical existence in an actual person in space and time (in Tillich's terms, the "miracle" side of an originating revelatory event); and it implies, on the other hand, the reception of that event, that is, understanding of it, acknowledgment of it, witness to it, and commitment in relation to it by the nascent community of disciples (the "ecstasy" side of an event of revelation).

It is important to emphasize the crucial importance for Tillich's Christology of *both* of these sides of the revelatory event: (1) the objective event, the actual personal life denoted by the name Jesus, as well as (2) the responding witness (*ST* II:97–99). The reason is that Tillich has frequently been interpreted as regarding that actual life as irrelevant to faith, as not only unknowable by us but even more as unimportant in comparison with the picture of the New Being in the Gospel records, a picture clearly created by the responding witness of the believing community. This misinterpretation has probably been caused mainly by Tillich's rather novel view of the roles of historical inquiry and faith in relation to this actual, personal existence. To that issue we shall now turn.

The correct question to ask initially, if we are to understand Tillich on the issue of the role of historical inquiry in Christology, is not, "Is there for Tillich a historical Jesus?" For as we note, he asserts unequivocally that there was an actual, historical person (Jesus) who was said to be the Christ (*ST* II:98–99, 107, 113–14). But "How do or can *we*, in the twentieth century, *relate* to this person or to this 'fact' who was said to be the Christ? How can we know of him, or be in any way certain of him, of the actual character of his life, teachings, destiny, and so on, if, as we agree, his actuality is essential to faith?" Pre-modern (pre-Enlightenment) Christians would have answered these questions by appeal to the infallible authority of the New Testament accounts or of the church, or both. In contrast, most post-Enlightenment Christians would probably say, "We can be sure of him only through historical inquiry, that same inquiry by which *any* historical fact is known if it is to be known at all." Since it is especially this last reply that Tillich finds inadequate, let us see how he proceeds to question and refute it.

Tillich first distinguishes two different meanings or referents for the phrase "the historical Jesus." The first referent is the actual, living person or individual life, "Jesus," who was received as the Christ, the person who inspired the movement and was the referent of the witness of the disciples or apostles, the historical figure "behind" the records of the New Testament. This referent Tilich affirms unequivocally. The second usage of the phrase "the historical Jesus" refers to the figure or picture reconstructed by historical inquiry out of and on the basis of the data present in the scant sources available to us today, "what we can know about him through scientific inquiry." Usually these two referents are fused into one: "What we can be sure of about Jesus is what historical inquiry can tell us about him." Tillich, on the contrary, wishes radically to distinguish them: the living person *behind* the texts, from the reconstructions by professional historians *out of* the text. For him, the first is crucial for the validity of the Christian message; the second, however, is of only preliminary, scholarly interest, and in no way essential to the message or to faith. "Christianity is not based on the acceptance of a historical novel; it is based on the witness to the messianic character of Jesus by people who were not interested at all in a biography of the Messiah" (*ST* II:105).

Let us begin with the second usage, the "historical Jesus" who is reconstructed by historical inquiry. Why is the historical Jesus in this sense only of preliminary, scholarly concern? The reason, says Tillich, is that no certainty or stability is ever possible here. Our records represent the believing witness of his followers, and so they portray Jesus *as* Christ; as is appropriate, they give us their *reception* of this event, not the historical event independent of their reception and witness. Thus the historical reconstruction of that event, *independent* of the believing witness, is a hypothetical and current, contemporary reconstruction, one necessarily created anew by each historian on the basis of his or her own theory with regard to the data. Like all historical reconstructions from the data, it is and can be only "more or less probable"; as are all hypotheses, it will be subject to ever-renewed critique because of new data, new perspectives, new theories. The shape, size, and certainty of this historical picture will continually shift, and every such account adopted at this or that time is in principle disprovable.

Historical reason, in other words, is "technical reason"; it can only achieve more or less probability; it is always in principle falsifiable. Hence, it can never be the vehicle either of certainty or of ultimate concern, of the personal, existential (participating) sort of knowing essential to religion. As Tillich frequently remarked to his classes: "I do not wish the telephone in my office to ring and to hear from some New Testament colleague: 'Paulus, our research has now finally removed the object of your ultimate concern; we cannot find your Jesus anywhere.' " For him, that phone call represented an obvious confusion of categories, a misunderstanding of different facets of reason, technical and ontological/ participating reason, and of the relation of each of these to religion. It represented the mistaken claim of autonomous, technical reason to be able to legislate through its knowledge of "the facts and their relations" for every realm of life: for morals, art, politics, philosophy, and religion—in the end, a false and dangerous claim because it dissolves all rational bases for ultimate concern and thus prepares the way for a new heteronomy.

If we cannot know Jesus, or of him, primarily through historical inquiry, then how can we be assured of a historical Jesus? Through "faith"? Can our faith be an authority for certainty about the historical details of Jesus' life contained in the Gospels? Can we say, "I believe he is the Christ; therefore, I know he lived, he said such-and-such, he did so-and-so"? Or can we say: "In the New Testament the Word of God has been heard; therefore, I know in the acknowledgment and obedience of faith that *its* historical account of Jesus' life and death is valid"? For Tillich, such certainty of a historical "happening" grounded in faith represents the reverse confusion (*ST* II:108). Here, ultimate concern or belief attempts to legislate as an authority in the realm of historical fact and in the place of historical inquiry; religious knowing makes the claim to impart "scientific," or at least "historical," information. Such a confusion represents heteronomy, the restrictive control or determination of autonomous reason about the facts and their relations by the claims of religious knowledge. Such a claim, when successful, is infinitely dangerous; when unsuccessful, it makes religion seem a game for blind fools. Religious knowledge of the *ground* of fact cannot be derived from, nor can it legislate for, scientific reason about facts and their interrelations. The essence of Tillich's answer, therefore, is the attempt to steer between these two opposite but interrelated confusions.

Faith, says Tillich, can be guaranteed or supported neither by historical knowledge nor by heteronomous belief. It can be guaranteed alone by *itself*, by its own experience or awareness of its object and its source or ground: the new reality or New Being (*ST* II:114). The basis for *my* faith has been the appearance of that New Being in my experience; the presence of faith is the direct result, the experiencing in consciousness, of the new reality in my existence, and therefore *in* existence. No historical uncertainty, no skepticism, can question this appearance of the New Being in existence, for it characterizes *my* existence. Behind my participation in the New Being, therefore, stands as its necessary source and ground a definitive participation in and through another historical existence, when essential humanity entered the conditions of existence and was not conquered by them. No hope by enthusiastic persons caught in existence, no picture imagined by the disciples or merely believed by them, in effect no *projection* of ours, could exert this transformative power, the power of a new reality, of which I am in my own awareness certain. Thus through participation, I can know that there is and was a historical reality, an actual life embodying the New Being. Once again, as in the appearance of courage and the knowledge of God, Tillich, as had Schleiermacher, has argued from (1) the *experience* of a New Being and (2) from the *impossibility* of human self-salvation to (3) a crucial theological conclusion, in this case the reality of a "historical" embodiment of that same New Being. *If* humans cannot extricate themselves from self-destruction, and *if* they experience such rescue, *then* the reality of the divine, the active presence of the divine, or (in this case) the appearance of divine redemption in and through a personal life, follows.

It is, moreover, not the case that we can, through our own experience of the New Being, be certain only *that* a historical embodiment has been actual. For this experience of the New Being has been mediated to us through the picture of Jesus in the New Testament and through the *whole* picture (Johannine and Pauline as well as Synoptic writings). The picture has functioned, therefore, as a *true* medium or symbol of the originating event, communicating the latter's power and meaning to us (*ST* II:114–16). Thus, there must be, Tillich reasons, a parallel, an analogy, between the picture as a true symbol and the historical ground. In this intriguing argument, one notes that Tillich (again like Schleiermacher) emphasizes the essential role of the community as the bearer of the picture and, even more, as the locus of the divine Spirit communicating through the picture the reality of the New Being to each succeeding generation. It is also evident that Tillich has sought to rescue the religious validity and power of the *whole* New Testament, including the Johannine and Pauline writings; for it has been this total picture that has communicated the New Being (*ST* II:117). As Tillich perceptively remarks, it is only when the historical Jesus of scientific inquiry has become crucial for faith that the Synoptic Gospels have more theological and spiritual importance than the rest, and this is to misunderstand them, for as Gospels they, too, are witnesses to Jesus as the Christ.

The picture of Jesus as the Christ in the New Testament is thus the definitive picture of the New Being, the criterion or norm, as we have noted, of Christian self-understanding, of religions generally, and expanded out into ecclesiology and theonomy, of Tillich's conceptions of church, of culture, and of their interrelations. It is a picture made up of two interwoven polarities: first, of essential humanity on the one hand and the conditions of existence on the other (the categories, polarities, and marks of estrangement). Jesus participates fully in the former (finitude) and, despite that participation, conquers the latter (estrangement). Secondly, there is the polarity of unbroken unity with God ("God-manhood") on the one hand and self-surrender and self-sacrifice on the other. For Tillich, this profound and moving picture, and its interwoven themes, can be summed up in the two symbols that dominate that picture, namely, the Cross (total participation in existence and self-surrender) and the Resurrection (essential humanity and unbroken unity with God, the ground of power and meaning [compare *ST* II:153–65]). Since Tillich's account of the further elements of this picture and the relation of those elements to the major events of Jesus' life as portrayed in that picture are straightforward, we shall cease our description at this point and move on to our final theme.

The Christian Claim to Universality

One of the most intriguing and, in view of our present acute consciousness of world religions, most relevant notions connected with Tillich's Christology is his resolution, or implied resolution, of the problem of universality. As the pointed question of Lessing shows, this question represents for Christian theology an old and extremely troubling issue: How can a particular religion, especially one based on a particular historical event, claim to embody a universal truth and so to be of universal relevance? We should note that the question raised by the Christian claim to universal relevance "offends" two quite different rival claimants to universality: philosophy and other particular religions. We shall, therefore, discuss Tillich's understanding of universality in relation both to philosophy and to other religions.

How is universal thinking and, as a consequence, a knowledge of universal truth possible for us? The most obvious answer is, of course, "through science," which abstracts from the particularity not only of the inquiring *subject* but also from the particularity of the various *objects* of any scientific inquiry. Thus appears the "universal language of science," a language apparently usable by members of any cultural or religious community. Scientists from another culture or religious community, however, must be "converted" to the general world view and epistemology presupposed by science before they can speak this universal language. By definition, this universal language of science deals with no issues of ultimate concern: with questions of ontology, of value or ends, of meaning, which science itself presupposes and with which any wider cultural life must perforce deal. If science seeks to deal with these questions, it can do so only if the scientist, in fact, takes on the role of philosopher or theologian.

We must, therefore, look beyond science to some other answer, and the answer obviously next in line is philosophy. Is it not the case that by abstracting from the particularity of the thinking subject (by its objectivity and "distance") and by seeking for the universal structures of being (not for particular entities within being) that philosophy has universal truth and relevance as its intentional object? It need not be stressed how committed Tillich himself is to this philosophical intentionality, how respectful he is of philosophy's claims to know the "universal structures of being," and how he views religious awareness or knowledge as *completed* only through the use of philosophical thinking. Nevertheless, for him the final path to universality (even by means of philosophy) is *religious* and not philosophical (and certainly not scientific). Because this claim (that through the religious the universal is apprehended) seems so bizarre in the modern world, it is deeply interesting and deserves explication.

For Tillich, while all philosophical thought aims at universality, it remains, in fact, relative to its cultural base and thus itself is incurably particular. Philosophy is the deepest and most universal cultural expression of the culture's substance, its "religious substance," that is, the particular and yet creative response of that culture to the manifestation of Being as reality, as truth, and as value. This religious substance represents the "mystical a priori" of all philosophy from which no philosophy can escape. Thus does "logos" have a *kairos*, a "fate" (*TPE*, chap. 1; *IOH*, part two); it is subject to the deepest presuppositions of its time and place, of its cultural epoch; and it cannot by the powers of abstraction transcend that particular base. Aristotle represents the spiritual substance of Hellenic culture; Hegel, the spiritual substance of modern European culture; Whitehead, the substance of recent scientific and democratic culture. Each surveys the universal structures of being from the perspective of a particular cultural point of view or epoch. If the cultural particularity is removed from such philosophical abstractions, the assumptions of Hellenism from Aristotle, of modern European culture from Hegel, of early twentieth-century science and liberal democracy from Whitehead, nothing is left. Even the process of abstraction, therefore, retains the marks of finitude (the particularity of time and space); and, since philosophy is confident it *can* become universal knowledge, more often than not these marks are compounded with the marks of estrangement (the self-elevating claim to an unconditional knowledge). Philosophy in existence is, in effect, *doubly* particular, once as finite and then a second time as claiming not to be (compare *IOH*, part two). Thus for Tillich, whatever the indispensability and value of philosophy for cultural and religious life, and despite its intentionality toward completion, philosophy is *not* the path to the universal any more than it is able, unaided, to achieve the knowledge that is its own fulfillment, namely, the knowledge of being-itself.

For these reasons (note they represent *reasons* and not merely an arbitrary adherence to a religious tradition), Tillich offers a *religious* path or way to the universal, or better, *toward* the universal, which, for him as for Kierkegaard, is about as far as a finite creature can go. This "path" involves the *recognition* of the finitude and so the relativity of one's own truth (scientific, social, philosophical, *or* religious), the *negation* of that particularity or the elements expressive of that particularity, and so the pointing *beyond* that particularity (beyond my truth or our truth) to the unconditional expressed in it. Since the attempt to transcend particularity through the abstractions of thought is regarded as futile (though useful for other purposes), the transcendence of particularity is here achieved existentially, personally, or subjectively, by the stance, the mode of existing and thinking, of the thinker himself or herself. Thus is this an *existential* resolution. It is a *religious* resolution since it points beyond the finite, beyond all rational elucidation or expression or categorization to the unconditional, to God. For Tillich, the universal lies there, in the unconditional, in God, which is a religious affirmation; we in turn can become "symbols" or "media" of that universality only as we point beyond ourselves, beyond our thoughts, our systems, our doctrines, to *their* infinite and transcendent referent, to God. But the medium of unconditional truth, the system of thought, of religious doctrine, even of scientific knowledge, cannot without demonic distortion or absurdity claim to be that to which it points. As Tillich recognizes and affirms (*ST* I:135–37, 150–53), it is the model of the *true symbol* (and of the New Being) that "negates itself without losing itself" (*ST* I:133) and in so doing points beyond itself and communicates the transcendent, that is to say, the picture of Jesus as the Christ, which lies in back of this novel and suggestive conception of the path to universality. As a self-negating and so self-transcending revelation, the revelation in Jesus as the Christ is a universal (and so final) revelation, of universal significance (*ST* I:133–37; II:150ff.); on its pattern, then, human being, thinking, and acting can approach universality.

For Tillich, this view answers or suggests answers to the issue of universality vis-à-vis both philosophy and other religions. For philosophy, its own culture, specifically the religious substance of that culture, is "the medium" through which being, truth, and good are manifested, and each philosophical viewpoint represents one specific form of that general medium. As noted, with regard to philosophy as such the question of the *sacrifice* of the medium, which is the basic question of finality and universality, (*ST* I:133), that is, the sacrifice of the elements of that culture's particularity, is an unresolvable one—except as philosophy becomes itself religious or theonomous. Only if philosophy participates in the religious, if its final revelation is located in the New Being, and so only if it can point beyond itself, can it transcend its particularity in the universal, can it become "theonomous" philosophy embodying ontological reason. To achieve union with its own ground, in other words, means, as it does for all true media, its sacrifice of its own particularity and its claims to possess universality; it means that it must point beyond its own systematic structure and conclusions in order to be transparent to the universal, to the unconditional. As Tillich has insisted from the start, only in religious philosophy ("theology," if the latter understands itself aright) can philosophy itself be fulfilled (*ST* I:150).

With regard to the question of universality vis-à-vis other religions, Tillich was also only suggestive; this was a subject he wished further to explore but for which he knew he had "no time." As noted, Tillich regarded the New Being in Jesus as the paradigm for the quest of culture and religion alike for universality. As Jesus "sacrificed" or "negated" all that was particular about himself, even "himself as Jesus" (*ST* I:136–37), that is, lifestyle, teachings, deeds, and pointed beyond even himself, so Christianity as a religion must sacrifice and negate its particularities (as a religion), that is, doctrines, laws, rites, polity. Christianity must point beyond itself to the New Being, to God as Spirit, and beyond even those theological expressions of New Being and of God as Spirit (*ST* I:136–37). Tillich has the greatest confidence (again on the model of Jesus as the Christ) that these concrete and particular media are not lost or dissolved in that sort of sacrifice; rather, that sacrifice is of the very *essence* of any final revelation (*ST* I:148). (One might remark that "the church" has never agreed with this, though many Christians have.) In any case, this sacrifice of all elements of particularity, while retaining "unbroken unity with the ground," represents the path, and the only path, to universality, to a transcendence of this or that religious tradition which results in neither a secular universality that is culturally particular, nor in a new religion made out of transcended elements of old religions. Only if each tradition negates itself in pointing beyond itself can the particularity of religion, and especially the estrangement embodied in that particularity, be "overcome." In this, for Tillich, Christianity shows its finality because its own center in Jesus who is the Christ represents precisely this process of self-negation and yet of unity with the transcendent ground.

9

The Nature and Work of Spirit

One of the most important and least discussed subjects in Tillichean studies is the symbol of spirit. That the Spirit was important to Tillich is undoubted: his largest volume of theology is almost entirely devoted to this subject, and I know he regarded his "doctrine of the Spirit" as not only Pauline but as the point "where," he once said, "my theology is entirely biblical." I shall by no means cover all the significant aspects of this rich doctrinal symbol. But I am interested in some of its fundamental elements, in part because they represent, so I believe, places where Tillich's theology has been sorely misunderstood or misinterpreted, and I wish to redress that balance a bit. The first is the way in which spirit, as the union of power and meaning, represents for Tillich the human and the personal, the principle of the *humanum*, the principle creative alike of self, of culture, of rationality, and especially of morality, of all that we associate with humanism. Secondly, I wish to show how this principle of spirit, the *humanum*, is intertwined for Tillich with the presence of the divine Spirit, the Spiritual Presence, and the implications of this for Tillich's concept of God. Finally, I am interested in the kinds of arguments Tillich uses to establish this relatedness of the human spirit and *humanism* to the divine Spirit, and hence to *theonomy;* for the unity of humanism and theonomy represents, I think, the essence of the Tillichean synthesis.

* * *

The moment Tillich begins, we can sense both how central and how dynamic this concept of spirit is. Life—which is, he says, (and this is a post-immigration remark!) a better word than process—is the negation of death, its overcoming; it represents the potentiality of certain beings to actualize themselves. Life is, therefore, the actuality of being (*ST* II:39). The fullness of life, in fact the power of life, its all-inclusive dimension wherein all its powers and its capacities come to actuality, is spirit (*ST*

III:21). Spirit is the unity of power and meaning (*ST* II:24, 249), the dimension in which being really and fully *is*, the *telos* of life as of being (what Whitehead would call the "satisfaction").

In a real sense, therefore, as we shall seek to show, spirit for Tillich defines being as its fulfillment. Thus, appropriately, life and spirit are for him primary symbols for the divine being, life being the first to be mentioned (*ST* I:241–49) and spirit being "the most embracing, direct, and unrestricted symbol for the divine life" (*ST* I:249). If, then, spirit represents the ontological basis for all we mean by the words "personal," "intentional," "purposive," "communicating," and "loving," then it is surely, in the light of this analysis, inaccurate to speak of Tillich's "impersonal" view of God. More than most theologians, Tillich gives a careful analysis of what he means by the "human," that is, by the personal and the spiritual; he applies this, as he says, "unrestrictedly," if of course symbolically, to God. This analysis of spirit as the principle of the *humanum* has, therefore, important implications for his concept of God.

Human being is the fulfillment of being, as it is of life; it represents the point where all the dimensions of being come together in awareness and in harmony, and thus, being now actual, are manifest (*ST* III:17–24). Human being is, therefore, the entrance into being, the point where its creaturely fullness and completion are revealed or uncover themselves and can thus be known (not, however, from the outside, but from within) in the experience of our own being and our own powers of spirit. Here we experience (or can experience) ourselves as a unity, a unity of inorganic and organic life, of psychological contents and spiritual self-direction. For Tillich, therefore, the body/mind dualism of our common cultural inheritance (*our* folk myth) is false to experience, as is the duality of power and spirit. Spirit is the unity of power and meaning, the dimension in which, via the appearance of spirit, *power* actualizes itself on every level, and correspondingly, the full potentialities of the human as *spirit* are realized.

Spirit is, for Tillich, the community and culture-creating power of the human (he called it "reason" in *ST*, volume one); it provides this power through its constitution of the centered self. Because of spirit, human beings are able, among other things, to know and transform their world; here *meaning*, or the awareness of it, becomes the basis of vitality and power. We can understand what Tillich means by "the unity of power and meaning," therefore, if we think of the human both individually and culturally; that is, as self, or better, selves together capable of cognizing and reshaping their world, capable of moral acts centering and controlling themselves, and of creative, artistic acts. Thus is the human a being who actualizes at once and together cultural and spiritual *power* (to be and to be creative) and cultural and spiritual *meaning* (to understand, to create, to reshape or transform, to enjoy). For Tillich, power and meaning support, generate, and control each other; they unite in the fullness of being that is spirit. There could hardly be a more drastic attack on dualism than this, or on an "impersonal" concept of being! To appreciate this further, let us see how this analysis proceeds.

Tillich begins his description of the appearance of spirit with the *centered self* (*ST* III:22). For full self-awareness and an act of knowing to take place, all the congeries of sense impressions, conscious and unconscious prehensions, traditions and authorities, must be penetrated by logical and methodological criteria: the cognitive act is dependent upon the transcendence of this material by a personal center so that a judgment about it is possible—this is a manifestation of spirit. Correspondingly, for a moral act, the vast and various materials of drives, habits, inclinations, conscious and unconscious, must be transcended and unified by the centered self if a *decision* is to occur. Deliberation and cognitive judgment, deliberation and moral decision alike presuppose a centered self, one in *that sense* "free," not free from influences (destiny) but free to organize, unify, and redirect destiny.

Concurrent with this inner analysis of centeredness, transcendence, and freedom, Tillich provides an analysis of the shift in our relation to our environment. With this centering, we step back from, gain distance from, our environment: it is organized into universals by language and thus becomes structured. As he puts it, through spirit and its language, environment becomes "world" (*ST* III:38), an ordered structure within which projects appear and so in which vocations or tasks are present; with them, an intentional and so vital life is made possible. Only in a coherent world of meaning does knowledge also become possible; only in such a world does the creative function of spirit, its reshaping of the world in line with the intentions, purposes, and decisions ("projects") of the self, become possible. Language and technology are the primal signs of spirit, of the *humanum:* they "create" the ordered and malleable world we know and form the materials for the culture that both *empower* the human in its quest to be and *express* the human in creating the realms of meaning. Spirit leads to power over self and over world *through* meaning; it is the union of power and meaning and, in that, the fulfillment of being.

I can already feel the slowly developing antipathy here. It runs something like this: "As we thought, Tillich unites power, meaning, and spirit into *power over* and offers little enough to us of the moral, personal, and communal or minimal consciousness of the dangers of technological, scientific, and cultural power."[1] As if many (if not all) of the voices that

---

1. That Tillich was very conscious at a very early point of the potential dangers,

prefer "personal religion" were not also happy with technology and missiles! In the midst, however, of the above analysis of centered self, cognition, deliberation and decision, language and technology—all associated for Tillich with spirit and freedom—is a concurrent analysis of the moral self-constitution of the self which is utterly central to his thought about human being. Tillich is quite explicit (as is Kierkegaard) that the centered self appears and integrates (unites) itself, that is, *becomes* a self, in the *moral* act: here "spirit comes into being. Morality is the constitutive function of spirit" (*ST* III:38). In moral decision, the self becomes a person: aware of itself *as* a responsible person, aware of the norms that direct and guide its freedom, and, above all, aware of its limits, that is, of its own finitude and partiality, of the limiting presence of "others" in its world.

As we have seen, the centered self, the cognitive and technical self, is able to know, assimilate, and reshape its world. So far, however, there has not yet appeared any limit to "man's attempt to draw all content into himself," as our technical and industrial culture, void of moral limitation, reveals. But there *is* such a limit, and only one such limit: the other self, the self encountered continually and inescapably in community (*ST* III:58). Such a self can be conquered physically; but its *spirit* "looks back"; it is free, *and* it constitutes *itself;* thus, the other cannot be made into an object and assimilated into oneself. We reach our ontological limit, that which finitizes each self and thus, in effect, creates it as a *finite* self, in the encounter with the other. "The experience of this limit is the experience of the ought-to-be, the moral imperative. The moral constitution of the self and so spirit begin in this experience. . . . Personal life emerges in the encounter of person with person and in no other way" (*ST* III:40).

To our scientific and technical culture, it is because of cognition, linguistic communication, and common technical competence that culture and human life flourish. For Tillich, however, it is in personal community that morality is born, that moral limits are disclosed, and that essential human being becomes possible. Surprisingly, it is precisely *here* that the grounds of a centered self, of a world, of community and freedom—of culture itself—arise. Finally, the norms encountered by freedom that limit and direct the power generated by spirit reflect the essential structure of humanity and so of all community. It is this essential structure of inter-relating, personal and social, calling for a union of justice, *arete*, and *agape*, that represents the essential *structure* of community and so the

---

as well as benefits, inherent in technological power over the world and ourselves, is shown in the excellent collection of his writings on this subject edited by J. Mark Thomas, *The Spiritual Situation in Our Technological Society: Paul Tillich* (Macon, GA: Mercer University Press, 1988).

conditions of community, that is, for a community that does not destroy itself. Moral self-constitution, an "act" that takes place in community, in encounter with the other, is thus the *foundation* both of spirit and of culture; it also represents the conditions for their culmination in justice and harmony. Strange as it may seem, in Tillich's ontology of spirit morality appears at the very center of the human, thus of being, and so, certainly, of the divine being, which is, after all, "Spirit."

A further and probably more familiar discussion of the union of power and meaning is found in Tillich's fascinating discourses on vitality, the power of life, and, therefore, the power of creative life: personal, political, economic, artistic, moral, and religious life alike (compare *CB*, 78ff.; *ST* III:56ff.). Vitality, says Tillich, is neither a biological nor a merely temperamental matter; it represents neither a physical nor a psychological "fate." Vitality expresses, rather, a relation to meaning, to some discerned good, deeply intended. "Man's vitality is as great as his intentionality" (*CB*, 81), as great as the eros that directs and fuels one's life. However biologically gifted, a life void of meaning finds no ground for the hard work of self-discipline; thus it quickly disintegrates into unorganized and undirected pleasures, is soon dominated by arbitrary pains, and finally evaporates or "fizzles out" in emptiness, self-pity, and despair. With no inner *telos*, life loses its fuel and so its power; as Casey Stengel said, "You've got to have *heart*." Meanings or purposes, or love of something as worthful, are as basic to personal vitality as is bodily health; of course, the two are interrelated. Correspondingly, in a culture where nothing is felt to be worthful, nothing will be accomplished, whether it be the tasks of essential labor, professional vocations, art, science, or governmental work. In human being, power is grounded, enhanced, and guided by *meanings*, in this case the achievement of commonly held values. "This makes man the most vital of beings," or "the more power of creating beyond itself a being has, the more vitality it has" (*CB*, 81). Thus, "in a man nothing is 'merely biological' as nothing is 'merely spiritual'. Every cell of his body participates in his freedom and spirituality, and every act of his spiritual creativity is nourished by his vital dynamics" (*CB*, 83). Nothing could express the nondualistic character of Tillich's thought more clearly than this notion of vitality and intentionality or clarify more helpfully what he means by the union of power and of meaning in spirit. And nothing, incidentally, could so clearly differentiate his thought from a mysticism that (like Buddhism) seeks to eliminate desire and vitality (and so all forms of power), rather than spiritualize, redirect, and reintegrate them with creative meaning.

Spirit is, then, the fulfillment of life and of the human. It grows out of an organic base and adds immeasurably to that base by transmuting it into the creative powers of cognition, decision, community building, and artistic expression. Its *essential characteristics* are the centered self, freedom, an ordered world, and valued meanings and goals; its *instruments* are language (universals), technology, and political and moral praxis. Its most *fundamental ground* is moral self-constitution in relation to an other; its *matrix*, therefore, is the personal community of individuals held together by love. Its unambiguous actualization comes when its being and its acts embody the norms of justice, *arete* (personal fulfillment), and *agape*, the modes, that is, in which humans come to be and reunite in both fulfillment and in harmony. Here, let me suggest, is a full-bodied ontological description of the personal, of the human, in all its embeddedness in the inorganic and the organic, and yet one articulating powerfully those characteristics that give power, creativity, and sublimity to that which is peculiarly human. Somewhat to our surprise, with this conception of spirit, Tillich reveals himself as a full-bodied humanist, even a personalist.

Tillich insists that spirit as so understood is symbolically applied to God and is the most important symbol for the understanding of God's being as it surely is for the understanding of human being. The analogical use of this symbol, unequivocally indicated by him (*ST* I:249–50), means that in some clearly discernible sense, centeredness and freedom, knowing and decision, moral self-constitution and intentionality are as applicable to God as is, for example, the more familiar category of being, which is also characteristic of finitude. As he has frequently reiterated, the norms of spirit for us, justice and agape, are as essential to God's reuniting power over and in us as they are to human relations with one another.

The only real point where there may be more than an analogical difference, so it seems to me, is with regard to the third function of spirit in us (self-integration and self-creativity are the first two). This third function he calls self-transcendence vertically to the divine (through which salvation is received), a symbol hardly applicable to God. Thus, applied to God, this third aspect is transmuted—as is reasonable it should be—to the initiating movement by the divine in the opposite direction, namely, the divine drive, which as we now know is also the divine intention, purpose, and decision, toward *reunion* with the separated or estranged, the divine agape and creative justice, on which our salvation is based (compare *ST* I:251, 179–86). It is in the Spirit or through Spirit that the Divine Life reunites itself with the estranged. Thus is the Spirit the principle of reunion, reconciliation, and salvation, that "aspect" of God decisively and unambiguously present in Jesus as the Christ, creating the New Being. Unquestionably, the Spirit is, as Tillich says, *the* central symbol for God: the basis for the articulation of the divine purpose and divine love so central to Christian faith, and the ground in God—if I may put it that way—for the saving activity of God on which that faith is based. Tillich is in truth a theologian of being; but what he means by being is quite misunderstood if he is not also seen as a theologian of the Spirit.

*   *   *

Tillich, we have noted, does not enlarge on the inescapable and interesting implications of the symbol of Spirit for the being of God.[2] So I must follow the path where he leads us on this theme, into the presence and working of the Spirit in our personal and historical experience: in culture, in the church, and in other religions. This is, of course, where Tillich is most at home (though he *does* know more about God than most of us!), namely, the theology of culture, of religious community, and of history. His range of subjects here is immense. I shall concentrate on the one that interests me the most, namely, the way he establishes the presence and significance of the *religious* dimension of the life of the human spirit, or, put in the reverse way, the modes in which the divine Spiritual Presence makes itself known in human experience (compare *ST* III:111–61).

The second half of this chapter, therefore, moves in an opposite direction from the first half, as Tillich's thought frequently does. In that half, I sought to show the way in which, under the symbol of spirit, Tilich developed a powerful interpretation of our human being that articulated the unique structures and powers of the *humanum*, that, in other words, presented itself as an example of a "high humanism." Human being as spirit is, we saw, the vital, free, centered, infinitely creative source of culture in all its vast range of powers, of meanings, and of expressions. Tillich could have, I know, fully affirmed that description ("high humanism") and seen it as a compliment. Yet he was, at the same time, the persistent, indefatigable opponent of humanism (when by the latter one means those champions of an autonomous, self-sufficient, and self-redemptive humanity). Hardly a line he wrote but presupposes the high

---

2. One can speculate endlessly on why Tillich did not, in volume three of *Systematic Theology*, explicate his analysis of the category of spirit when it is "symbolically" applied to God, as he did in much more deliberate form with the symbols of being and of life in volume one. Did he overlook this logically entailed part of the system? Did the implications of "spirit" applied to God (see *ST* I:249) seem too "personalistic" for him, a near capitulation to those theologians of God as Person or as Thou, which he found distasteful? Did it seem to offer a front to the secular critique of a personal or anthropological deity vulnerable to the accusation of human projection? One wonders.

humanism expressed in his notion of spirit; hardly any of these same lines but repudiates, and with devastating arguments, the notion that the human spirit is in itself *(a se)* capable of all this, that it can be understood either in its glory or in its depravity without the religious dimension of spirit. I need not add that it is precisely the juxtaposition of these two apparently contradictory themes that constitutes his central category of *theonomy*, the reunion of essential humanity with its own religious ground, and of secular culture with its authentic religious substance.

We are searching here for the focal point of unity between culture, morality, and religion—clearly *the* key to most of Tillich's thought. As we have seen, perhaps to our surprise, all the acts of culture, and so the "powers" of spirit, are based on the ethical, on the moral self-constitution of the self in encounter with the other (compare *ST* III:58). At this juncture, however, our point is the reverse, the ways in which for Tilich culture and morality find in turn their roots in the religious, in the spiritual principle of "freedom even from its own finitude" (*ST* III:31, 86), the principle of self-transcendence "toward ultimate and infinite being" (*ST* III:86), in what in volume one of *Systematic Theology* he calls the "infinite ground of reason." These ways to the infinite ground are many; many of them hearken back, now in the language of spirit, to the analysis of reason and its ground in part one and of finitude and its infinite ground in part two. As in those cases, they refer to ways in which the creative powers of our essential nature manifest themselves as permeated by and dependent upon the divine Spirit and ways in which the sufferings of our existence (what Tillich calls here the "ambiguities" of our life) register the absence of and so the need for the Spiritual Presence.

Tillich has outlined for us how the cultural powers of human being— language, technology, cognition, aesthetics, personal and social praxis— all arise because of spirit, the unique dimension of the human. At this point, then, we will retrace this route, making now an articulation of the "possibility of" or "conditions for" these powers (what Kant might have called a "deduction" of them) because of the religious dimension, because of the essential relation of finite spirit to the ultimate and infinite ground beyond itself. More specifically, these capacities are present only because, so to speak, at the beginning we have already experienced or apprehended (perhaps "prehended" is best) the divine act of *reunion* of the finite with the infinite, which is the act of the divine Spirit; in other contexts (volume three) Tillich refers to this reunion as the Spiritual Presence, and in volume two it represents what is called the New Being. Thus, as Tillich says explicitly, grace is the basis of culture (*ST* III:159). Without the renewing power of the New Being, human life would disintegrate through the self-destructive tendencies of existence and the ambiguities of life. As the divine power of being grasps, steadies, and secures our anxious finitude, so the Spiritual Presence heals and renews our existence and our life. Thus culture as such, not just *good* culture, becomes possible. Whitehead's God, so Whitehead tells us,[3] does not so much make an already real world orderly as he makes, first, *order* possible, and, second, through that ordering, a real world then becomes possible; so here, the Spiritual Presence makes self, world, and culture not just "good" but possible at all. The divine Spirit is the *ground* of culture and not only its fulfillment, though it is that as well. Let us try to see what Tillich means by these surprising (to our humanistic culture) statements.

At the very beginning of culture, the New Being (or Spiritual Presence) is present as the drive toward the reunion of the separated: reunion of subject and object, of self and world, of self and selves. Out of this reuniting drive, the union of perceiver and perceived, of naming and named, knower and known, shaper and shaped result. In "receiving" reunion, the self "grasps" the world and unites with it in cognition and in the aesthetic; and in active, shaping reunion, the world is molded by the self. Thus, language and technology, knowledge and art—the fundamental functions of culture—reflect as its finite effects the unifying power of the Spiritual Presence (*ST* III:64–68).

As we have noted, moreover, these cultural acts are themselves dependent upon the centered self as distinguished from its world by its own act of self-constitution. That fundamental act of spiritual self-creation, for Tillich, is in turn dependent on the *moral* encounter of self with self in which the self constitutes itself (*ST* III:58). For Tillich, however, the moral, which is that fundamental self-constitution in relation to the other, is itself dependent on the religious dimension present in all moral experience. For in that experience as *moral*, an unconditional element is experienced, an unconditional demand or requirement. The possibility of this unconditional requirement in the relation to the other, Tillich tells us, is that our essential being and that of the other are experienced as possessing infinite value, as participating in the transcendent union of the Divine Life (*ST* III:159), and only thus as making this unconditional claim on me. Again, grace is the basis of culture, since the unconditional element in the ethical relation to the other that establishes culture is itself a manifestation of the divine Spiritual Presence. Culture and religion, both inextricably locked to the moral, are united throughout history. The cultural existence that begins in the most rudimentary of taboos, verbal cries, and bodily signs, that is carried forward by tools, folklore and crafts, family and

---

3. Cf. A. N. Whitehead, *Religion in the Making* (New York: Macmillan, 1926), 119.

political relations, is, as we have seen, the artifact of spirit, of the ethical, and now of the religious. And that whole process culminates in explicit "faith," a conscious "being-opened-up-by" the same Spiritual Presence (*ST* III:133), and in *agape*, or enacted love, that is, "the ecstatic participation in the transcendent unity of unambiguous life" (*ST* III:136). At every stage of its self-constitution and so its autonomous and free development, the human is also the work, the *theonomous* work, of the Spiritual Presence.

Another perhaps more familiar theme in Tillich's theology of culture also shows culture's inescapably theonomous essential nature. Cultural life in all its ranges is dependent on deeply held meanings; our own analysis of vitality has shown this. Tillich reinforces this point when he outlines the necessity of an unconditional eros or ultimate concern at the base of every important cultural activity. The scientist who has no ultimate concern for the truth will manipulate the evidence, if sorely enough tempted by the lures of fame or tenure—and so science disappears. Meanings in cultural life, therefore, depend on an *infinity* or *ultimacy* of meaning; if such meanings have become merely relative or proximate, and so expendable, the institutions and activities of culture dry up and disintegrate, as do the people within that culture. This category of ultimate concern, basic to his analysis of culture, Tillich now describes as "moral": a commitment of self, a decision about existence, a self-constitution. This moral concern is, he says, what gives *seriousness* to culture, what eradicates the dilettante or detached attitude "untouched by eros" (*ST* III:100–101). It is, moreover, a *religious* concern, an ultimate concern to which one's life is surrendered.

Again, culture, morality, and religion are "theonomous," intertwined, and inseparable. Feuerbach, the great humanist, ridiculed the divine beings, the gods, and spirits, who were held to create and sustain each craft and its guild; slowly, he says, we have learned that these are powers of *humanity* and not of the gods; our powers have projected themselves into the latter and falsely given *them* the credit and the glory.[4] Tillich powerfully reverses this argument. The human cultural powers we celebrate—as does he—are themselves dependent upon the religious dimension of spirit, the Spirit's touch with an unconditional meaning and an unconditional demand. It is this relation and dependence that has been, with some discernment, expressed through these sacral founders and keepers of the guilds.

The Spiritual Presence, the divine Spirit reuniting the world to itself, is

---

4. Ludwig Feuerbach, *Lectures on the Essence of Religion*, trans. Ralph Manheim (New York: Harper and Row, 1967), 212–13.

never absent from culture and history (*ST* III:138–140). Thus, the manifestations in ordinary experience of this sacred basis of community are
legion, wherever the aura of an unconditional power or meaning appears:
for example, in the founding principles of reality around us, in the fertility
on which the community's continuing life depends, in the hero, or in the
uniting political center of the community, its government, on which it
also depends. Power, life, and order—and slowly with this, justice—
become the major media or symbols through which this unconditional
base of communal and so of individual life is expressed. Each is a symbol
of ultimate power and meaning, of life itself; yet each—power, life, order,
and justice—establishes and orders an essential aspect of cultural life.
Together, they constitute the "religious substance," the unity of power or
existence and meaning on which that culture lives; and of course, each set
of these appears in the particular symbolic forms of its own historical
culture's life. Central, therefore, to the life of culture is this religious
substance made up of these essential media between ultimacy and culture
as well as the particular symbolic structures through which they are
expressed.

Cultural life cannot exist without access to these ultimate powers of life
and security, that is, without a consistent system of ultimate concerns, on
the one hand, and without a coherent universe of meaning, on the other,
within which these concerns are ordered and the promise of fulfillment
expressed. In other words, cultural life is impossible without an articulated "religious substance" at its core. Thus, it cannot function without
language capable of expressing these grounds and horizons of our activities of finite spirit. Such language is "symbolic" or "polysemic" (in
Paul Ricoeur's usage). It refers at once to an experienced aspect of the
subject-object world: water, mountain, tree, hero; life, power, order,
justice; but it does so "symbolically" so as to refer also beyond that finite
reality or principle to the infinity of power and meaning communicated
through that medium. Religious language, the language of myth, is as
basic for cultural and moral existence as is the religious dimension of spirit
in relation to which culture arose. Thus, Tillich speculates that, possibly,
religious language expressive of the relations of creatures to the ultimacy
or ultimacies that ground them antedates the technical language of the
subject-object world (*ST* III:59), as the actions of rite and cult parallel, if
not precede, the technical and practical activities of early culture. Thus,
he found himself quite without patience for a secular culture that thought
it could articulate its experiences of reality without such a language. The
essential nature of culture, as of spirit, is to be grounded in the infinity of
power and meaning, which is its source and goal. Even, therefore, where
communities thrash about in self-destructive existence and frustrating

ambiguity, as they do in history, evidences of this religious dimension, of the Spiritual Presence, abound all around us. Here is the first half of his argument against humanism.

* * *

Tillich's heavier argument for the presence and reality of the divine Spirit, however, is not the pervasive, positive presence of the Spirit in life, grounding, supporting, and fulfilling every human aspiration and achievement. Far more central, far more emphasized—both formally in the construction of the system and materially in the concerns about which he writes—is what we could call the argument from the negative. This argument, which we might say represents Tillich's "neo-orthodox" side, dominates the first and second volumes of *Systematic Theology*: it is *the* way that Tillich moves our thought from the finite before us, which we can analyze philosophically, to the divine, which is not before us and of which we speak theologically. Interestingly, in neither volume does he, as he well might have, present to us as an argument the pervasive, continuing, and essential presence of the transcendent ground in all our experience, as we have shown him to have done in the third volume.

There are two forms or phases to the "neo-orthodox" argument from the negative. For obvious reasons, since this *is* his neo-orthodox side, Tillich does not wish to call either one an argument. He denies, we may recall, that arguments get anywhere in this connection. But I think they *are* arguments, even if they do argue through and over negativity, much as Kierkegaard's did. The first is a *real* argument. As we know, Tillich uses philosophical analysis, so to speak, like a dentist's drill, to penetrate into the *structure* of our finitude in order to uncover there the theological core of pain, namely, the *meaning* of finitude for us, and that meaning is anxiety. As he lucidly shows, this anxiety is so essentially tied to the structure of our finitude that there is, on the one hand, absolutely no escape from it, and, on the other, there is no way finitude alone can provide any solace for it. Finitude, felt from the inside, *is* anxiety; there is thus no answer *in* finitude. That rescue he calls *courage*, the courage to be, even if we are, and must remain, temporal, spatial, caused, and so on. Now, here comes the argument: although such courage cannot come from finitude, nevertheless, such courage *is* there, and it appears everywhere. Therefore, in this universal fact of courage we experience, and must do so, the infinite power and ground of being. If that is not an argument, I do not recognize one!

The second move from the finite to the infinite has much the same form, but is more accurately, I think, described as witness than as demonstration. The negations of life, says Tillich, call for rescue, a rescue—as he has elegantly shown—that our finite and estranged condition cannot provide. A distraught reason calls for revelation; an anxious finitude calls for God as power of being; and a self-destructive existence calls for the New Being. Faith knows that these calls *are* answered; in fact, receiving that answer and assenting to it—being "grasped by it"—is precisely what faith is. Thus, theology takes this question and answer form in order to reflect faithfully the structure of faith, the structure of desperate need and of unexpected and undeserved answer. This is, as I noted, more a witness to the coming and the presence of the Spiritual Presence than it is an argument. Still, it represents, as does the other, the way, so to speak, to the divine *through negation*, which, as I suggested, is a major way for Tillich of proceeding from here to there, from surface to depth, from us to God.

My point in outlining these forms of argument is partly because I find their variety and roles fascinating in Tillich, but even more to emphasize my original point, namely, the pervasiveness and sheer weight of his argument against naturalistic humanism. The reiteration of these themes page after page—reason *cannot* overcome disruption, finitude *cannot* conquer anxiety, existence *cannot* overcome its suffering and self-destruction—shows how aware he was of this "struggle," as he would have called it. Humanity, even essential humanity, however creative and sublime its powers and accomplishments, is *not* self-sufficient; nor can it alone escape the lethal and dark nemesis that moves inexorably forward to engulf it. Without the infinite ground and power of being, without the renewing power of the New Being, without the Spiritual Presence—without "God"—endless suffering and despair would engulf finitude from the inside, and disintegration and conflict would overcome it from without. There is no heavier analysis of human ills than Tillich's; correspondingly, there is no more powerful polemic against secular humanism than this one.

With regard to the presence of the divine Spirit, we find the same fundamental form of argument as with finitude and existence, only now it is a bit more complex, or more "confused," if you do not like it. In this part of the system, Tillich speaks of the "ambiguities of life" as the representatives of the negative pole of this relation we have described: "Questions arising out of man's finitude are answered by the doctrine of God. . . . Questions arising out of man's estrangement are answered by the doctrine of the Christ. . . . Questions arising out of the ambiguities of life are answered by the doctrine of the Spirit and its symbols" (*ST* III:286). It is not easy to know *theoretically* just what "ambiguities" are, although when Tillich describes them, we recognize each one of them quickly enough. Let us, however, outline such a theoretical description and then give one illustration.

Life for Tillich—and recall, life *is* being in its fulfillment—is a multi-faceted thing, a "many" in unity. It *must* have unity to be at all, and yet because it is multifaceted or "many," that unity is infinitely precarious. On the one hand, being is *polar* in a number of ways, a unity of divergent principles and tendencies which appear to oppose one another and can quickly become actually opposed. But, like a wondrous organism, they can, because they are polar, also come into a supremely effective harmony: individual-community, dynamics and form, freedom and destiny. At any point, these can move apart and "struggle against each other," and they usually do. Added to the problem of this delicate equilibrium is the fact, now brought out in volume three, part four of *Systematic Theology,* that life always risks itself and must do so; it moves forward out of unity into a new diversity. Although it has to integrate itself into a "centered unity," it also must, says Tillich, go out from itself to create the new, in fact to *become* something new. It risks its delicate balance lest it sink. But in moving on, it risks itself totally: Can a new unity be established out of all this, plus the novel, often strange, element? One can feel here the deep sense that Tillich felt of the precariousness as well as the creativity necessary to the dynamic life. Dewey and Whitehead had also felt that need for growth, for continual movement into the new, and the danger (yes, the death), of complacent reiteration in mediocrity and sameness. Neither felt, as did Tillich, the utter precariousness to all values of every such passage out of the past and into the new, necessary as that passage clearly was. Growth—personal, social, historical—is not just progress; it is also quite possibly nemesis.

To this innate precariousness of life we must add further the category of existence or estrangement: the demon of disruption that characterizes all aspects of our existence and, so to speak, actualizes these negative possibilities of our essential structure every time we aim at these positive goals. It is part of our essential structure as spirit to be "free," as we saw; an aspect of freedom, the self-transcending aspect that relates us to the infinite, is, paradoxically, to be free even of freedom; "to be free from itself, from a total bondage to finitude" (*ST* III:86). Thus are we capable of denying our essential nature by separating ourselves from our ground, our true selves, and from the other; we are free to "fall" into estrangement.

"Ambiguities," then, are not inherent in essential structure: they are, to be sure, ever-present *possibilities* of that dynamic, complex unity. Nor are they the mere result of "existence" with its inexorable drive to self-destruction. They represent the risks, unavoidably there, which the complex unity that is life inevitably faces when it, as it must, rushes precariously forward while it is at the same time continually jostled or sideswiped by existence. The complex and dynamic structure of life, precarious in any case, plus existence, equals ambiguities.

Let me quote a helpful passage: "The three functions of life unite elements of self-identity with self-alteration. But this unity is threatened by existential estrangement, which drives life in one or the other direction, thus disrupting the unity." Thus result our ambiguities: "Self integration is countered by disintegration, self-creation . . . by destruction, self-transcendence by profanation" (*ST* III:32). Ambiguities are negative possibilities of our structure rendered actual by estrangement as we realize the positive, creative fulfillment that our essential being requires of us. Now let us turn to our examples among the many kinds of ambiguities that Tillich describes.

We shall consider the ambiguities of the self-creativity of life as they appear in the creation and recreation anew of culture, especially with regard to "communal transformation," that is, politics (compare *ST* III:77–84). Tillich lists three such ambiguities. First, "exclusion and inclusion": a group *is* because it includes certain kinds of people and not others, and yet this basic principle of its existence leads (thanks to estrangement) to endless ambiguities. Second, "competition and equality": we are each different and yet also equal. Justice requires that both of these "facts" be recognized and creatively dealt with. Thanks to estrangement, countless ambiguities arise here, examples of unfairness. Third, "the ambiguity of leadership": leadership in a group is essential; it stands for the centering unity necessary for all life, in order that life exists and persists in existing. Yet no leader or leading group *is* that center essentially. The leader represents a mere part: a class or a family or a person *within* the larger group; thus, his or her power as center, again thanks to estrangement, can become intrinsically unfair and can lead to vast ambiguities. None of these *is* sin or even directly results from it; all are disruptive possibilities of our essential nature. And all result, thanks to the disruptive effect of estrangement, whenever life in the spirit realizes its potentialities and fulfills itself.

As these and all the other examples show, ambiguities are always there, and they are also destructive: "Life always includes essential and existential elements; this is the root of its ambiguity" (*ST* III:107). In turn, "all creatures long for an unambiguous fulfillment of their essential possibilities"; thus, among humans who are aware of this, "the quest for unambiguous life arises; this quest is for a life which has reached that towards which it transcends itself" (*ST* III:107). This is the "quest" or, as

Tillich calls it, "the question": not (to me) as desperate a cry as that which issued from either the anxieties of finitude or the self-destruction and despair of existence, but nevertheless an urgent and essential quest. For Tillich, the divine Spirit, the Spiritual Presence grasping us and uniting us to the unambiguous life of the divine, is the answer. This answer is universally given in all the religions, but its decisive presence, and thus the continuing criterion of that unambiguous and so renewing presence, was in the New Being in Jesus as the Christ.

As we see, Tillich has marshalled almost all of life's negatives—the essential ones of finitude, the absolutely destructive ones of estrangement, and the frustrating ones of life's ambiguities—and he has shown how the many names of the divine serve to answer these, our deepest needs. This form of "argument" is illustrated throughout his works and the various parts of his system, but nowhere more clearly than in this discussion of the Spirit. This question and answer, need and its fulfillment, represented for him the basic form of religion as it was of the *humanum*—finite spirit seeking the theonomy from which it has become estranged and in which all its powers and glories are fulfilled. In this sense, form and content, method and message, and, perhaps most important, his personal being and his reflections, were uniquely and powerfully united in Paul Tillich.

Part Three

Retrospective

10

The Role of the Theologian in Contemporary Society

This chapter is an exercise in retrospective and then imaginative extrapolation. Its purpose is to describe the role of the theologian in our contemporary situation as Tillich would (or might) have seen it. Since I have long found Tillich's view of this role both helpful and persuasive, this account will sail pretty close to my own view of that role—though unfortunately, it took Tillich to embody and enact it! Still I shall seek to steer as close to Tillich's emphases and categories as I can, as *he* might have used them in *our* context.

We must begin, as all Tillich's thought did, with the keystone of his system: God (the supreme object of religion) equals or is identical with being-itself (the ground of all finitude and so of the whole range of common experience). From this center flow the principles that determine and structure the theologian's role. First of all, with this identity is entailed the interrelatedness of religion and culture (of creative human being), for thus is "God" the depth of every aspect of cultural life. As a consequence, religion enacts itself in and through the forms of culture, and culture is characterized by an essential religious dimension. Secondly, from this identity there also stems the interrelatedness and interdependence of *theology* (as reflection on religion, on the *meaning* of being) and *philosophy* (reflection on the *structure* of being). From these two principles follows the correlative form of theological reflection: on the one hand, thought begins with a philosophical/theological analysis of the *structure* of finite existence (philosophy), including culture, in order to uncover its problematic, its "questions," so to say its *negative meanings* (theology). On the other hand, there follows a theological/philosophical description of the received "answers" to those questions, that is, a reflection on the religious symbols expressive of that answer (theology) and a reflection structured by the categories of finitude (philosophy) analogically and mythically used (*ST* I:59–66; II:13–16).

The important point is that, as we have seen, contrary to most simplistic and incorrect interpretations of Tillich (correlation means philosophical questions, theological answers), philosophical and theological elements lie on *both* sides (philosophical/theological questions and theological/philosophical answers). In turn, this understanding of correlation is crucial for the role of the theologian. He or she does *not* saunter through a distraught cultural scene passing out theological answers at each corner; Tillich never saw his own role in this way. More than most theologians, he was aware that culture in all its aspects, including philosophy, was fairly bristling with "answers" as well as wracked with problems. His point was, rather, that the answers which characterized culture, even a secular culture, whether in politics, law, art, morals, or philosohy, had as their deepest ground the *religious* dimension of the culture in question, its religious substance (in philosophy its "mystical a priori"), and that these answers were structured by the "mythos" of the culture and enacted in its common rites. As a consequence, one of the important cultural roles of the theologian was to uncover, analyze, and critique those answers. In other words, there were *theological* elements on both sides of the correlation represented by *philosophy* (some important questions of philosophy are questions of *meaning*, and all ultimate answers of philosophy have a *religious* source and mythos), as there are *philosophical* elements on both sides of the correlation represented by *theology*.

All profound and significant thought (embodied ontological reason) is a combination of philosophical and theological elements, of analysis of structure and uncovering of meaning, of reason and the depths of reason. Separated out into mere philosophy (autonomy) and unphilosophical theology (heteronomy), both lose their power, depth, and significance, and fail utterly. Then culture is, on the one hand, cut off from its own religious substance, and, on the other, religion is cut off from its possibilities of reflective power. Only in concert together can philosophy and theology either ask important questions or find healing answers, whether in cultural or religious matters, in "philosophy" or "theology" (compare *TPE*, chap. 6). There are, to be sure, differences between a secular community implicitly built around a religious substance and a religious community explicitly concentrating on its religious center, and so in reflection between a "theology of culture" and Christian systematic theology. In neither is it a simple case of cultural and philosophical questions receiving Christian or theological answers; in both theology of culture and in systematic theology, questions of structure and meaning, and so philosophical and theological elements, are intertwined.

The role of the theologian is, therefore, a dual role, a cultural as well as an ecclesiastical role; in this sense, too, she or he is "on the boundary." As philosophical analyst of the structure of finitude and theoretician of the religious dimension and of religious symbols, he or she is, if Tillich be right, as much relevant and at home in culture with its religious substance as in *ecclesia* with its religious center. In the end, in a *theonomous* culture and in a *true ecclesia* (i.e., in the Kingdom as the norm for both), theology of culture and systematic theology would in principle coalesce into one enterprise, each of the *kairoi* or creative epochs of culture or of history now being centered about *the Kairos* to which the Christian community witnesses. Thus is the role of the theologian "public" as well as "churchly." By this, Tillich would *not* mean that the theologian should seek to defend theology or theological conclusions by the criteria of culture (a sort of natural theology). Such self-defense on the part of theology would, I suspect, have represented for him a relatively insignificant enterprise and a bit narcissistic in character; on a deeper level, it would (at least in our age) also have to submit ontological (philosophical/theological) reason and its conclusions to the barren and profanizing criteria of technical reason.

On the contrary, the public task of the theologian is the analysis of public life and communal experience with regard to its religious issues and dimensions (e.g., not with regard to its economic, sociological, or psychological dimensions though each of these has a religious basis and ground). As noted, while by no means representing all the important issues and dimensions there are, those that are religious are important; and they are "ultimate." That is to say, these issues involve questions of our being and nonbeing, the security and insecurity of our being, and our courage in the face of this contingency, the deepest threat to and the deepest supports of our common life. The public task of theology is thus desperately significant even if its voice is not often heeded.

Every aspect of culture has its ground in the culture's religious substance. Art, science, morals, law, and economic and political structures each reflect and depend upon a particular apprehension characteristic of *that* culture of the unconditioned. Consequently, the history as well as the forms of a culture, its sequence of developments and events, takes its shape as much from the character and career of this religious dimension as from its sociological, economic, or political developments. Both the negativities of a culture's life, its "structures" of contradiction, disintegration, and destruction *and* the positive possibilities of that culture's life are, therefore, functions of the culture's relation to its religious substance, of its continuing temporal relation to eternity; they are to be understood fully *only* if this religious substance is also taken into account. For example, the *World Situation* is a typical Tillichean analysis of the relevant recent public history of the West. Reason, the culture-creative power of men and women, can only understand itself, in its relativity as well as in its forms of alienation, in relation to the *depths* of reason. And socialism, as an example of a cultural possibility, can only understand itself, its distortions, and its genuine possibilities as *religious* socialism. Theological analysis and critique are as essential for cultural and historical self-understanding as they are for religious self-understanding. To recall our starting point, if "God is being-itself," then the career of *being* must be understood through "God" (culture in terms of its religious dimension) as well as "God" through the structure, the contradictions, and the possibilities of being (religion in terms of philosophy).

Granted, then, the important public role of the theologian for Tillich, what in our day might a theologian, understanding his or her task in Tillich's terms, contribute to our common self-understanding? Tillich's own analyses penetrated with illuminating power into an amazing variety of areas of culture: art; economic, social, and political life; psychological existence, both individual and social; science and technology; law and morals as well as organized religion. Since, therefore, the Tillichean theologian in our day might well discourse with effect on any number of presently relevant themes, any selection is fairly arbitrary. I shall choose five such themes.[1] With most of these five themes Tillich himself was deeply concerned; and because, since his time, each of them has if anything become more significant, I have chosen to represent them here. In each case we see a problematic area of current cultural existence illuminated by the kind of philosophical/theological analysis that Tillich was wont to provide. In offering to the wider public these "theological" interpretations of culture, the theologian fulfills a significant part of his or her role in contemporary society.

1.

First, the problem of the *unity* of the diverse realms of personal and cultural existence was a question reflected frequently in Tillich's thought. The apprehension of this unity, he thought, was particularly weak in our time; as a consequence, on many levels a destructive sense of disunity

---

1. The most important theme, both to Tillich and to our own day, is the political-social one, that of communal justice and so, for him, of religious socialism. Since we have dealt with this aspect of Tillich's thought in chapter 1, I will more or less omit it here.

prevails. The consequence of this in intellectual or reflective life is the disunity of the university; the noncommunication between disciplines; the lack of common categories or language bridging the physical, the psychological, and the social sciences, between the sciences and humanistic studies; and, finally, all of these cognitive or theoretical disciplines with the practical, shaping, and so normative disciplines concerned with technical development, political action, legal practice and reformation, and the moral obligations of life.

This disunity on the linguistic, conceptual, and theoretical level, crippling enough to be sure, indicates a deeper disunity in our personal and social existence. How is the self which, as a body, sleeps, eats, exercises, makes love, shops at the market, and goes to the doctor related to the professional self who has a job, the political self who votes, the mortal self that sees a lawyer about its will, the anxious self late for an appointment with its analyst, the self in love or desolately rejected—the self who asks about the meaning of its life? Is there any possibility of unity, of identity within *one's own* self, amid these diverse functions and activities of daily life; is there only the same body in all of them, and if so, how is *it* related to its own interests and activities? The disunity of the university is a theoretical reflection of this same disunity of each self in culture and of the professions and functions of the wider culture itself. It represents estrangement of body from spirit, of desiring from willing, of knowing from valuing and doing, of individuals from themselves and from each other. Its personal terror, as Tillich often referred to it, is that of "falling apart into a hundred pieces" (*ST* II:61); its social and political threat is the separation of expertise and purposes, of means and ends, of *techne* and of norms, of rational knowledge and political decisions. A part of Tillich's own amazing significance for American culture as a whole was his role in providing in all he said a deep sense of the unity of human being and of being generally and of supplying a philosophical language for expressing that unity in categorical form.

This task is, of course, primarily philosophical. It is the precise task and aim of ontology (or "metaphysics" in Whitehead's sense of that word) to provide categories "in terms of which every aspect of our experience may be interpreted" (*ST* I:166). For Tillich, however, the unity of finite being and the unity of the reflective interpretation and so expression of it stems from the *depth* of reason in which subject and object, self and world, thought and external reality find their common ground and so point of unity. Thus a *philosophical* explication of the unity of finite being is itself dependent on a *religious* apprehension of the depth of reason. Again, both philosophy and theology unite and complete themselves in the union of

these two elements, namely, philosophical/theological thinking. The first
public role of the theologian is the explication, nurturing, and preservation of the unity of personal existence and in that the unity of cultural life.

2.

The second area in which for Tillich theology would make a significant
contribution is the issue of *rationality*, in our epoch the question of
technical rationality. For Tillich, "reason" did not represent, as it does for
most of us, only one aspect of creative spiritual power, opposed to or at
least differentiated from imagination, valuing, or the moral, the artistic,
the emotive, or even from self-giving and self-dedication. Rather (and
again that powerful drive toward unity manifests itself), reason represents
the total creative spiritual power or capacity of human being. Thus as a
consequence, this realm encompasses not only cognitive and organizational capacities—science and technology—but every other realm or dimension of cultural life as well: morals, law, political and economic
structures, art, even religion. As it is found at work in us, reason, even in
its most objective cognitive endeavors, evinces elements not usually recognized as aspects of the rational: deep, even "ultimate" concern (for the
truth); an emotional attachment to an end and to the community devoted
to that end (as in science); dedication to the moral norms of that community and its aims; a degree of empathetic participation in its object, and
so on. To separate these elements from "reason," to strip the rational
down to bare cognitive capability and technical organizing, is, therefore,
to divest it of characteristics essential to its *own* functioning, to endanger
its own creative exercise. Above all, it is to subject a now purely technical
rational expertise, unguided by its own norms and directionless without
its own ends, to the lethal risk of itself being used for other, nonrational,
even demonic, purposes. For reason, having been confined to the laboratory, the planning office, and the factory—"technical reason"—is now
itself alienated from the larger issues, questions, and decisions of culture:
political, moral, existential, and religious. These latter, therefore, now
bereft of rational norms, rational goals, and the capacity of rational
assessment and decision, tend toward irrationality and absolutization.
Thus can a "pure" science and a merely instrumental technology become
the potent instruments of economic or political purposes (of large corporations, fascist and communist ideologies, even religious fanaticism) that
are now *themselves* utterly irrational, absolutist, and oppressive. In this
way, autonomous rationality pushed far enough finds itself meta-
morphosed into its dialectical opposite, a demonic religious heteronomy.
Such was Tillich's own view of the "fate" of rationality if an unimpeded

autonomy was allowed to run its course: from a powerful, creative, originating, and probably rebellious (against a previous heteronomy) theonomy (ontological reason), through an autonomy centering more and more on technical reason, to a final oppressive and self-destructive heteronomy. To him, the development of modernity since the Enlightenment and down to his own experience of the Germany of the 1920s, '30s, and '40s more than justified empirically this speculative/historical (a kind of mirror-image of Hegel) schema of creative synthesis, unravelling thesis, and final destructive antithesis. The even greater relevance of this schema to developments since the '40s into our present seems uncontestable. Philosophy has become even more non-ontological since Tillich's day. (He never really believed that positivism, language philosophy, and analytic philosohy could be serious.) Political science and social and psychological theory tend more and more toward "science" and away from theory; technical and vocational rather than liberal or humanistic patterns of education rule more and more college and university curricula; politics is more and more directed by the requirements of the dominance of *instruments* and *their* needs over the humans who use them and their purposes. It is obvious that the understanding of the rational as the capacity or use of a tool or skill (expertise) has enlarged and grown dramatically away from such categories as insight, imagination, understanding, and wisdom—capacities not only rational but also necessary for cultural health. Whereas in Tillich's day fideism, nationalism, fascism, and an authoritarian communism represented to him almost apocalyptic signs of a coming heteronomy, of the end of an era, in our own day two even clearer, if not more dramatic, signs have appeared of the lethal consequences of technical rationality and of the deepening split between the dwindling forces of rational autonomy and the advancing evidence of a new religious heteronomy.

The first, which we shall briefly mention, is the crisis in the relations of a scientific and technical culture to nature. Tillich had been well aware of the political and social dangers of a technical reason that made "objects" out of the human beings it sought to know, categorize, and manipulate; in knowing them thereby and using them as mere objects, technical reason, he said, not only does not know its object but destroys the very object it seeks to know. Recently, it has become clear that a merely instrumental knowledge of nature, and so a merely manipulative use of it, also fails in the end to understand it and culminates by destroying it—and in destroying it, it destroys us. Nature is *misunderstood* as merely an object over against us, as are we, its knowers, if we understand ourselves as merely objective knowers and manipulators of its forces.

What is lacking here is the *correlation* of objective logos (system) and subjective logos (knowing and policies), the *participation* of subject and object in one another, as well as their difference and distance—in this case, the necessary participation of human culture in, and its fostering of, the system of nature if either one is to survive. A Tillichean philosopher/theologian has much that is relevant to say about the spiritual origins of the present ecological crisis and a good number of categories to offer that may be helpful in the rethinking of the relation of human being to nature. An ontological and a religious understanding of the unity of the natural and the human world (and on what other grounds could that unity be comprehended?), long scorned by the empirical sciences as representing the dying vestige of a primitive, animistic view of nature, may well in our day provide the best opportunity in the West for the retrieval of that lost unity. Technical reason can only know the human as an object, as an objective product of nature, and it can only know nature as objective and so separated from the human subject; thus, it loses both humanity and nature. With his background in German romanticism and *Lebensphilosophie*, Tillich's approach is now relevant in an area for which his generation had little direct concern since the problematic of that area had not yet surfaced: the correlation of logos in human being *and* in nature and the unity of human being with nature in the ground of being.

I will add here one further word on the subject of the technical, industrial, and commercial culture. In the last decade, this worldwide "modern" culture has revealed itself to us as a veritable predator of nature's resources, not only of fuel, but of air, water, and soil, of fecundity itself. Human being here manifests itself as infinitely greedy, as seeking to use and to use up everything there is, in Tillich's colorful phrase, to "take the whole world into itself" for its own well-being and ultimately for its own self-destruction. Certainly there are elements of pride or hubris in this demonic process, pride of knowledge and of expertise and, above all, pride of power, the economic power evidenced by exploitation. There can be little doubt, however, that Tillich's category of "concupiscence," of infinite and so inordinate desire (*ST* II:52), desire to grasp and use the whole world (a category he lifted right out of Augustine) hit the nail squarely on the head long before the ecological crisis made its appearance. As Tillich would put it, this demonic use and using up of nature bespeaks a deep alienation of human being from itself, from nature, and from its own infinite ground; consequently, it seeks that infinity of meaning, and so seeks itself and its unity, through taking the infinite into itself, by possessing and using the finite *infinitely*. To a post-Freudian generation, "concupiscence," oriented as it had been exclusively to sexuality, had long gone out of fashion as a primal form of sin. Tillich has, in reinterpreting it, given it a much wider meaning as the prime symptom of the estrangement of human being from the whole world of goods and so of nature—and as the key "sin" of our technical, commercial culture.

The second new "sign" of the progressive disintegration of an autonomous rational culture into one split into technical and heteronomous elements is the appearance in the last decade of religious cults and of the religious right. These developments would not have surprised Tillich. A technical culture does not eradicate the depth of reason nor the need of the culture for it. On the contrary, ends, meaning, and hope remain as essentials for existence; myth and cult remain as the only verbal and behavioral forms in which these, and the tragic elements of life, can be expressed; and the infinite and holy ground of all is continuously apprehended. Fifteen years after his death, all this has been amply confirmed. Religious cults have mushroomed among the middle classes and the intelligentsia, especially, one may note, around the great university centers. For the individual, and so for religious communities that are "set apart," these religious cults, structured in theory by mythical language and in practice by trans-rational meditative rites, provide principles of personal moral discipline, of personal goals and ends in life, of meaning in wider history, and of religious union totally omitted from the secular, technical, and commercial culture and yet desperately needed by the inhabitants of that culture. A Tillichean analysis can help immensely to illuminate the social and spiritual conditions that prepared the way for the "new" religious movements, in providing anthropological categories that may mediate the present split between an official autonomous, scientific, and technical culture and these new separated religious elements in it, and in providing theological categories that can express and thematize the positive healing powers without question present in many of these movements.

3.

The central theme, as we noted, of Tillich's theology of culture was the interpenetration of religion and culture, the presence of a religious dimension or substance in each aspect of cultural life. Thus, whenever religious elements are officially excluded from daily life in secular culture, ultimate concern, myth, and cult manifest *themselves* in new and "unreligious" forms. They reappear in exotic, "set apart" religious communities and even as the threat of a new theocracy. One of the more significant levels of this same manifestation of "religious substance" illuminates a prominent trait of our contemporary political epoch, namely, the "ideological" character of our fundamental politics. This provides the third theme we shall address.

By ideology here I refer to the subtle transformation of political and economic theory into a "religious" symbolic structure, that is, into myth, when the "theory" begins to function as the uniting, shaping, and guiding ethos of a social community. This is what has happened to capitalistic and democratic social theory as they have been reshaped into, say, the "American way of life"—that set of social, economic, and political symbols which in turn shape fundamental American aims, norms, institutions, vocations, education, and many patterns of behavior and judgment. To the Marxist, this whole symbolic structure is, of course, a "capitalistic ideology," that which *claims* to be "science" but which (1) actually sanctifies and so justifies the capitalistic social structure, (2) provides a moral cloak for imperial self-interest, and (3) serves the sole interests of the ruling bourgeois classes. Interestingly, this is *also* what has happened to Marxism as it moved from a critical social theory to becoming "embodied"; it recently functioned (or sought to do so) as the constitutive ethos shaping, directing, sanctifying, and justifying the structural elements of Russia's economic and political life, its patterns of vocational and educational life, and its most fundamental policies. To the western social scientist, certain that his or her own theory is "objective science," this Marxist symbolic structure is by no means science but pure ideology. By their use of this word, western commentators mean a symbolic structure (1) assented to on the grounds of authority and not of evidence, (2) asserted because of faith, not rational assessment, and (3) functioning as the cloak for the predatory aims of world Communism and of party rule. Probably both are in large part right about the other, though not in their flattering estimates of their own "scientific" objectivity!

In any case, as many commentators have pointed out, the appearance and dominance of powerful ideologies, of national, racial, religious, as well as political and economic ideologies, mark our epoch. The systematic denial of ideological elements in the science of each bloc—because "we are empirical and pragmatic" if we be bourgeois, and because "we are proletarian" if we be communist—indicates the pervasive importance of ideology. In turn, criticism of the ideological elements of modern theory, so that communication between communities can become possible again ("ideology critique"), has become a major enterprise for philosophers and social theorists alike.

My point is that the dominant presence of ideologies in our epoch and this active current interest in them provide an opportunity for a significant public role for the Tillichean theologian/philosopher. For such an analyst has something unique and helpful to add to a philosophical/ epistemological, economic, sociological, anthropological, political, or psychological interpretation of these phenomena. That is because, as Tillich reiterated, ideologies express and thematize the mythic structure, the religious substance, of the culture—as in traditional societies organized religion provided that mythic structure. It is, therefore, no accident that the fact of ideology (and the word itself), a secular, symbolic structure unifying a community, appears just after the French Revolution, when organized religion was officially removed from the center of public life.

The religious dimensions of ideologies consist not only in the fact that they *function* as traditional religions once did, though that is surely significant. On the contrary, on the objective side these religious elements consist in the intrinsic constitutive traits of ultimacy, universality, and meaningfulness that characterize each ideology. Each ideology appears for its adherents as *the* truth about *all* of history and society; in so doing, it answers all the most pressing problems of *meaning* in communal life; and it provides the most fundamental *moral* norms and *social* goals for that common life. On the subjective side, individual persons relate to these ideologies through commitment and assent ("faith"); each ideology requires or entails an ultimate loyalty, obedience, and, in the end, self-sacrifice; and in "doctrine" they generate the polarity of orthodoxy and heresy or deviationism. "America, love her or leave her" expresses an advanced ideological attitude that implies all of the above, as do countless elements of recent Russian life. The dominance of ideology in cultures seeking to base themselves solely on autonomous rationality *also* calls for a Tillichean theological hermeneutic if the full dimensions of our ideological age are to be uncovered and understood.

4.

The return of the unheeded and forgotten religious dimension has not, however, been confined either to the so-called cults or to the "religious" character of "secular" politics. Perhaps just as culturally, politically, and spiritually significant has been the dramatic rise in American culture of ultraconservative Protestantism to public as well as private prominence, religiously the fundamentalist wing of evangelicalism and politically the powerful "religious right." This represents the fourth theme. In the last two or three decades the charismatic and fundamentalist movements have, in and out of the major denominations, represented by far the fastest growing segment of American religion. Further, they have progressively entered (or re-entered) the American public scene, and in a movement and depth utterly surprising both to a "secular" and to a liberal religious culture that thought orthodox religion to be on its way out of history. Fundamentalist "Christian" schools, colleges, and even universities have sprung up. Television and radio programs devoted to fundamentalist evangelism and healing dominate large segments of the communications industry; such programs raise incredible volumes of money, and their leaders have become notorious public and even political figures. In the sphere of public law, moreover, fundamentalist groups have embarked on moral-political crusades against abortion, homosexuality, and sex education, not to mention near misses in the attempt to legislate, via creation science, their own theological teachings in public education, on the one hand, and to capture the grass roots of the Republican Party, on the other. The leading American military (and diplomatic!) "hero" of the last decade, Colonel North, is a declared member of the evangelical right, and on the desk of one of the most revered coaches in professional football, Thomas Landry, sits a book by the Reverend Jerry Falwell.

Fundamentalist religion at the end of the '80s is thus by no means an esoteric, fringe phenomenon, a carry-over of horse and buggy revivalism into an alien modern age. On the contrary, it is a "modern" phenomenon, fully at home in the technical, commercial, political, and social scene and making its disturbingly effective claims to dominate that scene. It is perhaps too much to say that it now defines "mainstream America," but insofar as it represents a coherent religious, moral, and political movement, it is making as credible a claim to define the "Moral Majority" as does any other segment of American life. As our scientific, atomic age has matured, orthodox religion, in fact (as in Israel and the Islamic world) the *most* orthodox forms of religion, has not receded but advanced steadily forward, not only as a movement taking increasingly conservative theological and moral positions, but, as was quite unexpected, even more as one advancing in ever new areas its theocratic claims to dominate the legal, political, and moral life of "Christian America."

To anyone who has worked their way through Tillich's thought, or this volume, this fundamentalist movement, uniting as it does ultraorthodox belief and theocratic political ambitions, represents a classic example of Tillich's category of heteronomy: dogmatic, exclusivist, intolerant, and oppressive of alternative views either in the religious or cultural spheres; nationalistic, militaristic (in fact bellicose!), latently racist (compare Falwell and Robertson vis-à-vis South Africa and segregated schools), and externally intensely "pious" or "religious." Its perceived enemy is the mature *autonomy* of modern culture, with special emphasis on the latter's relativism, pluralism, skepticism, and implicit atheism ("secular humanism"), not to mention those whom it regards as the liberal hangers-on, both humanistic and religious, and their "perverted" saints (Darwin, Marx, and Freud) and long-standing alliance with communism. As if they had read Tillich, they see themselves as rescuing the original "theonomy" of American life with its purported union of Bible, democracy, free-private enterprise, and technology from this secular relativism and pluralism, and reintroducing—as all heteronomies claim to do—the "original" bases of American life: the "values" of God, family, liberty. And to do this they are, again like all heteronomies, quite willing to dispense with the cultural, political, and religious *autonomy* that they feel to be alien both to our historic tradition and our present needs. Historical myths about "Protestant America" (most of them quite false) abound, communicated via the "cults" of evangelical preaching. Their allies are the conservative capitalists, though neither Wall Street nor the New York neo-conservatives are happy with allies robed in polyester! And their enemies are the liberals among academics, writers, and clergy. As a leading creation-scientist (a Ph.D. in biochemistry from Berkeley) said to me in 1985: "Gilkey, you may have the academy, but we have the White House." I had to admit he was right!

Again it is quite clear how helpful Tillich's analysis of the dialectic of theonomy, autonomy, and heteronomy is to the enterprise of interpreting this disturbing history. Perhaps the major cultural and political task for the theologian of our day is to undertake in convincing form this Tillichean analysis: how the deep anxieties of our time combine with the relativism and skepticism of developed autonomy to render unbearable a situation without spiritual ground or discernable meaning (in certainty, in norms, in confidence); and how as a consequence a heteronomous "faith," expressed in renewed myth and cult, can then *re-enter* the modern scene with terrifying power and destructive results.

5.

We have cited and analyzed four elements of our current cultural scene which a Tillichean analysis, based on the philosophical and theological presuppositions intrinsic to his thought, might vastly illuminate. This illumination of the theologian's surrounding culture through creative theoretical interpretation of cultural developments and problems, possibilities and perils, constitutes *one* of the major public roles of the theologian in the Tillichean tradition. It represents part, and a major part, of what he meant by a theology of culture. This is, however, not the only public role of the theologian. For surely the central theological task is the creative and contemporary self-interpretation of the message of the religious community itself and the setting of that message in terms of the present cultural "situation," namely, the task of systematic theology. This will be our fifth theme.

This theological task also represents a public as well as an ecclesiastical role, and for two reasons. First, because systematic theology is constituted by the correlation of cultural and religious elements, of philosophy and of theology, theology possesses a common ground with every theoretically alert member of that culture and so presents to us a public rather than esoteric set of materials. Second, the church is an institution with a mission *to* and, therefore, *in* history and within the cultural communities of history. Ideally (eschatologically), the church would bear, represent, express, and mediate the Spiritual Presence to the wider cultural community; it would express and manifest the theonomous center of the culture, its religious substance; it would be the religious center of the "Kingdom" in the same way as a fully theonomous culture would be the Kingdom's historical manifestation. In actuality, because of the alienation or estrangement *both* of the culture *and* of the church, no such theonomy is ideally actual, nor is the Spiritual Presence anything but fragmentary, even in the church. The present church, therefore, is suffused with ambiguity as well as with grace, and it must await its own redemption before it can fulfill fully its own historical task.

Nevertheless, the role of the church is *in* the world, united with culture both in estrangement, in grace, and in promise. The New Being, to which it witnesses, is a gift to the *world*, to the world's *entire* life, and so to culture. The problems or contradictions which the New Being heals are the *world's* problems and contradictions; its promises are promises for the world. The present task of the church is, therefore, within culture, not apart from it. It is as much the task of nurturing, criticizing, and reshaping the religious substance of *culture* closer to the New Being which the church seeks to bear and to the Kingdom it proclaims as it is the task of nurturing and fostering the community of the *ecclesia*. (The many *kairoi* of cultural history are submitted by the *ecclesia* to the criterion of the *Kairos* or center of history in the New Being; the Kingdom as a symbol refers to that point where history and New Being are united in an eschatological theonomy.) Thus the church retrieves, nurtures, and fosters the "Catholic substance" of *culture* as well as its own "substance," and it enacts over against *culture*, as well as over against itself, the Protestant principle of criticism and judgment. As the one whose task is the theoretical self-interpretation of the *ecclesia*, itself a cultural-religious institution, itself "on the boundary," the theologian *qua* systematic theologian has, therefore, also a cultural role. In the following brief comments

I shall try to describe five elements of that role today, that is, the ways that the development of a contemporary and relevant *systematic theology* can—if heeded at all—contribute to the present wider contemporary cultural and social situation.

First, the most direct and central task of the theologian is the creation of a systematic theology, a unified, encompassing, and intelligible statement of the Christian message. As noted, as a correlation of situation and message, this statement is couched within the terms and categories of the cultural situation. It seeks to answer the culture's problems and contradictions; and it states its positive, redemptive message through the categories of the culture's self-understanding. A systematic theology so constructed is, therefore, also a contemporary *cultural* document, a part (the Christian part, to be sure) of the culture's self-interpretation. It unites the religious and the intellectual (scientific, social scientific, psychological, historical, artistic, literary, and philosophical) traditions of that culture, and in uniting them it brings each "up-to-date" in terms of a novel interpretation in contemporary terms. This *reinterpretation* of a given historical destiny in terms of new perspectives on new problems represents precisely Tillich's view of creative cultural and historical activity, of the way the new can creatively enter into passage as a union of tradition and new possibility. Thus, systematic theology unites past and future, "through the Eternal Now," into a new synthesis, as well as the other often disparate elements of a separated present cultural life referred to earlier. This temporal as well as spatial unifying task must take place in every area and discipline of culture; in systematic theology, it occurs in that area closest to the religious substance of the culture, in the fostering and the criticism of that substance. A classic statement of the eternal message in contemporary and novel form represents the paradigm of historical creativity for Tillich, a model, if done well, of creative spirit.

Second, systematic theology begins with the analysis of the *structures* of our finitude (philosophy), and its aim is to uncover the *meaning* for our being and nonbeing of those structures (theology). By "meanings" here we refer to *(a)* the crises and possibilities with which being finite and yet free (i.e., being human) seem to present us, *(b)* the deep, ineradicable modes of anxiety that accompany this finitude, and *(c)* the possibilities of courage that are open to us and that alone can overcome ("conquer") that anxiety. The point *theologically* of this philosophical/theological analysis of our finitude is, of course, to show in the "answering" section what in our experience God is, and so that to which this central word in religious discourse refers, namely, as the infinite power of being conquering the experienced nonbeing of our finitude and so as the source of the courage common to all creative human existence. It is, however, evident that this theological point, central as it is, does not exhaust the value, for believers and unbelievers alike, of this philosophical/theological analysis. To uncover and illuminate the structural sources of our deepest and most pervasive anxieties, granted the latter are there, is of great value to all.

To be aware of the unconscious but always effective terrors, as well as the possibilities, of our temporality, spatiality, and contingency, and to face realistically in the context of the divine ground the overwhelming threat of death, presents to culture as a whole, which also groans under these anxieties, one creative way, the Christian way, through which these anxieties can be borne. This form of theological analysis brings to consciousness the *religious* (existential) problems involved in our human being as such and brings to awareness and so into real possibility one answer to them. Since these are problems fully as characteristic of ordinary persons in culture as of ordinary persons in church, this sort of analysis has a most creative cultural role to play. For example, the particular forms that anxiety about space take will shift with each cultural context; they are of *one* sort in a nomadic culture, of *another* sort in a high-rise apartment in Chicago. Thus, the analysis of the meaning (theology) of spatiality (philosophy) must be continually renewed with an eye to each particular social situation, but the value of this theological/ philosophical enterprise as a most creative form of religious reflection is constant.

It might also be added that this sort of ontological, theological analysis, an analysis of the structures of our finitude and of the religious problems involved in those structures, is particularly relevant to American religion. Stemming from the Calvinist and evangelical traditions, most American Protestantism has been primarily concerned with the *moral* problems of being human, as if these were the only issues in which true Christianity should be interested. Insofar as death remained an important issue, it was understood under and comprehended within moral categories: a "bad" life resulted in eternal death after death, a "good" life in salvation from death. Thus, vast regions of genuine and devastating spiritual problems were left unaddressed, problems as debilitating to Americans as to any other humans: growing older, loss of place, radical contingency or insecurity, utter dependence on undependable factors, and so on. To be sure, selfishness and inordinate desire add to these problems of our finitude; they do not, however, create them. In fact, as Tillich pointed out, it is more often than not in despairing *reaction* to these ineradicable sources of anxiety in our finitude that we go morally sour, that is, become overly selfish or inordinately concupiscent. Thus an ontological, theological analysis of a Tillichean sort can open up many significant areas left unexplored by other types of American religious witness and theology.

Third, I shall be brief about the most important facet of the role of the Tillichean theologian in contemporary society, for this facet is obvious and well covered in other volumes on Tillich. This concerns the political role of the church and so of theology, a role that quite dominated Tillich's early career in Germany and which he continued to take very seriously to the end of his life.

The grounds for this political concern have already appeared and reappeared in these chapters: the interweaving of religion and culture, an interweaving that penetrates to every aspect of both culture and theology. Thus, on the side of culture, the health of culture depends on the character of its religious substance, on its capacity for self-affirmation and courage, and so the character of its fundamental aims and norms; further, its health is a function of the justice of its structures, a function of its capacity for self-criticism and self-judgment; lastly, it depends on its courage and hope in the face of the future. All of these capacities represent "religious" issues intrinsic to creative cultural life; each of them appears in relation to the eternal ground of being and meaning, to the divine; each is compromised if politics seeks to remain autonomous and not the-onomous. Thus are religious and theological dimensions necessary for passage toward a healthy culture and so for a creative politics.

On the side of theology, the gospel (and so theology) becomes esoteric and possibly heteronomous when it is unrelated to culture; it loses its touch with the structures of life and becomes empty and irrelevant. It loses its claim to justice and becomes fatuous or ideological. In centering solely on the individual, it loses both community and history and so becomes meaningless to the individual who lives in both. In sum, the categories of history and the Kingdom drop out as relevant to the New Being and so as religious and theological concerns. Such an omission is untrue both to the original message and to the human situation. The drive toward justice and so toward the Kingdom is, therefore, as essential an aspect of any theological statement of the message as is any other aspect; thus is theology essentially political if it is to be theology at all.

Possibly more than any other of the issues essential to theology, the political aspect changes as the cultural situation changes. This Tillich discovered when he moved to America; political problems and require-ments now took a different form than they had in Weimar Germany. He wisely and humbly chose to be largely silent on these issues until late in his career. The factor of change of the political situation, both domestic and international, is even more evident since his time. Vast historical and social transformations have occurred from the '30s, '40s, and '50s, changes that require at every point reformulations of socio-theological theory, some of them radical. The problems of justice in economic life, in social status and opportunity, and among the races and nations remain, of course; but in the following areas quite new issues have arisen.

The dominance of the West, both in political and in cultural power, has all but vanished. Socialism has joined capitalism/democracy in showing deep, actual, and so theoretical ambiguity (in economic creativity as in politics) and thus as also in need of essential rethinking and reformulation. The international rectitude of the liberal democracies has been sharply put in question by their economic dominance of other cultural centers, especially Africa and South America, and the assumed virtue of their domestic institutions challenged by the black and feminist movements. The Third World has appeared as an originative, autonomous part of the common world with its own needs, values, and aims. Finally, a common ecological crisis has suddenly appeared (since 1970) that dominates every political and social question for the future. Each of these new appearances requires a different formulation from the religious socialism of Tillich in the 1920s, and even (one suspects) from some of the more simplistic socialist aims of much recent liberationist theology. Yet with all this need for reformulation, the crucial role of the theologian in political matters remains, and for all the reasons Tillich so clearly stated.

Fourth, as the above makes clear, ours is an age not only of dramatic change for the West but of apparent decline, a "time of troubles" when few of our established institutions seem able to cope with a mounting sequence of crises. Tillich realized all this deeply; but the reality of the appearance in power of *other* cultural traditions to near dominance as well as the fissures in our own cultural house was not part of his world as it is of ours. Thus, the sense of dismay at the present and of despair over the future is perhaps deeper now, and the grounds for hope in the future less certain. For now much less depends on *us* than in his day, when only the western powers seemed to be able to make important decisions. Added to these historical changes is the ecological crisis, looming darkly and menacingly over every political and economic possibility for the future. In this historical situation, courage, hope, and confidence in relation to the future are very important, for the culture as a whole as well as for the church. If a nation becomes anxious, increasingly insecure, with little remaining confidence in its destiny and little hope for new possibilities in its future, then it becomes a danger to all at each new threat. Thus the theological message of promise, of a *kairos* to come, even if it is not what we expect or want, is of very great significance. The theological analysis of the forms of our estrangement is constantly crucial, else we understand neither our problems nor ourselves. But in our contemporary situation, it is the promise of Providence "in spite of" all the visible facts, of a new *kairos* developing out of the contradictions of the present, that is most important.

Fifth, the final contemporary cultural issue to be noted is one to which the theologian can make a significant contribution. The recently achieved "oneness" of the world economically and politically has made the continual and deep interrelation and interaction of cultures more and more of a reality, increasing even since Tillich's time. Added to this is the crucial aspect noted, the "shaking of the foundations" of western culture itself and as a consequence the disappearance for westerners and non-westerners alike of any sense of western superiority, and so of the superiority of western religions. This latter point (not the first one) has opened the West to the influence of "alien" cultures and religions in a way undreamed of before, except among esoteric circles. Thus non-western religions have appeared in *power* amongst us, that is, as traditions obviously possessing both truth and grace. No modern western theologian can possibly deny this powerful presence or fail to take account of it in his or her systematic theology. Tillich felt deeply this new set of relations between religions in his last years and wished above all that he could live to deal creatively with this new situation. He knew well that the easy ways by which Christian theology had previously demoted its rivals were now irrelevant or impossible and that a new understanding of "religions" and of their relation to Christian (and western philosophical!) claims was necessary. This is one of the two or three major inescapable theological problems of our time, one that has appeared in a quite new and radical form in our present generation.

Anyone familiar with Tillich's carefully articulated view of revelation and with his sense of the immanent presence of the divine power of being and meaning to every creature, culture, and religion will see at once the immense possibilities latent in his thought with regard to this problem. To him, being grasped by the divine power gave courage to every creative human existence, and an apprehension of some facet of the divine meaning founded every cultural *Gestalt*. To him, each religion embodied answers as well as questions and so reflected, in however fragmentary a form, the New Being. All of this offers immense opportunity for understanding the truth and grace present in other religions. Tillich's doctrine, moreover, of the true "medium" that sacrifices itself and its own particularity in pointing beyond itself, can provide one way of understanding how a religion can relate creatively and humbly to other religions and yet preserve its own characteristic witness.

My main point, however, is the contribution of a theological analysis of this problem to culture as a whole. That an understanding on the deepest level of other cultures is now imperative for us in the West is obvious to all. It is equally obvious (at least in relation to *them!*) that each of these other cultures contains a "religious substance" that must be understood first: How can an Islamic land, India, China, or Japan, be understood at all without comprehension of its religious heritage? Tillich helps to explicate this point elegantly and provides categories that mediate between that *religious substance*, to be comprehended by the methods appropriate to the study of religion (among them a *theological* understanding), and the *cultural substance* in question: its history, economic and political institutions, art, morals, and so on. Area studies departments concerned with the Middle East, with India, China, and Japan have begun to recognize this point and to give important place to an analysis of the relevant religious heritage alongside of analysis of other elements of the culture. Insofar as the religion in question (or, as noted, a current ideology) is central to the shape of the entire culture, a *theological* analysis like Tillich's, uniting the religious center with its cultural expressions, is also necessary for intelligibility; otherwise, all else will be understood through the psychological or economic aspects of that culture alone. Thus, in a world of interacting and now of interlocking cultures, that is to say, *our* world, a theological analysis of a Tillichean sort, but reworked to fit this very new situation, is necessary. As is evident, there is a great deal for a Tillichean theologian to do in our age!

11

Pathos and Comedy: Recollections of Tillich

Paul Tillich was a lovable as well as an awesome man. There was something childlike about him, a hint of vulnerability, of near help-lessness, that made even much younger persons, like graduate students or assistants, feel protective about him. He seemed (even if he may not have been) barely able to cope, near at times to panic, subject himself to the terrifying modes of angst of which he spoke with such familiarity. I always felt much more able to handle the world than he did. No one even remotely ever felt this way in relation to Reinhold Niebuhr! This vulner-able aspect of Tillich, of course, united with his vast intellectual power and the strange magnetic vitality that emanated from him to give him extraordinary personal presence, a kind of dialectical *coincidentia op-positorum* which, like the universe of being he reported to us, combined at once dynamics, form, and alienation, in short both depth and mystery. His was a power of personal being that was also accessible, almost "cuddly," and so a numinous *power* united with a *pathos* and *comedy* that were infinitely attractive.

As his writings show, Tillich's intellectual capacities were formidable indeed; but this was never, to his friends, the side of Tillich that shone forth from him and encountered the friend. It was his smoldering vitality, united beneath the surface with his angst and pathos, that one first apprehended in his speech and in his entire being. Only slowly did his all-encompassing, all-ordering mind appear, but always it was in unity with this opposite, his fragmentary and vulnerable finitude.

In him, therefore, spirit in all its matchless, universal power was starkly embodied, finitized, incarnate in estrangement, and so vulnerable, subject always to the potentiality of disarray, disorder, and disintegration. Tillich was—so it seems now to me—conscious of this at each moment. And this apprehended unity of power and of powerlessness gave his speech its own rare power. Needless to say, an unconscious (or perhaps conscious) apprehension by his hearers of this unity of opposites in his person added to that power of his speech. Still, what was rare about Tillich's public speech—his addresses and especially his sermons[1]—was his ability to communicate with his whole audience on the deepest existential level as well as on the intellectual, conceptual level. He understood and could speak to the hidden but menacing lostness, alienation, loneliness, unacceptability, helplessness, and terror among his hearers as well as provide categories for comprehending these frightening depths and open up ways to conquer their terror. Not all of his audience could understand the grandeur of his philosophical and theological vision; but few of them failed to hear and respond to his at-oneness with them in his angst and yet in his courage and faith. I remember a woman saying in amazement after hearing one of his Cole lectures in Nashville, where he filled the great Vanderbilt auditorium every night for a week: "I did not understand a word of what that man said, but he was speaking directly to me every moment of the lecture."

Stories gathered naturally around Tillich. This was not because he was "funny," either a natural comic or an experienced raconteur—anything but. It followed, rather, from this rare union of power and pathos, of supreme intellectual strength with a sort of inner frailty and outer vulnerability. Funny things happened to him. He was just helpless enough to be continually buffeted here and there; and he was strong and powerful enough so that this buffeting was funny and neither pathetic nor tragic.

I remember when I was a graduate assistant going into his office and finding him sitting there softly wringing his hands; he looked up relieved to see me. "Oh Langdon, tell me, v'ere is the Grand Central Station?"— this in 1948 at least a dozen years after his arrival in New York and when he was fast becoming a dominant, if not *the* dominant, force among the New York intelligentsia! He came once to preach at Vassar while I was teaching there. After his magnificent sermon in the chapel, I went up to congratulate him and take him to Sunday lunch at President Blanding's house. He looked at me as if he were being pursued and said, tensely yet eagerly: "Langdon, v'ere is the vhisky?" Such little yarns were repeated endlessly among his students.

---

1. Cf. Tillich's own comment on this: "Many of my students and friends outside the Seminary have told me of the difficulty they have met in trying to penetrate my theological thought. They believe that through my sermons the practical or, more exactly, the existential implications of my theology are more clearly manifest" (*The Shaking of the Foundations* [New York: Scribner's, 1948], Preface).

I remember him impishly telling a story about himself and Wilhelm Pauck. These two old friends were lodged for the weekend at a minister's conference in the Cathedral Close (grounds) in Washington. As in its medieval prototypes, so there one had, if one came home after eleven, to ring the porter and rout him out of bed, if one were to be let in. Apparently, the two *bon vivants* were more than a little late, and, as we say, neither one was feeling any pain. They rang the bell loudly over and over again; finally, a sleepy porter poked his head out the window above and called out: "Who is there?" Tillich, giggling with his hand over his mouth, said that he replied to the porter: "Vee are ze bad boys!"

One never knew which side of Tillich would manifest itself. What did reveal itself was, therefore, always a surprise and, as I have noted, almost always—for some reason or other—extremely funny. When Tillich was at the very height of his real prominence—recently on the cover of *Time*, called upon to address the American Psychoanalytic Society, main speaker at the opening of a new wing at the Museum of Modern Art—he was invited to preach during Holy Week at the noon services at one of the collegiate churches downtown. Each noon the church was packed. At the conclusion of one service, Tillich was standing in the narthex beside the dominie, greeting a very long line of awestruck and certainly admiring New Yorkers. An elderly and apparently slightly deaf lady in line made her way to the dominie and addressed him in a stage whisper that could be heard throughout the narthex: "Who was that dear, sweet professor who spoke to us today?" Tillich, horrified, jabbed his elbow into the ribs of the dominie and said: "Show ze lady de program!"

*   *   *

Tillich came to Vanderbilt in Nashville to deliver the Cole lectures in the late 1950s. Several faculty persons closely connected with southern church circles were worried that the audience to hear this "philosopher" would be minuscule and thus far outclassed by the overflowing con-gregations coming to hear a well-known evangelist from Florida. Why not put Tillich in our small Divinity School chapel and the evangelist in the University auditorium? As I noted above, this anxious prophecy was far off the mark. Tillich drew immense crowds each night, the auditorium being more crowded at the end than it was on the first night. Since I had largely initiated the invitation, I was concerned that Tillich have a good and pleasant time while he was there ("worthwhile experience" is too un-Tillichean to write here).

In early April, Nashville is ablaze with floral beauty. Gardens, clearly loved and so well cared for, proliferated everywhere and in vast variety. Nashville iris were world famous, and the exploits of the garden clubs represented one of the most significant social concerns of the city's prominent residents. In expectation of his visit, therefore, I planned an itinerary of the most famous gardens; carefully, I made all the right arrangements with their fortunately flattered proprietors for his visit to their gardens. My plan was to begin with two of the most renowned "city" gardens on the properties of old mansions within the city limits, then to move further to two famous "suburban" gardens on estates in Belle Meade, and finally to conclude in the hill country south of Nashville where I had begun payments on some wooded property quite outside both the city and suburban limits.

I was very much excited by the whole grand plan, especially its culminating point in the "real" country. This was not only because the property was someday to be mine—no small factor, indeed. It was also because Tillich, to all of us, was the one "nature mystic" among the then great theologians. We all knew, of course, of Tillich's concern for history, for religious socialism and the renewal of alienated society in the present *kairos;* but we were also certain that if any present Christian thinker could experience the sacred within nature and so express theologically the religious dimension of our relatedness to the natural order, it was Tillich. We also knew from repeated references of his own how intensely meaningful it was for him to be near and so to feel the presence of the sea, to experience, as he once put it, its unconditional power and meaning, its infinity, calmness, depth, and awesome terrors—all of these being manifestations for him of the sacred, of infinity, of the holy.[2] I looked forward, therefore, to being with him when he experienced the beauty of the wooded hills, "nature's garden," so to speak, where dogwood and rhododendron covered the wild woods and fields of uncut Tennessee.

To reach this property we drove beyond the suburban development south of Nashville about ten miles into the country; then we turned off onto a dirt road that wound another two miles or so into the hills. The property itself lay along that road on a slight rise: a field of tall grass sloped down into woods about a hundred yards away and then continued on down through the woods to a stream and then up to another field on a hill on the other side. The woods were aflame with flowering trees and shrubs; there were well-worn paths, and so it was a joy to walk there and look and sniff.

I pulled up the car on the edge of the narrow dirt road and jumped out. As I came around to open the front door for Tillich, I noticed he was a bit

---

2. *IOH,* 7–8; Paul Tillich, *On The Boundary* (New York: Scribner's, 1966), 18.

flustered, even nervous. "Are zere *zerpents* here, Langdon?" This was vintage Tillich. He was never fully at home in our language, but for that very reason he could use it with great originality and power, pulling out new words to give potent expression to his own meaning. He did not say, "snakes," a secular beast at best; he said "zerpents," a much more formidable and mysterious sort of creature, a creature transparent to the unconditional power of life and of death in nature. Not yet aware of all that was afoot, I laughed and said:

"Of course, Paulus. There are rattlers all over the place in these Tennessee hills, but they don't bother us here. I've walked here dozens of times and never encountered one; they don't want to trouble us unless we trouble them. Oh yes, the lady who lives in that cabin over there"—and I pointed to a bungalow with a front porch about a quarter of a mile away where a middle-aged lady was rocking—"told me that she saw one near her back porch the other day and had to kill it with her shotgun. Come on, let's walk to the woods." Tillich stood still and looked soberly ahead down the road—not once over at the high grass in the field.

"Zen I get back in ze car."

"But Paulus, don't you want to see the beauty of these woods and hills, the real glory of untouched nature?"

"No, Langdon, I am a zity boy, and I get back in ze car."

With that Paulus climbed hastily into the front seat, put his two hands on his knees as he was wont to do, and with back erect, continued to stare steadily, if a bit gloomily, forward out of the windshield, waiting for me to join him. I was at once disappointed and entranced, sorrowful and deeply amused. Who would ever have thought that *this* would happen? That night he gave a wonderful lecture on the unconditional in art, science, and law, a masterpiece of feeling and of intellect.

* * *

Graduate students and teaching assistants know relatively little about the actual relations between the professors with whom they work and observe from the outside; like messengers for the gods, they are hardly privy either to the intimate councils of the latter nor to their private wars. Thus I was never at all conscious during my four years at Union Theological Seminary (1946–50) of any signs of the so-called conflict between Paulus and Reinhold Niebuhr. To us in the late 1940s—or at least to me—both represented divergent versions of the exciting new theology that I discovered first through Niebuhr in the spring of 1940, a theology in marked and conscious contrast to the "liberal," optimistic religiosity of my own youth. For each emphasized what were to me the central, exciting, and valid themes of that new movement: a deep sense of the alienation of ordinary historical existence, which made intelligible the war that had just engulfed us; a dependence on special manifestations of renewal and of grace, which fitted our own experience of rescue from meaninglessness; and a central experience of transcendence as the resource of new life, of obligation, and of hope. To be sure, these two theologians provided differing, even contrasting, versions of these common "neo-orthodox" or "dialectical" theological themes, but to us the unity of the two (over against, for example, the faculty at Columbia or even President Van Dusen) far outweighed their divergences. Later, when this new theology ("neo-orthodoxy") became the norm, the established interpretation of Christianity, and liberal theology was an almost forgotten relic of the distant past, the differences between these two leaped into new prominence. But then these were mainly exciting variations within a new and shared viewpoint.

We were always conscious of Tillich's disdain for Brunner's theology. It was Brunner's I-Thou, relational theology that he had in mind most frequently when he spoke distastefully of naming God as "the highest being," or as "an absolute person over against us" (*ST* I:235). And we were well aware that to Barth, as probably to Brunner as well, Tillich was "merely a liberal," a representative of *Kultur Protestantismus*. But to those of us then at Union (1946–50), Tillich and Niebuhr (and probably H. Richard Niebuhr at Yale as well) occupied a kind of healthy, vital, and relevant center in theology. They shared a common concern with culture and with social renewal that separated them from Barth and the Barthians; and yet they sought to ground their theologies on the extracultural sources of revelation and faith, and so were differentiated from Boston's personalism and Chicago's process theology. Of course, it was commonly understood that Tillich's frequent arguments against a "mainly" biblical symbolism and for ontology in theology were also directed at Niebuhr. And we all were familiar with the latter's usually gentle chiding of "those who depended too much on the abstractions of philosophy" in doing theology, and we knew he meant Tillich. But it was also understood how long they had been friends, how active Niebuhr had been in securing Tillich a place on the faculty at Union, and, as noted, how much theologically and politically they had in common.

I recall two occasions that illustrate to me the essentially friendly and certainly respectful rivalry—if we can call it that—of those years.[3] At a retreat of the Fellowship of Socialist Christians (about 1947–48) on the possibilities for continuing peace and increased justice in the post-war

---

3. These incidents have been reported in the review article of Fox's biography of Niebuhr in the *Journal of Religion*, April 1988.

world, both were present as speakers on the program. After the first evening session we all gathered in the sizable lounge before a fire and sat on the floor, the two leaders occupying large armchairs. One could not help but be aware that all the attention of the assembled students was directed at Reinnie, and questions were continually flung at him about the current international and domestic political situations. Finally, one thoughtful student—it was not I—turned to Tillich and asked him a question. Quietly and seemingly quite without rancor, he replied: "Why ask me a question in politics when you have a veritable *(echte)* genius sitting right here among us?" And he subsided again into attentive silence.

On another occasion Tillich got the better of Reinnie. It was some meeting at Union, again sometime in 1947–49, where methods in theology were under discussion. Reinnie had been chiding Tillich for deserting a "mythical" account of Creation and Fall, which kept Creation and Fall clearly separate, and for embracing a philosophical interpretation ("the impersonal and necessitating abstractions of ontology"), which inevitably "identified" Creation and Fall, the ultimate and baleful evidence of a philosophical pantheism. (Niebuhr to me never understood, or wanted to understand, how Tillich avoided, as I think he did, this pantheistic doom, but that is an issue that has been discussed in chapter 7 of this volume.) Tillich smiled, recognizing a familiar argument in their continuing debate, and then stood up. Pushing back the sleeve of his suit jacket, Tillich looked carefully at his watch and then up at Reinnie.

"Alright, Reinnie. You vish to separate Creation and Fall. Good. Zen how long vas it, Reinnie?" Tillich pointed to the face of his watch: "Vas it from twelve noon to five after twelve, Reinnie, or perhaps a little longer? How long did ze good Creation, separate from ze Fall, last? And, Reinnie, if you do not, in fact cannot, say to me how long it lasted, then how can we *separate* zem as you wish to do? And what does it *mean* to try to separate zem in myth if zey cannot be separated? Must we not hold zem together as one event, even if we distinguish zem as different aspects of that event of coming to be? But that is ontology united to myth, is it not Reinnie?"

Niebuhr may not have understood clearly how Tillich escaped pantheism, but he certainly understood when someone had gotten the better of him! Thus he laughed that delighted if somewhat embarrassed laugh that appeared naturally whenever he realized the joke was on him, shrugged hs shoulders, and muttered something about the obscure labyrinths of philosophy. We all agreed later that Tillich had more than won that exchange. Neibuhr may later, when I had left Union to teach at Vassar (after 1951), have become more petulant and outspoken about Tillich's philosophical theology—as stated, for example, in Fox's strange book on Niebuhr.[4] All I can say is that I never felt between them the hostility reported there. On the contrary, their differences seemed to me more than transcended by their common affection and respect.

Barth was neither much studied nor much discussed at post-war Union. Most of our interests in "biblical theology" were absorbed by Niebuhr, Bennett, and the Old Testament professors, Meilenberg and Terrien, and for many by reading Brunner; the remaining energies with regard to theology were devoted to Tillich, to Kroner, and, of course, to David Roberts's early introduction of Kierkegaard and of psychoanalysis onto the American scene. Nevertheless, Barth was, like Mount Everest, *there*, and we were all more than aware of that immense presence, alien as it was to our innate "Union" concern with culture and with renewing the social world. Thus it was natural that one evening in Tillich's apartment at a *Privatissimum*, as he called them, we asked Tillich to tell us about his relation to Barth. After Tillich had carefully opened the bottle of Moselle wine and we had ceremoniously sipped it, he settled back, and, deeply clearing his throat, began to answer our questions.

"Venn you're fighting against a tyrant, zen Barth is ze best man to have on your side. He drives a sharp wedge between heaven and earth, between the gospel and culture. And zat is good venn culture becomes demonic and claims ze authority and power of heaven. With Barth's sharp *diastasis* (separation), he gives to us ze power to resist ze tyrant who then represents *Kultur*, has in fact swallowed *Kultur* whole, and there is zen *in Kultur itself* no place to stand. Zat is why Barth's theology had such power in these days. It gave power to all those who wanted to resist Hitler and found in German culture no place from which to resist. Barth's message was appropriate for zat *Kairos*—more appropriate zan mine. I respect and have always respected Barth, not only for the originality and power of his theology but also for the clarity of his insight into the idolatry of Hitler and his courage for declaring it." Tillich paused, and then began again in an even firmer voice:

"*But*," and here Tillich was silent once more and looked at each of us with weighty seriousness and yet also with great vulnerability, as from one who had been vastly misunderstood and had suffered therefrom. He spoke with deliberate emphasis, pausing with great care at each point:

"But, I was *right* about the relation of culture to theology, even a theology of resistance against culture, and Barth was wrong, even about his own "revelation theology" which is *full* of culture. *And* I resisted for

---

4. Richard W. Fox, *Reinhold Niebuhr: A Biography* (New York: Pantheon, 1986).

the right reason, justice for the Jews rather than the freedom of their *evangelische* pulpit. *And* I left on an earlier train!"

For us Tillich had spoken, and spoken a final word. Later he added that while Barth had left *for* home on that train, he, Tillich, had left his home.

But then, lest we misunderstood him in that last reference, he went on to say how *much* he had learned in the United States.

"It vass a shock to an antibourgeois socialist to be rescued by a bourgeois, by *the* bourgeois, nation! I understood as I had not understood at all before that democracy can, though it often does not, balance the inequality and injustice of capitalism. Above all, I learned here that no concept or word has meaning unless it refers to experience. I learned I must think, and how to think, *experientially*, and that I learned here—something no one, *no one*, understands in my homeland!" Unlike many unwilling immigrants or refugees, Tillich balanced his private critiques of American culture with a reasoned, deeply felt, and publicly expressed appreciation of the assets of American life.

* * *

Although the next two stories do not concern Paulus directly, he was a prominent actor on the scene in both of them. Anyway, they are each extraordinary enough to justify the telling.

The first took place at Union in the spring of '48. The final volumes of Arnold Toynbee's great work, *A Study of History*, had been published that year, and, when he made his triumphful pilgrimage to the United States, he was feted and honored everywhere in New York. For some interesting reason, Henry Luce particularly admired Toynbee and his work; as a consequence, Toynbee appeared on the cover of *Time;* and when he was given an honorary degree by Union Theological Seminary, Luce, as chairman of the Seminary's board, was at the center of all the ceremonies. An impressive banquet was held in the large, high-ceilinged, gothic refectory at Union attended by most, I should imagine, of the elite intellectuals and church leaders of New York. I was there only because they needed a host of waiters for the banquet, and as a graduate student, I was a first-string member of the refectory cafeteria team, being in charge that year of the cash register.

It was an elegant, glistening affair. The long refectory tables were covered with white linen and filled with guests in formal attire; subdued lights and candles on the tables gave elegance to the scene; and the portraits of Union's saints and heroes were dimly visible on the wall and lent the significance of an important tradition. We all felt then that if the theological world had a center, this was surely it. The refectory was built on the style of an English college hall, with a raised portion at the end where the "high table" was placed. This, we had to admit, was itself an impressive sight. There in a row at the center of the long speakers' table sat, in sequence, President Pitney Van Dusen, Paul Tillich, Henry Luce, Arnold Toynbee, and Reinhold Niebuhr. At the close of the dinner, after we waiters had cleared away and were standing there in the back holding our trays at our sides, the hall quieted in expectation. Henry, as chairman of the board, rose to open the ceremonies.

Henry was a handsome, forceful man; his presence and his commanding voice drew everyone's attention sharply to himself. After welcoming the visitors and introducing most of the head table, he began with a good deal of charm to extol the achievements and brilliance of the guest of honor. I remember noticing from the back of the hall the benevolent smiles of interest and approbation on the faces of the two theologians whom we knew so well, seated on either side of him, both looking up at him with comfortable satisfaction as he warmed to his task. I do not remember all he said or exactly how he said it, except its crucial center; but it went something like this:

"With this study of history, Toynbee has clearly shown himself to be one of the veritable geniuses in our century, to be ranked with Einstein, Thomas Mann, Rachmaninoff, and Picasso. For he, as no one else before him, has opened up for us the mystery of the processes of history. If still only in part, we now understand that which was quite obscure before. I refer, of course, to the springs of the rise of great cultures, and then especially to the causes of their strange breakdowns. Who in history heretofore has understood, much less controlled, the terrible decline, decay, and disappearance of even the mightiest of nations? Now at last in understanding, we may, *Deo volente*"—and Luce smiled at his audience's surprise—"begin for once to control these processes of history." Even from the back we could see the small signs of somber disapproval, like tiny dark clouds on a sunny horizon, beginning to appear on the faces of Tillich and of Niebuhr.

Luce was, however, by no means finished. After continuing on about the sheer brilliance and extraordinary value of this inquiry into history, he paused again so as to draw everyone's attention to himself:

"But"—and he raised his finger high—"there is one thing Toynbee does *not* understand about our common human history!" At that he had everyone's eye completely riveted upon him. I noted that the largely benevolent and still partly somnolent satisfaction on the faces of Tillich and Niebuhr had suddenly changed to surprised attention and expectant curiosity as Luce's voice boomed forth:

"The one thing Toynbee does not understand is that the United States of America has *solved* the problem of the breakdown of cultures!"

At this, the graduate students at the back of the refectory—long made aware by almost everyone of importance at Union of the imminence of the divine judgment on the slightest sign of hubris—expected at the least a thunderbolt to cleave the great hall in two. All of us, of course, looked immediately at Tillich and especially at Niebuhr, infinitely curious to see how these two, undoubtedly the leading prophets of their age, would be reacting to Luce's heedless blasphemy—if not against God, at least against the reigning theology at Broadway and One Hundred Twenty-Second Street! I remember as if it were yesterday and not forty years ago, the way Niebuhr and Tillich first stared directly ahead in sheer amazement, and then each went into what turned out to be a quite characteristic pose. Niebuhr clasped his head in his large hands and bent his head down so that it almost touched his knees and stared, hands over his bald pate, at the floor. Tillich put his hands on his knees, half closed his eyes and, tilting his head way back, looked partly in disbelief, partly in sorrow, at the ceiling. Delighted with this scene as far surpassing my wildest expectations, I whispered fiercely to the five other waiters (Durwood Foster was among them), "Look—neither one of them is looking at God! Paulus is looking up, and Reinnie is looking down, and for neither one is there any God in *that* direction!"[5]

I must admit that I cannot remember anything else that happened that evening.

*   *   *

The last story took place twenty-five years later when my wife, Ram Rattan, and I came to the University of Chicago in 1963. Since my young wife as a European was as yet not quite used to the American academic world, much less the American "seminary" environment, we agreed that we would not try to invite faculty colleagues to our home until we both were considerably more acclimatized. As one exception, I suggested that we have the Tillichs over for dinner. I knew that she would feel at home with them as Europeans and also that she would find both of them quite fascinating, and I wanted very much to renew my own relation to them.

Meanwhile, a very energetic group at the Divinity School had been trying eagerly, almost desperately, to enlist the active support of my wife.

---

5. It is well known that Niebuhr's "biblical God" is "up there," in the heavens over us," while Tillich's God, as the source and ground of our being, is "under" us.

This was a group, now long since gone to its reward, called the Divinity Dames, student and faculty wives who as at most seminary centers met together frequently for Bible study, prayer, and discussion of the common problems besetting the wives of ministers. They hoped, nay expected, the wife of the new professor of theology to join them and perhaps to lead a session or two in the study of the Scriptures. Since my wife had recently come from living on the Left Bank in Paris, and before that had been brought up in a Dutch business family with few church ties, she was quite baffled by all this: "What *is* this group, Langdon; what is it they want *me* to do, and *why?*" It was clear that she felt not a little nervousness and even some dread over this whole matter.

As quickly as I could I got on the phone with the faculty wife advisor of the group, the spouse of a colleague in the theological field, and began to explain my wife's situation to her. I thought in my innocence that the whole matter was quite simple. "My wife is extremely inexperienced in American church life and church customs, Mrs. . . . ; she is *not at all* ready for what they ask her to do. *Please* take her name off your list and wait for her to get in touch with you if she becomes interested."

I thought this was perfectly clear, but no; invitations to come to subsequent meetings, to speak at a gathering in December, to lead in prayer sessions, and so on kept coming. So I called again and repeated my message in an even firmer voice. Finally, they took the oft tried and frequently successful American recipe when someone seems "too shy" to come forward by themselves and to join in with the community. They sent her a letter telling her she had just been made vice president!

It was just after we had in utter astonishment opened this last letter that the Tillichs came to dinner. I was delighted to see them both again, but I had not expected the warmth with which Hannah and my wife greeted one another. Despite the difference in their ages, their common northern European background immediately drew them together; each answered at once a deep need in the other. Hannah could seem from the outside (to a graduate student) to be a formidable woman indeed; erect, handsome, often indrawn and alone, obviously very intelligent and strong-willed, she appeared too aloof and self-contained to be approached with mere American chatter. But not now; she greeted Ram Rattan so warmly that the latter apparently felt she could immediately ask her advice on this most recent problem facing her in the unknown American environment.

"Frau doctor Tillich—no, I mean Mrs. Tillich, have you ever had any dealings with a group called the Divinity Dames?"

"Oh, ze Divinity Dames!" Hannah's voice shook in horror as she raised her hands above her head in a gesture of combined unbelief and disdain. "Zey were ze bane of my life veen vee first came to Union! Zey asked me—*me!*—to read vis zem ze sacred Scriptures und to pray mit zem. I could not belief my ears! But do you know vatt I told zem?" And here Hannah leaned toward Ram Rattan with a gleam in her eye: "I told zem zat venn you go to the East Indies as a missionary, you must *love* ze natives, but"—and here she grasped her nostrils between her thumb and forefinger—"you do not have to wear ze ring in ze nose!" At this, Tillich laughed a deep laugh, I stared and wondered, and Hannah and Ram Rattan slowly embraced each other. Hannah *was* formidable indeed! I have never been able again to view our strange antics, particularly, perhaps, those of American church life, without thinking of them as tribal customs looked at with no small wonder by visitors to our shores.

Indexes

SUBJECTS

211

VanBuren, Paul, xii

Whitehead, Alfred North, 23,
  25n, 27n, 28, 29, 57, 58, 60,
  71, 72, 82, 82, 83n–84n, 85n,

86, 87, 88n, 90n, 91, 100,
106–107, 108, 119, 155, 159,
166, 171, 181
Williams, Tennessee, 131